JOHN ROBERTSON

Accounting Principles for Non-Accounting Students

© Roger W. Mills and John Robertson, June 2000

Design and Typesetting: Mars Business Associates Ltd

Printed and bound in Great Britain by: The Bath Press/Bookcraft

---

LIBRARY OF CONGRESS CATALOGING IN PUBLICATION DATA

Robertson, John

Accounting Principles for Non-Accounting Students

Included bibliographies and index

ISBN   1 873186 17 7

1. Financial Accounting, Cost Accounting, Management Accounting

I. Title

Mars Business Associates Ltd

62 Kingsmead, Lechlade, Glos. GL7 3BW

Tel: + 44 1367 252506

Email: john@marspub.co.uk

Preface

This book has been written specifically with the non-accounting student in mind. Such students we know from our experience are following programmes where accounting is not a major element of the degree. Students simply require an appreciation of accounting both to understand its unique language and to use certain elements in their studies. With this in mind we have constructed each chapter to provide a blend between explanation and actual examples. At the end of chapters 2 to 12 there are additional exercises with answers to the arithmentic components of each exercise at the end of the book. Our aim is to offer an interesting excursion into the accounting world; perhaps it might be re-visited again, during the development of their careers.

The book is organised in the twelve chapters shown in the following illustration:

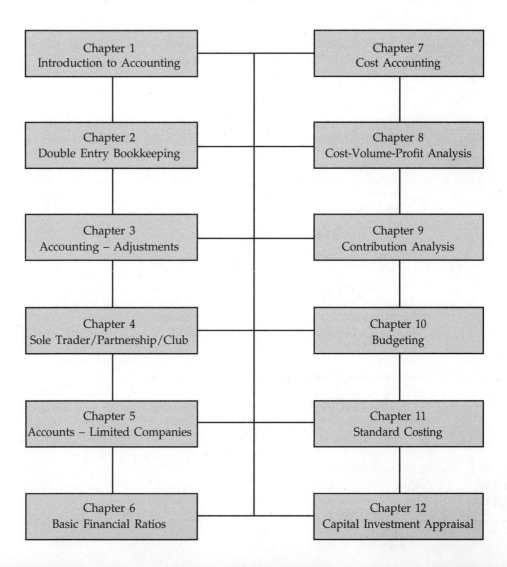

Chapter 1 Introduction to Accounting	Chapter 7 Cost Accounting
Chapter 2 Double Entry Bookkeeping	Chapter 8 Cost-Volume-Profit Analysis
Chapter 3 Accounting – Adjustments	Chapter 9 Contribution Analysis
Chapter 4 Sole Trader/Partnership/Club	Chapter 10 Budgeting
Chapter 5 Accounts – Limited Companies	Chapter 11 Standard Costing
Chapter 6 Basic Financial Ratios	Chapter 12 Capital Investment Appraisal

The relationship between the chapters is as follows:

Chapter 1 provides an introduction to the profit and loss account and the balance sheet. It assumes that you have had little formal exposure to the main financial statements used within an organisation and the rules and conventions used in drafting them. It will take you through these and the working capital cycle, quite gently.

Chapter 2 introduces you to double entry bookkeeping. A simple concept i.e. that each transaction affects two accounts, hence the principle of double entry. However, many students initially find this concept difficult to grasp. We would recommend – persistence; it will reward you in the end, since double entry bookkeeping is similar to the ABC of a language it acts as a foundation to begin to understand accounting processes.

Chapter 3 provides an introduction to the main accounting 'adjustments' such as depreciation, revaluation, disposals, goodwill, accruals and prepayments. Chapters 4 and 5 build on the previous chapters with the preparation of the main financial statements used by sole traders, partnerships, club/societies and limited companies. Chapter 6 is concerned with financial ratio analysis covering profitability, liquidity, gearing and employee ratios.

Chapter 7 introduces cost accounting. Here we focus on the contentious issue of the apportionment of overheads and take you through a comprehensive example. We also consider the development of product costs and complete the chapter by introducing activity based costing. Chapter 8 examines the relationships between cost, volume and profit including the concept of relevant costs while Chapter 9 contiunes and develops the contribution approach to short-term decision making. Here we provide examples on closing a business (dropping a product/service), best use of scarce resources, the make or buy decision, competitive tendering, accept/reject a special order and complete the chapter with an example on marginal v absorption costing.

In Chapter 10 we introduce budgeting through the budget environment. Also a range of budgeting techniques such as fixed/flexible budgets, incremental or zero based budgets, rolling budgets, forecast/outturn and activity based budgets. The preparation and purpose of cash budgets is also covered. In Chapter 11 we continue with the 'budgets' for products/services i.e. standard costing. The emphasis of the chapter is on variance analysis covering, sales, materials, labour and variable overheads.

Chapter 12 is concerned with capital investment appraisal. It covers the basic principles through examples dealing with the development of cash flows with a comprehensive example covering the traditional and discounted cash flow techniques associated with capital investment appraisal including the use of annuity tables.

John Robertson   August 2001

Contents

CHAPTER ONE

INTRODUCTION TO ACCOUNTING

When you have finished studying this chapter you should be able to:

❑ Understand the relationship between the three main financial statements, Cash Flow Forecast, Profit and Loss Account and Balance Sheet.

❑ Understand the structure of a Balance Sheet both vertical and 'two sided', interpret and show the effect of single transactions.

❑ Prepare Profit and Loss accounts, describe their relationship between the opening and closing Balance Sheets and comment on the differences between profit and cash.

1.1   Introduction

The successful study of accounting and finance is dependent upon the assimilation of a number of basic principles. Rather than deal will all of these by way of a comprehensive introduction, in this chapter, we have selected only those needed for the earlier chapters of the book. In these earlier chapters, the particular focus of attention is upon the principles, content, layout and interpretation of the main financial statements.

This chapter provides an overview of accounting both for those with little or no background in the subject and for those with some background who wish to review some fundamental principles. Specific reference will be made to important terminology and to what financial statements do and do not portray. To know what financial statements do not communicate is just as important as knowing what they do communicate.

Fundamental principles are discussed in the chapter without employing some of the specific accounting techniques (like double entry bookkeeping) and jargon (like debit and credit). It is directed at answering two important questions often asked by managers and other parties with an interest in an organisation: How well did it or will it perform over a given time period? What is, or will be the financial position at a given point of time? The accountant answers these questions with two main financial statements which we shall consider at length in this chapter – the profit and loss account and the balance sheet.

Our focus of attention in the chapter is directed at 'for-profit' organisations and, in particular, limited liability companies. Such organisations typically revolve around a similar, usually regular, cycle of economic activity. For example, retailers and most businesses buy goods and services and modify them by changing their form or by placing them in a convenient location, such that they can be sold at higher prices with the aim of producing a profit. The total amount of profit earned during a particular period heavily depends on the excess of the selling prices over the costs of the goods and services (the mark-up) and the speed of the operating cycle (the turnover). However, as we shall demonstrate, profit is not the only important focus of attention. Cash is equally important and must be carefully monitored as well. Quite how profit, cash and financial position can be monitored and the relationship between them will be demonstrated in this chapter.

Financial statements are used by organisations to summarise aspects of past, present and expected or likely or anticipated future performance. These financial statements are the result of applying certain principles, like double entry bookkeeping and some are reliant upon accounting conventions, a basic knowledge and understanding of which is essential in most of what follows.

One vital feature of the profit and loss account and cash flow statement for you to be aware of is that different principles are applied in drafting each of them. The application of these different principles means that for the same period cash and profit results will rarely be the same, hence the importance of having the two statements to convey the necessary information required for managing a business.

1.2   Introduction to Balance Sheet, Profit and Loss Account and Cash Flow Statement

Our discussion in this chapter will focus on three main financial statements and the difference in the information conveyed by each of them:

1.   The Balance Sheet

2.   The Profit and Loss account

3.   The Cash Flow Statement.

In the rest of this section we will introduce the main components of the Balance Sheet and show its relationship to the Profit and Loss account and Cash Flow Statement. In *Section 1.3* we will show the development of a Balance Sheet over a number of periods; this will include the relationship with the Profit and Loss Account. In *Section 1.4* we will follow a worked example showing how the three main financial statements can be used in a system of forecasting.

1.   Balance Sheet

The balance sheet is the financial statement used to illustrate an organisation's financial position. It can be likened to a snapshot because it is a static representation of an organisation's financial position in the form of its total assets and total liabilities at a particular point in time.

The balance sheet is reliant upon the following simple principle:

TOTAL ASSETS = TOTAL LIABILITIES

In developing this principle in this chapter our focus of attention will be upon those liabilities and assets to be found in the balance sheet of a limited liability company. However, in principle, though not the terminology used it is also applicable to most types of organisation. What are assets and liabilities? We provide a short review of each of them.

Total Assets

These are those resources obtained from the sources of finance which are expressed in monetary terms. Assets to be found in a company balance sheet are those in its possession, whether owned or controlled, and which are expected to yield future economic benefits. As shown in *Figure 1.1*, assets are usually referred to as being 'fixed' or 'current'. Fixed assets are those like land and buildings, machinery, vehicles, which are intended for use in the business and are not intended for sale as part of normal trading activity. Current assets form part of the working capital of a business and are instrumental in the generation of profit within the business. The main items of current assets include stock, debtors and cash held for use within the business.

Figure 1.1   Total Assets

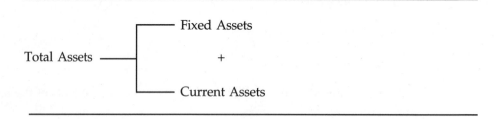

Total Liabilities

These are monetary obligations arising from past events and can be thought of as being the sources of finance used by the business. They include 'liabilities' to the owners, known as shareholders' (owners') funds or equity, which is usually categorised as share capital and reserves (such as retained profit), and liabilities to external sources of finance in the form of long-term loans and short-term sources like trade credit (creditors) and bank overdrafts. The sources of finance and how they may be generally categorised is illustrated in *Figure 1.2*.

Figure 1.2   Total Liabilities

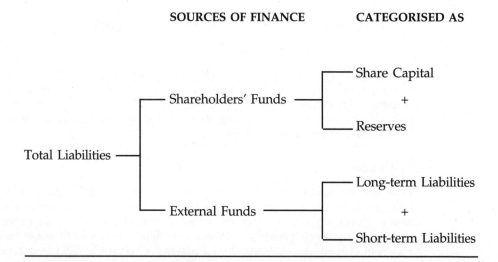

2.   Profit and Loss Account

The profit and loss account summarises the revenue generated and the costs incurred in the trading period between two balance sheet dates. Where the revenue exceeds the cost there is a profit and where the costs exceeds the revenue a loss is incurred.

In a profitable environment the result of recording accounting transactions will be that the assets of the business will increase automatically. On a regular basis, at least annually for publication purposes, companies prepare profit and loss accounts to determine the amount of profit generated by and retained in the business. The amount retained is added to the shareholders' fund under the sub-heading *Profit and Loss Account*, (please note that Profit and Loss Account in the balance sheet refers to the accumulated profits retained in the business over time, thereby increasing the total liabilities section). In this way the benefit to shareholders from profitable activity is recognised in the form of growth in the assets.

Profit that is retained in the business forms an important link between successive balance sheets. In *Figure 1.3* we show the relationship between the opening balance sheet, the profit and loss account for the period and the closing balance sheet at the end of the period (often a period will relate to one year).

Figure 1.3   *Relationship between Balance Sheet and Profit and Loss Account*

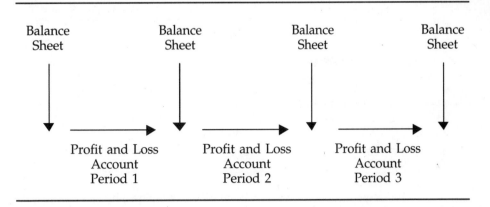

In *Figure 1.3*, moving from left to right we have:

❏   The Opening Balance Sheet for Period 1, the Profit and Loss account for Period 1 and the Closing Balance Sheet for Period 1.

❏   The next day, the Closing Balance Sheet for Period 1 becomes the Opening Balance Sheet for Period 2 and the process repeats itself.

3. Cash Flow Statement

In its simplest form, the cash flow statement will record sources and uses of funds generated for the period under review. This requires taking:

1. the profit before taxation for the period, adding back non-cash transactions such as depreciation to obtain the profit generated from the operations.

2. the opening and closing balance sheets, extracting the differences between the two and recording them as a source of funds or a use of funds. For example, an increase in an asset is a use of funds while an increase in a liability is a source of funds. This subsidiary statement is known as a Balanced Report. In *Figure 1.4* we show this process.

Figure 1.4   Process for Determining Sources and Uses of Funds

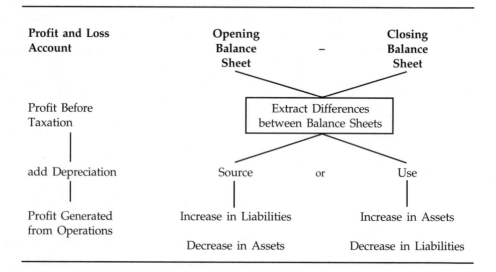

From the figures produced above we can prepare a number of different cash flow statements. One common statement is the Residual Form Report which takes say the Opening cash balance, adds all sources of funds to obtain an interim balance, then deducts all uses of funds; the resulting figure will be the Closing cash balance. This form of statement provides answers to the question 'What has happened to all our cash'?

1.3   Example – Main Financial Statements

In the following example we will show 'snapshots' of a business by comparing two Balance Sheets. To start, we will invest £50,000 in our business. How will this be shown in our opening Balance Sheet?

Balance Sheet 1.

	£		£
Current Assets		**Subscribed Capital**	
Cash	50,000	Share Capital	50,000
	50,000		50,000

In Balance Sheet 1, we show the £50,000 cash under a subheading Current Assets; this is what the company owns. On the Liabilities side of the Balance Sheet we show the £50,000 as Share Capital i.e. owners share capital; this is what the company owes. If the company were to be liquidated, it would simply take the £50,000 cash and pay it back to the owners (shareholders).

Balance Sheet 2.

	£		£
Fixed Assets		**Subscribed Capital**	
Land and Buildings	15,000	Share Capital	50,000
Plant and Machinery	10,000		
Current Assets			
Cash	25,000		
	50,000		50,000

It is now a game! Called 'spot the difference'. You are required to spot the difference between Balance Sheet 1 and Balance Sheet 2. These are the confidence builders!

In this case we can see that the company has bought Land and Buildings for
£15,000 and Plant and Machinery for £10,000. We can also see that the Cash has
reduced by the same amount i.e. (£15,000 + £10,000). This is a good example of
the principles of double entry book keeping; every transaction affects two
accounts; in this case Land and Buildings and Cash, and Plant and Machinery
and Cash.

Balance Sheet 3.

	£		£
Fixed Assets		**Subscribed Capital**	
Land and Buildings	15,000	Share Capital	50,000
Plant and Machinery	10,000		
Current Assets			
Stock	15,000		
Cash	10,000		
	50,000		50,000

Still with the confidence builders. Now spot the difference between Balance
Sheet 2 and Balance Sheet 3. Yes, we have bought Stock and paid for it by Cash.
This is typical when companies commence trading since it is unlikely that they
will be able to obtain stock on credit. Many small companies find themselves
squeezed for cash flow by having to give credit to their customers while their
suppliers are reluctant to extend similar credit to them.

Balance Sheet 4.

	£		£
Fixed Assets		**Subscribed Capital**	
Land and Buildings	15,000	Share Capital	50,000
Plant and Machinery	10,000	Profit	4,000
Current Assets			
Stock	7,000		
Debtors	20,000		
Cash	2,000		
	54,000		54,000

Now this is more like it. The difference between Balance Sheet 3 and Balance Sheet 4 shows that some trading has taken place. This is evident by the figure for Debtors. Debtors are our customers to whom we have sold goods on credit. We can also see that there is a figure for Profit i.e. we have 'made' a profit on the sale of the goods. Finally, the Stock and Cash figures have also reduced.

Therefore, Balance Sheet 3 can be viewed as our opening Balance Sheet, we will construct a Profit and Loss Account to show the trading, while Balance Sheet 4 is our closing Balance Sheet for the period. We will now construct a Profit and Loss account (which should explain all the changes from the two Balance Sheets).

Profit and Loss Account for the period ending xx/xx/xx

		£	£
Debtors	Sales (assume all credit)		20,000
Stock	less Materials	8,000	
Cash	less Wages and Overheads	8,000	
	Cost of Sales		16,000
	Profit		4,000

Why is Profit shown as a Liability? It is important to recognise that the physical profit is achieved through trading; i.e. when goods move from Stock and are sold to customers. The profit element is added at this point although it is not physically received until the customer pays for the goods. If we left it at that, the Balance Sheet would not balance. It would have more on the Assets side of the Balance Sheet i.e. the profit. Therefore, we have to put a corresponding entry on the Liabilities side of the Balance Sheet. To whom does the profit belong. The shareholders of the business. If the business were to be liquidated at this point and we obtained book values, the original share capital and the profit would be returned to the shareholders (owner).

We might ask at this point 'how successful is the company, so far'? In pure profit terms, profit as a percentage of sales £4,000 ÷ £20,000 x 100 = 25% which would be considered very good in most cases. However, here we have an example of a company which is selling goods profitably but is running out of cash. Quite simply, it doesn't have enough cash to convert its remaining stock into a saleable state. Furthermore, it is also unable to buy further stock. Is the position the company finds itself in purely the result of selling goods on credit (i.e. its Debtors) or is there other important messages here?

The position is similar to many start–up companies. In this case, we started the company with £50,000 in cash. This should have been sufficient funding until we achieved a foothold in our particular market. However, what did we do? We went out and purchased premises (Land and Buildings) and equipment (Plant and Machinery). This immediately took away half of our cash. What should we have done? Perhaps we should have rented our premises and rented or leased our equipment. This would have conserved our cash which could then have been used in trading.

Balance Sheet 5.

	£		£
Fixed Assets		**Subscribed Capital**	
Land and Buildings	15,000	Share Capital	50,000
Plant and Machinery	10,000	Profit	4,000
Current Assets		**Current Liabilities**	
Stock	17,000	Creditors	10,000
Debtors	20,000		
Cash	2,000		
	64,000		64,000

The difference between Balance Sheet 4 and Balance Sheet 5 introduces Creditors. Creditors are our suppliers who have supplied us goods on credit. In this case, our Stock has increased by £10,000 and we now have Creditors with a £10,000 balance (owing).

We are now relying on our suppliers to supply us goods on credit and our customers to pay their bills.

At this point we will suspend this activity and consider the main components of the working capital cycle. In Balance Sheet 5 above the working capital cycle is represented in the lower section i.e. Creditors to Stock to Debtors to Cash to Creditors. We will now examine each of the components within the working capital cycle with the focus on internal control systems.

Working Capital Cycle

The Working Capital Cycle helps to highlight the financial controls i.e. Stock Control, Credit Control and Cash Control. There is no recognised control system for Creditors. The Working Capital Cycle can be shown as follows:

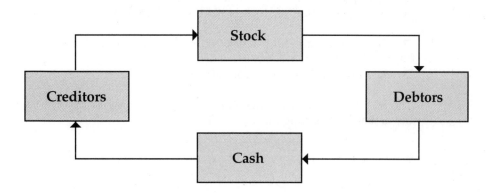

A control system

What is a control system? What do we mean by control? In its simplest form, a control system will have three elements:

1. **Record**: to set a standard, limit or plan

2. **Analyse**: to compare actual against standard, limit or plan and identify any deviation

3. **Correct**: to take corrective action, if required. Sometimes referred to as feedback.

The following diagram shows a typical control system. Most business systems use feedback based on measuring the output.

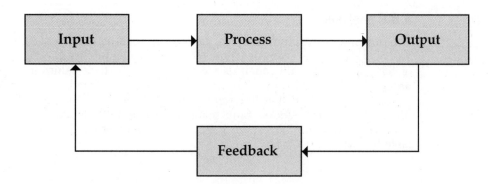

Pareto – a system of prioritising control

The Pareto curve, or more commonly referred to as the 80 : 20 rule suggests, for example that:

❏   80% of a companys sales comes from 20% of its customers.

❏   80% of the value of stock is held in 20% of the lines.

❏   Consultants can show a 80% return for a 20% effort!

❏   80% of problems come from 20% of staff.

The 80 : 20 is a generic statement, is not an exact measure. You may find that the actual figures range from 70 : 30 to 90 : 10.

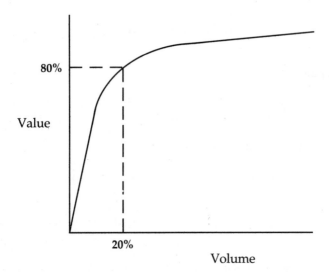

A B C analysis

The principle underpinning Pareto can be extended by the use of ABC analysis. Taking the previous example where 80% of the value (of Stock) was held by 20% of the volume. In ABC analysis we would list all stock values in descending order. If we moved down the list until we had accounted for say 60% of the value, we might find that this represented 15% of the stock held. This would become our A class stocks. Similar movements would be taken to determine B class stocks with the remainder being the C class stocks. This is shown in the table below:

	A	B	C
Volume	15	25	60
Value	60	25	15

Stock Control

Stock control is the process by which a company ensures that it has sufficient stocks to meet its operational requirements. A typical system of stock control should include the following levels:

1. Maximum.

2. Reorder.

3. Minimum.

Stock control - problems

Too high:

❑ Ties up limited working capital.

❑ Cost of holding stock.

❑ Obsolescence.

Too low:

❑ Might interrupt operations.

Credit Control

The aim of Credit Control is to minimise bad debts. A company will not be able to trade without experiencing a certain level of bad debts. What are the elements of a Credit Control system?

1. Credit control policies.

2. Credit rating.

3. Collection.

Credit Control - problems

High debtor days:

❐ Ties up limited working capital.

❐ Shift in marginal debtors.

Low debtor days:

❐ Could lose customers.

Cash Control

Many profitable companies go out of business because they run out of cash. An important element in the working capital cycle, the control of cash requires that a company prepares annual cash budgets together with daily, weekly or monthly cash flow forecasts.

The aim of Cash Control is to highlight:

1. **Cash surpluses**. To forward plan investments of cash for a short-term; benefit, interest received.

2. **Cash shortages**. To reduce the disasterous effects of running out of cash; modify our plans.

Creditors

There is no recognised control for Creditors. It would seem that it requires the mirror treatment we give to Debtors i.e. do unto others. Creditors are our suppliers, they supply us goods on credit, all they ask is that we pay their invoices on time. In times of expansion, suppliers will often provide a substantial portion of the financing requirements of a company. If the company had to go to the bank to obtain short-term financing it would have to pay interest on the loan.

Therefore, the treatment for Creditors is similar to that of our Debtors i.e. obtain as much credit from our suppliers as we can afford – but pay their invoices on time. Prompt payment of the suppliers invoices will build up a good credit rating for our company.

We will now continue with the company snapshots, with the difference(s) between balance sheets 5 and 6.

Balance Sheet 6.

	£		£
Fixed Assets		**Subscribed Capital**	
Land and Buildings	15,000	Share Capital	50,000
Plant and Machinery	10,000	Profit	4,000
Current Assets		**Current Liabilities**	
Stock	17,000	Creditors	10,000
Debtors	10,000		
Cash	12,000		
	64,000		64,000

The difference between Balance Sheet 5 and Balance Sheet 6 shows that we have received £10,000 in cash from our Debtors. Therefore, the Debtors balance has reduced by £10,000 and the Cash balance has increased by £10,000.

We now have the means (cash) to convert further stock for resale.

Balance Sheet 7.

	£		£
Fixed Assets		**Subscribed Capital**	
Land and Buildings	15,000	Share Capital	50,000
Plant and Machinery	10,000	Profit	4,000
Vehicles	5,000		
Current Assets		**Current Liabilities**	
Stock	17,000	Creditors	10,000
Debtors	10,000		
Cash	7,000		
	64,000		64,000

The difference between Balance Sheet 6 and Balance Sheet 7 shows that we have spent £5,000 cash on a Vehicle. At this point in our trading activities this does not seem to be a good idea. Balance Sheet 7 clearly shows that we have taken £5,000 out of our Working Capital Cycle and put it into Fixed Assets i.e. Vehicles. This often occurs when companies make capital investment decisions, either for new plant or vehicles or to acquire another business – in the short-term the company is vulnerable to the reductions in working capital.

The differences between Balance Sheet 7 and Balance Sheet 8 shows a number of movements; Stock, Debtors, no Cash, Bank Overdraft and Profit. In fact we have completed another trading activity. Balance Sheet 7 being the opening Balance Sheet, the trading in the form of a Profit and Loss Account and Balance Sheet 8 being the closing Balance Sheet.

Balance Sheet 8.

	£		£
Fixed Assets		**Subscribed Capital**	
Land and Buildings	15,000	Share Capital	50,000
Plant and Machinery	10,000	Profit	11,000
Vehicles	5,000		
Current Assets		**Current Liabilities**	
Stock	5,000	Creditors	10,000
Debtors	40,000	Bank Overdraft	4,000
	75,000		75,000

In this example, Debtors have moved from £10,000 to £40,000 indicating a sale of £30,000 on credit. Stock has reduced from £17,000 to £5,000 indicating usage of materials of £12,000. Cash has reduced from £7,000 through zero cash into a Bank Overdraft of £4,000 a spending of £11,000 on wages and overheads. Profit has increased from £4,000 to £11,000 indicating a profit on the transaction of £7,000. These movements are now shown in the Profit and Loss Account, below.

Profit and Loss Account for the period ending xx/xx/xx

		£	£
Debtors	Sales		30,000
Stock	less Materials	12,000	
Cash	less Wages and Overheads	11,000	
	Cost of Sales		23,000
	Profit		7,000

Balance Sheet 9.

	£		£
Fixed Assets		**Subscribed Capital**	
Land and Buildings	15,000	Share Capital	50,000
Plant and Machinery	10,000	Profit	8,000
Vehicles	5,000		
Current Assets		**Current Liabilities**	
Stock	5,000	Creditors	10,000
Debtors	40,000	Bank Overdraft	4,000
		Dividend Payable	3,000
	75,000		75,000

The difference between Balance Sheet 8 and Balance Sheet 9 shows that the (retained) profit has reduced from £11,000 to £8,000 while an entry for a (proposed) Dividend payable of £3,000 is shown in the Current Liabilities section. We might be concerned regarding the possible future of this company. So much relies on collecting in amounts owing from its customers. For example, £10,000 of the Debtors figure is outstanding from the previous transaction. How can we obtain more stock from our suppliers? How can we convert stock for resale? How can we pay our creditors? Are we concerned that we have a bank overdraft?

The fact is, this game has been a fairy story. And like all good fairy stories they all start off 'once upon a time' and finish 'they all lived happily ever after'. This is the case for this small company. Wish it were true in practice.

Balance Sheet 10.

	£		£
Fixed Assets		**Subscribed Capital**	
Land and Buildings	15,000	Share Capital	50,000
Plant and Machinery	10,000	Profit	8,000
Vehicles	5,000		
Current Assets		**Current Liabilities**	
Stock	5,000	Creditors	2,000
Debtors	15,000		
Cash	10,000		
	60,000		60,000

We will leave you to make up your own minds regarding the fortunes of this company. What we have shown is the build-up of a Balance Sheet to show the main components. Also the Profit and Loss account and its relationship with the opening and closing balance sheets.

While the two sided Balance Sheet does have an appeal i.e. Total Liabilities equals Total Assets this is not the format used in published accounts throughout the UK and Europe. On the next page, we produce the final Balance Sheet (10), in one of the accepted UK formats. This is a vertical layout where the Assets are followed by the Liabilities rather than shown side by side and the two categories of working capital, Current Assets and Current Liabilities, are placed together within the first section.

Balance Sheet 10 – Vertical format.

	£	£
Fixed Assets		
Land and Buildings		15,000
Plant and Machinery		10,000
Vehicles		5,000
Total Fixed Assets		30,000
Current Assets		
Stock	5,000	
Debtors	15,000	
Cash	10,000	
	30,000	
Creditors: amounts owing within one year		
Creditors	2,000	
Net Working Capital		28,000
Total Assets less Current Liabilities		58,000
Subscribed Capital		
Share Capital		50,000
Profit and Loss Account		8,000
Shareholders' Fund		58,000

Note:

Creditors: amounts owing within one year is the same as Current Liabilities

1.4   Accounting Concepts

The following provides an explanation of these generally accepted principles:

- ❒ **Entity:** An organisation is deemed to have a separate existence from its owners. This means that personal transactions are excluded from business accounts.

- ❒ **Going concern:** An organisation is assumed to continue in operational existence for the foreseeable future.

- ❒ **Money measurement:** Accounting only records those events that may be described and measured in money terms.

- ❒ **Timing of reports:** A time period is fixed as a basis for measurement of profit or loss.

- ❒ **Realisation:** Accounting recognises only those profits that have been realised in the accounting period. Other than in certain specific situations profit is only accounted for when the earning process is virtually complete.

- ❒ **Consistency:** The accounting treatment of particular items should be the same from period to period; if changed, the difference should be revealed.

- ❒ **Prudence or conservatism:** Provision should be made for all potential costs whereas, as indicated, profits should not be accounted for until realised. This means that a far more conservative approach is adopted towards accounting for profit than is the case for costs.

- ❒ **Accruals/Matching:** Accounts have to ensure that costs are matched with their associated revenues.

- ❒ **Materiality:** Non standard usage in accounting practice is permissible if the effects are not material.

CHAPTER TWO

DOUBLE ENTRY BOOKKEEPING

LEARNING OBJECTIVES

When you have finished studying this chapter and completed the exercises you should be able to:

❑ Understand the principles of double entry bookkeeping from basic transactions through to trial balance.

❑ Prepare accounts from basic transactions using double entry principles.

❑ Prepare a trial balance from accounting records.

2.1   Introduction to Double Entry Bookkeeping

In this chapter we will describe the double entry bookkeeping process by means of a number of examples. Should you wish to become proficient in this area we suggest that you work through the same examples until 'the penny drops'. Yes, while it is a simple process it often takes time before one becomes familiar with the system.

We will start by explaining the basic rules of double entry bookkeeping. A tip, do not try to bring your own logic into these rules – just follow them to the letter and you will succeed. From experience, we know that many students find it difficult to apply these rules without question, but if you continue to rework the same example you will eventually understand the rules/process.

The main aim of this chapter is to provide an example of the double entry bookkeeping process from initial transactions through to the preparation of a trial balance. In later chapters we will use a trial balance as the starting point to produce final accounts – these are the Trading Account, the Profit and Loss Account and the Balance Sheet.

2.2   Rules

In accounting, each transaction affects two items (or accounts). The main rules used to determine the actual positions are as follows:

Debit	Credit
IN	OUT
RECEIVER	GIVER

These two rules simply state,

> Debit what comes in   Credit what goes out
>
>   and/or
>
> Debit the receiver   Credit the giver

Please note, it is possible to mix and match the two basic rules.

2.3   Example 1

On the 1st January U.N. Welcome started a business, the initial transactions were:

Jan 1   Started a business with £1,000 cash

Jan 2   Purchased goods £250 on credit from G.Ashley & Co

Jan 3   Bought display equipment and paid £200 cash

Jan 5   Sold goods for cash £400

Each transaction affects two accounts. Here we show the two accounts and apply the rules to the above transactions.

	Debit	Credit
1. Started a business with £1,000 cash	Cash	Capital
2. Purchased goods £250 on credit from G.Ashley	Purchases	G.Ashley
3. Bought display equipment and paid £200 cash	Equipment	Cash
4. Sold goods for cash £400	Cash	Sales

1.   Jan 1   Started a business with £1,000 cash

The first transaction requires us to open two accounts. One for cash and the other for capital. Try to follow the posting. You will see that we have debited the cash account with £1,000. Notice we say capital, this refers to the other side of the transaction. In the capital account we have entered a credit of £1,000, this time it refers to the other side of the transaction which is cash. The posting to the accounts would be:

Cash

Dr.				Cr.
Jan 1	Capital (1)	1,000		

Capital

Dr.				Cr.
			Jan 1 Cash (1)	1,000

2.   Jan 2   Purchased goods £250 on credit from G.Ashley & Co

In this transaction we debit what comes in i.e. Purchases and we credit the giver i.e. G. Ashley & Co. G. Ashley & Co is a supplier of goods to the business on credit, therefore a creditor.

Purchases

Dr.					Cr.
Jan 2	*G. Ashley & Co (2)*	250			

G. Ashley & Co

Dr.					Cr.
			Jan 2	*Purchases (2)*	250

3.   Jan 3   Bought display equipment and paid £200 cash

In this transaction we debit what comes in i.e. Display Equipment and we credit what goes out i.e. Cash. There is an assumption that the display equipment is for use within the business i.e. an asset, therefore, not the goods in which the business trades.

Display Equipment

Dr.					Cr.
Jan 3	*Cash (3)*	200			

Cash

Dr.					Cr.
Jan 1	*Capital (1)*	1,000	*Jan 3*	*Equipment (3)*	200

4. Jan 5 Sold goods for cash £400

In this transaction we debit what comes in i.e. Cash and we credit what goes out i.e. Sales. Sales can either be for cash (as in this example) or sold on credit to a customer. Note that Purchases (in transaction 2) has a debit balance while Sales (below) has a credit balance; this will *always* be the case.

Cash

Dr.					Cr.
Jan 1	Capital (1)	1,000	Jan 3	Equipment (3)	200
Jan 5	Sales (4)	400			

Sales

Dr.					Cr.
			Jan 5	Cash (4)	400

Balancing off the accounts.

We will take the Cash Account to provide an example of balancing off the accounts. The balancing amounts are shown in italics.

Cash

Dr.					Cr.
Jan 1	Capital (1)	1,000	Jan 3	Equipment (3)	200
Jan 5	Sales (4)	400	Jan 7	Balance c/d	1,200
		1,400			1,400
Jan 8	Balance b/d	1,200			

a. Check to see which side is greatest. In this case it is the debit side with £1,000 + £400 = £1,400.

b. Add the two entries on the debit side then take the total across to become the total of the credit side i.e. £1,400.

c. Deduct any amounts on the credit side from the total to obtain the balance i.e. £1,400 less £200 that gives a balance of £1,200.

d. Finally, transfer the balance down to the debit side.

Example 2

In this example we have introduced a number of other transactions. We also show the two accounts for each transaction and the rule.

	200X	Transactions
1	Aug 1	Started business depositing £20,000 into bank
2	Aug 3	Bought goods on credit from G. Marsh £3,000
3	Aug 4	Withdrew £3,000 cash from bank
4	Aug 7	Bought Motor Van paying £2,000 cash
5	Aug 10	Sold goods on credit to T. Barr & Co £500
6	Aug 21	Returned goods to G. Marsh £400
7	Aug 28	T. Barr pays the amount owing by cheque
8	Aug 30	Bought Furniture from B. Wise Ltd £1,500
9	Aug 31	Paid £2,500 by cheque to G. Marsh

We will now post each of the transactions, balance off the accounts and produce a trial balance. Please note, we will show each initial posting in italics; postings already in the accounts will be in normal typeface.

1.   Aug 1   Started business depositing £20,000 into bank

Accounts	**Transaction rules**
Bank	Debit what comes in
Capital	Credit the giver

Bank

Dr.			Cr.
Aug 1	*Capital (1)*	*20,000*	

Capital

Dr.					Cr.
			Aug 1	Cash (1)	20,000

2.   Aug 3   Bought goods on credit from G. Marsh £3,000

Accounts	**Transaction rules**
Purchases	Debit what comes in
G. Marsh	Credit the giver

Purchases

Dr.					Cr.
Aug 3	G. Marsh (2)	3,000			

G. Marsh

Dr.					Cr.
			Aug 3	Purchases (2)	3,000

3.   Aug 4   Withdrew £3,000 cash from bank

Accounts	**Transaction rules**
Cash	Debit what comes in
Bank	Credit what goes out

Cash

Dr.					Cr.
Aug 4	Bank (3)	3,000			

Bank

Dr.					Cr.
Aug 1	Capital (1)	20,000	Aug 4	Cash (3)	3,000

4.   Aug 7   Bought Motor Van paying £2,000 cash

Accounts   **Transaction rules**
Motor Van   Debit what comes in
Cash   Credit what goes out

Motor Van

Dr.			Cr.
Aug 7 *Cash (4)*	2,000		

Cash

Dr.			Cr.
Aug 4 Bank (3)	3,000	*Aug 7* *Motor Van (4)*	2,000

5.   Aug 10   Sold goods on credit to T. Barr & Co £500

Accounts   **Transaction rules**
T. Barr & Co   Debit the receiver
Sales   Credit what goes out

T. Barr & Co

Dr.			Cr.
Aug 10 *Sales (5)*	500		

Sales

Dr.			Cr.
		Aug 10 *T.Barr & Co (5)*	500

6. Aug 21 Returned goods to G. Marsh £400

Accounts	Transaction rules
G. Marsh	Debit the receiver
Returns out	Credit what goes out

G. Marsh

Dr.					Cr.
Aug 21	Returns Out (6)	400	Aug 3	Purchases (2)	3,000

Returns Outwards

Dr.				Cr.
		Aug 21	G. Marsh (6)	400

7. Aug 28 T. Barr pays the amount owing by cheque

Accounts	Transaction rules
Bank	Debit what comes in
T. Barr & Co	Credit the giver

Bank

Dr.					Cr.
Aug 1	Capital (1)	20,000	Aug 4	Cash (3)	3,000
Aug 28	T. Barr & Co (7)	500			

T. Barr & Co

Dr.					Cr.
Aug 10	Sales (5)	500	Aug 28	Bank (7)	500

8. **Aug 30**   **Bought Furniture from B. Wise Ltd £1,500**

Accounts   **Transaction rules**
Furniture   Debit what comes in
B. Wise Ltd   Credit the giver

Furniture

Dr.						Cr.
Aug 30	*B. Wise Ltd (8)*	1,500				

B. Wise Ltd

Dr.						Cr.
			Aug 30	*Furniture (8)*		1,500

9. **Aug 31**   **Paid £2,500 by cheque to G. Marsh**

Accounts   **Transaction rules**
G. Marsh   Debit the receiver
Bank   Credit what goes out

G. Marsh

Dr.					Cr.
Aug 21	Returns Out (6)	400	Aug 3	Purchases (2)	3,000
Aug 31	*Bank (9)*	2,500			

Bank

Dr.					Cr.
Aug 1	Capital (1)	20,000	Aug 4	Cash (3)	3,000
Aug 28	T. Barr & Co (7)	500	*Aug 31*	*G. Marsh (9)*	2,500

Trial Balance as at 31st August 2000X

	Dr.	Cr.
Bank	15,000	
Cash	1,000	
Motor Van	2,000	
Furniture	1,500	
Purchases	3,000	
Capital		20,000
B. Wise		1,500
Sales		500
G. Marsh		100
Returns Outwards		400
	22,500	22,500

In the above Trial Balance we have determined the balances on each of the accounts without going through the process of balancing off. We would suggest that you use pre-lined paper, write up each of the transactions, balance off the accounts and produce a trial balance.

2.4 Expenses

So far, we have concentrated on buying and selling goods mainly for resale. Another important element is the expenses incurred, or additional income received.

Expenses include rent, rates, heating, lighting, wages and salaries. They could also be grouped, for example, administration expenses, marketing and selling expenses. Additional income will include, for example, interest received, rent received, discounts received.

An alternative rule:

Debit	Credit
Expenses	Cash or Bank
	or Creditor

Example

The following balances are brought forward from the previous period; Bank £14,000 Dr., Cash £1,000 Dr., Equipment £3,000 and Capital £18,000

1. Jun 1   Paid rent £300 by cheque

2. Jun 4   Interest received on bank deposit, £500

3. Jun 8   Paid wages £2,500 by cash

4. Jun 9   Paid electricity bill by cheque £400.

In this example there are starting balances brought forward from the previous period. Therefore, we have to open up accounts for Bank, Cash, Equipment and Capital.

Bank

Dr.						Cr.
Jun 1	Balance b/d	14,000	Jun 1	Rent (1)		300
Jun 4	Interest Received (2)	500	Jun 8	Cash (contra) (3a)		2,000
			Jun 9	Electricity (4)		400

Cash

Dr.					Cr.
Jun 1	Balance b/d	1,000	Jun 8	Wages (3b)	2,500
Jun 8	Bank (contra) (3a)	2,000			

Equipment

Dr.			Cr.
Jun 1	Balance b/d	3,000	

Capital

Dr.					Cr.
			Jun 1	Balance b/d	18,000

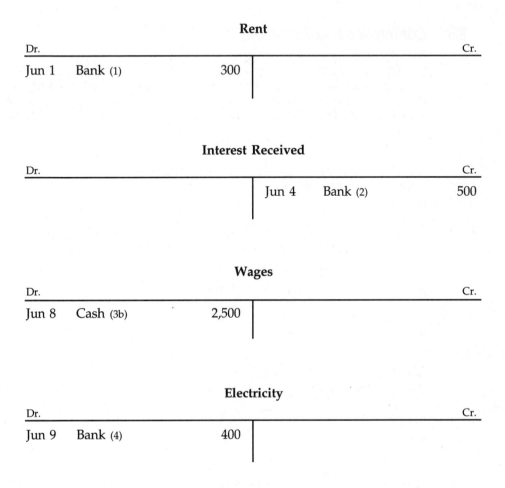

Rent

Dr.			Cr.
Jun 1	Bank (1)	300	

Interest Received

Dr.			Cr.
		Jun 4	Bank (2)	500

Wages

Dr.			Cr.
Jun 8	Cash (3b)	2,500	

Electricity

Dr.			Cr.
Jun 9	Bank (4)	400	

In each of the above transactions we have debited the expense account i.e. rent, wages and electricity and either credited bank or cash. In the case of interest received we credited the income account and debited (in this case) bank.

For the payment of wages, there was insufficient cash. Typically, a cheque would be made out to cash and presented to the bank. The accounting transaction is debit (what comes in) cash and credit (what goes out) bank, this is know as a contra entry; see transaction (3a) 8th June. We can then pay the wages from cash; see transaction (3b).

In the next example, we will balance off all the accounts and produce a Trial Balance.

2.5 Comprehensive Example

We will now take you through a comprehensive example, posting transactions to the accounts, balancing off and extracting a closing Trial Balance. For this example and for the sake of simplicity, we will show each account once e.g. the Bank Account has all the transactions and is not shown being built up as previous examples.

Enter up the books from the following details for the month of March, and extract a Trial Balance as at 31st July.

1	Mar 1	Started business with £80,000 in the bank
	Mar 2	Bought goods on credit from the following persons:
2		K. Henry £7,600
3		M. Hymers £2,700
4		T. Bulmer £5,600
5	Mar 5	Cash sales, £8,700
6	Mar 6	Paid wages in cash, £1,400
	Mar 7	Sold goods on credit to:
7		H. Elmer £3,500
8		L. Locke £4,200
9		J. Tenor £7,200
10	Mar 9	Bought goods for cash, £4,600
	Mar 10	Paid the following by cheque: (see note at end of example)
11		M. Hymers £2,400 Cash Discount £300
12		T. Bulmer £5,200 Cash Discount £400
13	Mar 12	Paid wages in cash, £1,400
	Mar 13	The following customers paid by cheque:
14		L. Locke £4,000 Cash Discount £200
15		J. Tenor £5,000 Cash Discount £200
16	Mar 15	Bought shop fixtures on credit from Betta-Build, £5,000
17	Mar 18	Returned goods to K. Henry, £2,000
18	Mar 21	Paid Betta-Build a cheque for £5,000
19	Mar 27	Goods returned by H. Elmer, £500
20	Mar 30	J. Dent lent us £6,000 by cash
21	Mar 31	Bought a motor van paying by cheque, £12,000

Work through the example then repeat a number of times only referring to the answer when in difficulty.

Balancing the accounts is shown in italics. Initially, you should ignore this until you have worked through all the transactions. We have balanced off each account for completeness, check each of the balances against the listing in the Trial Balance (at the end of the example). You will notice that some of the accounts don't have any balance; therefore, they are not shown in the Trial Balance.

Bank

Dr.						Cr.
Mar 1	Capital (1)	80,000		Mar 10	M. Hymers (11a)	2,400
Mar 13	L. Locke (14)	4,000		Mar 10	T. Bulmer (12a)	5,200
Mar 13	J. Tenor (15)	5,000		Mar 21	Betta-Build (18)	5,000
				Mar 31	Motor Van (21)	12,000
				Mar 31	*Balance c/d*	*64,400*
		89,000				89,000
Apr 1	*Balance b/d*	*64,400*				

Capital

Dr.						Cr.
Mar 31	*Balance c/d*	*80,000*		Mar 1	Bank (1)	80,000
		80,000				*80,000*
				Apr 1	*Balance b/d*	*80,000*

Purchases

Dr.						Cr.
Mar 2	K. Henry (2)	7,600		*Mar 31*	*Balance c/d*	*20,500*
Mar 2	M. Hymers (3)	2,700				
Mar 2	T. Bulmer (4)	5,600				
Mar 9	Cash (10)	4,600				
		20,500				20,500
Apr 1	*Balance b/d*	*20,500*				

K. Henry

Dr.					Cr.
Mar 18	Returns Out (17)	2,000	Mar 2	Purchases (2)	7,600
Mar 31	*Balance c/d*	5,600			
		7,600			7,600
			Apr 1	*Balance b/d*	5,600

M. Hymers

Dr.					Cr.
Mar 10	Bank (11a)	2,400	Mar 2	Purchases (3)	2,700
Mar 10	Disc. Received (11b)	300			
		2,700			2,700

T. Bulmer

Dr.					Cr.
Mar 10	Bank (12a)	5,200	Mar 2	Purchases (4)	5,600
Mar 10	Disc. Received (12b)	400			
		5,600			5,600

Cash

Dr.					Cr.
Mar 5	Sales (5)	8,700	Mar 6	Wages (6)	1,400
Mar 30	J. Dent (20)	6,000	Mar 9	Purchases (10)	4,600
			Mar 12	Wages (13)	1,400
			Mar 31	*Balance c/d*	7,300
		14,700			14,700
Apr 1	*Balance b/d*	7,300			

Wages

Dr.					Cr.
Mar 6	Cash (6)	1,400	Mar 31	Balance c/d	2,800
Mar 12	Cash (13)	1,400			
		2,800			2,800
Apr 1	Balance b/d	2,800			

Sales

Dr.					Cr.
Mar 31	Balance c/d	23,600	Mar 5	Cash (5)	8,700
			Mar 7	H. Elmer (7)	3,500
			Mar 7	L. Locke (8)	4,200
			Mar 7	J. Tenor (9)	7,200
		23,600			23,600
			Apr 1	Balance b/d	23,600

H. Elmer

Dr.					Cr.
Mar 7	Sales (7)	3,500	Mar 27	Returns In (19)	500
			Mar 31	Balance c/d	3,000
		3,500			3,500
Apr 1	Balance b/d	3,000			

L. Locke

Dr.					Cr.
Mar 7	Sales (8)	4,200	Mar 13	Bank (14a)	4,000
			Mar 13	Disc. Allowed (14b)	200
		4,200			4,200

J. Tenor

Dr.						Cr.
Mar 7	Sales (9)	7,200	Mar 13	Bank (15a)		5,000
			Mar 13	Disc. Allowed (15b)		200
			Mar 31	*Balance b/d*		*2,000*
		7,200				7,200
Apr 1	*Balance b/d*	2,000				

Discount Received

Dr.						Cr.
Mar 31	*Balance c/d*	700	Mar 10	M. Hymers (11b)		300
			Mar 10	T. Bulmer (12b)		400
		700				700
			Apr 1	*Balance b/d*		700

Discount Allowed

Dr.						Cr.
Mar 10	L. Locke (14b)	200	*Mar 31*	*Balance c/d*		*400*
Mar 10	J. Tenor (15b)	200				
		400				400
Apr 1	*Balance b/d*	400				

Shop Fixtures

Dr.						Cr.
Mar 15	Betta-Build (16)	5,000	*Mar 31*	*Balance c/d*		*5,000*
		5,000				5,000
Apr 1	*Balance b/d*	5,000				

Betta-Build

Dr.					Cr.
Mar 21	Bank (18)	5,000	Mar 15	Shop Fixtures (16)	5,000
		5,000			5,000

Returns Outwards

Dr.					Cr.
Mar 31	Balance c/d	2,000	Mar 18	K. Henry (17)	2,000
		2,000			2,000
			Apr 1	Balance b/d	2,000

Returns Inwards

Dr.					Cr.
Mar 27	H. Elmer (19)	500	Mar 31	Balance c/d	500
		500			500
Apr 1	Balance b/d	500			

J. Dent (Loan Account)

Dr.					Cr.
Mar 31	Balance c/d	6,000	Mar 30	Cash (20)	6,000
		6,000			6,000
			Apr 1	Balance b/d	6,000

Motor Van

Dr.					Cr.
Mar 31	Bank (21)	12,000	Mar 31	Balance c/d	12,000
		12,000			12,000
Apr 1	Balance b/d	12,000			

Selected Transactions (mainly transaction 11)

M. Hymers

Dr.					Cr.
Mar 10	Bank (11a)	2,400	Mar 2	Purchases (3)	2,700
Mar 10	Disc. Received (11b)	300			
		2,700			2,700

We bought goods from M. Hymers on 2nd March worth £2,700. M. Hymers has a credit balance on the account of £2,700.

On 10th March we pay M. Hymer £2,400 (Bank transaction (11a)). This still leaves a credit balance of £300 which is transferred to a Discount Received account (transaction (11b)). The £300 is a 'cash discount' (i.e. that £300 less cash is spent to clear the debt owing to M. Hymers) that M. Hymers has allowed for prompt payment.

Transaction 12 follows the same process while transactions 14 and 15 are cash discounts that we give to our customers i.e. Discount Allowed i.e. to Locke and Tenor.

Please note that we open separate accounts for Discount Received and Discount Allowed and Returns Inwards and Returns Outwards. If at a later date, we want to net these accounts then we can do so; we can't do the reverse e.g. having netted off say returns into one account it is difficult to find out the level of returns inwards and returns outwards.

Trial Balance

Finally, we now show the Trial Balance as at the end of March. Here we take all the balances in the accounts, listing all the debit balances first followed by all the credit balances. If all the transactions have been posted correctly then the total of the debits should equal the total of the credits. It is possible that the total of the debits equals the total of the credits but does not reveal errors e.g. posting to the wrong account.

Trial Balance as at 31st March 200X

	Dr.	Cr.
Bank	64,400	
Purchases	20,500	
Cash	7,300	
Wages	2,800	
H. Elmer	3,000	
J. Tenor	2,000	
Discount Allowed	400	
Shop Fixtures	5,000	
Returns Inwards	500	
Motor Van	12,000	
Capital		80,000
K. Henry		5,600
Sales		23,600
Discount Received		700
Returns Outwards		2,000
J. Dent (Loan Account)		6,000
	117,900	117,900

2.1   On the 1st March B.E.Good started a business, the initial transactions were:

Mar 1   Started a business with £10,000 cash

Mar 6   Purchased goods £2,500 on credit from R.Matthew & Sons

Mar 7   Bought Equipment and paid £3,500 cash

Mar 9   Sold goods for cash £3,000

2.2   On the 1st October P. Green started a business, the initial transactions were:

Oct 1   Started a business depositing £20,000 cheque into bank

Oct 2   Purchased goods £3,200 on credit from F. Ewart & Co

Oct 5   Bought Motor Van and paid £2,500 by cheque

Oct 8   Returned goods to F. Ewart & Co worth £300.

2.3   On the 1st May R.E. Joyce started a business, the initial transactions were:

May 1   Started business depositing £3,000 into bank

May 4   Bought goods on credit from DottyCom Ltd £3,000

May 5   Withdrew £500 cash from bank

May 8   Bought Motor Van paying £1,500 by cheque

May 11   Sold goods on credit to U. Candoit £2,500

May 14   Returned goods to DottyCom Ltd £500

May 15   U. Candoit pays the amount owing by cheque

May 22   Bought Furniture on credit from B. Wise Ltd £1,500

May 31   Paid £2,000 by cheque to DottyCom & Co

2.4   On the 1st May R.E. Joyce started a business, the initial transactions were:

Aug 1   Started business depositing £8,000 into bank

Aug 3   Bought goods on credit from I.T. Digital & Co £6,000

Aug 4   Withdrew £2,000 cash from bank

Aug 7   Bought Furniture paying £1,500 cash

Aug 10   Sold goods on credit to M. Istaken Ltd £4,500

Aug 21   Returned goods to I.T. Digital & Co £300

Aug 28   M. Istaken Ltd pays the amount owing by cheque

Aug 30   Bought goods on credit from U.N. Wise Ltd £1,500

Aug 31   Paid £4,000 by cheque to I.T. Digital & Co

2.5   The following balances are brought forward from the previous period; Bank £20,000 Dr., Cash £2,000 Dr., Motor Van £6,000 and Capital £28,000

Nov 1   Paid rent £800 from cash

Nov 5   Interest received on bank deposit, £450

Nov 13   Paid wages £1,400 by cash

Nov 16   Paid insurance policy by cheque £1,200.

2.6   The following balances are brought forward from the previous period; Bank £8,000 Dr., Cash £1,400 Dr., Motor Van £7,000 and Capital £16,400

Aug 1   Paid wages £600 from cash

Aug 3   Rent received by cash, £300

Aug 6   Paid motor expenses £500 by cash

Aug 10   Paid telephone bills by cheque £300.

2.7 Enter up the books from the following transactions for the month of August, and extract a Trial Balance as at 31st August.

Aug 1 Started business with £50,000 in the bank

Aug 2 Bought goods on credit from the following persons:

R. E. Turn Ltd. £30,000

L. Last Ltd £12,000

C. Cooke & Co £22,000

Aug 5 Cash sales, £32,000

Aug 6 Paid wages in cash, £4,400

Aug 7 Sold goods on credit to:

Sid Spice £14,000

K. Krankie £19,000

N. Nettle £30,000

Aug 9 Bought goods for cash, £18,000

Aug 10 Paid the following by cheque:

L. Last Ltd £11,400 Cash Discount £600

C. Cooke & Co £20,900 Cash Discount £1,100

Aug 13 Paid wages in cash, £4,400

Aug 14 The following customers paid by cheque:

K. Krankie £18,500 Cash Discount £500

N. Nettle £25,000 Cash Discount £800

Aug 15 Bought shop fixtures on credit from Betta-Build, £8,000

Aug 18 Returned goods to R.E. Turn Ltd., £5,000

Aug 21 Paid Betta-Build a cheque for £8,000

Aug 27 Goods returned by Sid Spice, £1,200

Aug 30 J. Jones lent us £12,000 by cash

Aug 31 Bought a motor van paying by cheque, £15,000

2.8   Enter up the books from the following transactions for the month of June and extract a Trial Balance as at 30th June.

June   1   Started business with £60,000 in the bank and £5,000 cash in hand.

    2   Bought goods on credit from D. Duval £50,000

    3   Credit sales to the following:

T. Woods	£6,600
F. Couples	£2,500
P. Mickleson	£4,300

    4   Goods bought for cash £2,300

    5   Bought motor van paying by cheque £8,000

    7   Paid motor expenses by cheque £120

    9   Credit sales to the following:

C. Montgomerie	£2,400
L. Westwood	£2,600
D. Clarke	£6,500

    11   Goods bought on credit from the following:

N. Price	£24,000
E. Els	£6,200
G. Norman	£4,600

    13   Goods returned to N. Price £2,500

    15   Paid motor expenses by cash £50

    19   Goods returned by F. Couples £1,100

    20   Cash taken for own use (drawings) £1,000

    21   Paid the following suppliers by cheque:

E. Els	£5,500	Cash Discount	£700
G. Norman	£4,000	Cash Discount	£600

    23   T. Woods paid account in cash £6,200, Cash Discount £400

    25   P. Mickleson paid by cheque £4,300

    26   Cash sales £3,400

    27   Cash taken for own use £2,400

    28   Goods returned to N. Price £4,200

    29   Paid for postage stamps by cash £40

    30   Credit sales to the following:

F. Couples	£4,300
P. Mickleson	£6,700
L. Westwood	£4,500

CHAPTER THREE

FINANCIAL ACCOUNTING – ADJUSTMENTS

LEARNING OBJECTIVES

When you have finished studying this chapter and completed the exercises you should be able to:

❏ Understand the adjustments made to fixed assets and their affect on the profit and loss account and balance sheet e.g. depreciation, disposal, revaluation, goodwill.

❏ Describe the main components of current assets including stock (valuation), debtors (bad debts written off, provision for doubtful debts) and prepayments.

❏ Describe the main sources of long-term financing.

3.1   Introduction

In *Chapter 1* we introduced the Balance Sheet from the start-up of a business through a number of transactions. Our aim was to provide an easy entry into the terminology of accounting and show the main sections of the Balance Sheet together with its interrelationship with the Profit and Loss account.

In this chapter we intend to use the Balance Sheet as our structure. We will take each section and explain the adjustments that have to be made (e.g. Depreciation, Bad Debts, Provision for Bad and Doubtful Debts, Accruals, Prepayments) and how they are treated in the accounts. We will also explain some of the other items that find their way onto the Balance Sheet (e.g. Share Premium, Revaluation Reserve, Goodwill, Brands).

In Appendix A to this chapter we have included the bookkeeping entries for depreciation, bad debts, provision for doubtful debts, accruals and prepayments.

Please note that we will continue to use a two sided balance sheet throughout this chapter, showing the assets on the left hand side and the liabilities on the right hand side, hence, the balance sheet equation: *total assets equals total liabilities*. Once you become familiar with this layout you will find it easier to cope with balance sheets using vertical layouts.

Table 3.1   Outline Balance Sheet

Fixed Assets	**Share Capital and Reserves**
Land and Buildings	Issued Share Capital
less Depreciation	Share Premium
Plant and Machinery	Revaluation Reserve
less Depreciation	Profit and Loss account
Vehicles	Shareholder's Fund or Equity
less Depreciation	
Other Fixed Assets	
Investments	Long-Term Loans
Current Assets	**Current Liabilities**
Stock	Creditors
Debtors	Accruals
less Provision for Doubtful Debts	Bank Overdraft
Prepayments	Taxation
Short-Term Investments	Dividend
Cash/Bank	

3.2   Fixed Assets and Adjustments

We saw in *Chapter 1*, that fixed assets were those assets that had a life greater than one year. These are the assets that a company acquires before it can carry out trading. They consist of Land and Buildings, Plant and Machinery, Equipment, Vehicles, Furniture and others. There are two main treatments for accounting for fixed assets, these are:

❏   Depreciation. Since the assets extend over an accounting period (normally one year) we have to find a method of attaching a portion of their cost to each accounting period; this is referred to as depreciation i.e. the wearing down of an asset.

❏   Disposal. We also have to recognise that assets will be sold, either at the end of their useful life or part way through their useful lives.

❏   Another asset in the fixed assets section of the balance sheet is Trade Investments. Trade investments normally consist of a portfolio of shares held of companies in the same line of business, major suppliers or major customers. These differ from short-term investments since we cannot say with any certainty that we will be able to sell trade investments (i.e. shares) at the time we might wish to.

We will now deal with:

1.   each of the main classes of fixed assets and the adjustments for depreciation;

2.   the disposal of fixed assets; and,

3.   trade investments.

1.   Depreciation

The purchase a company makes can fall into two categories. The first is as an expense (or cost), for example wages, telephone, electricity. These items are written off in the profit and loss account for the period in which they are incurred. The second is when an asset is bought for use in the business and has an estimated useful life exceeding one year, that is there is an 'unexpired' part of the cost which is reflected in the balance sheet as a fixed asset. These assets are written off in future profit and loss accounts over their estimated useful life by a process known as depreciation.

Depreciation is a measure of the wearing out, consumption or other loss of value of a fixed asset whether arising from use, passage of time or obsolescence through technology and market changes.

The most common methods are, (i) **straight line** where an fixed amount is taken to the Profit and Loss account each year (ii) **reducing balance** where a fixed percentage is applied to the remaining balance, in this case the amount taken to the Profit and Loss account will start higher than the straight line method but will reduce each year.

The annual figure for depreciation is treated as a deduction of profit in the Profit and Loss account, (thereby reducing the profit for the period) while the accumulated figure for depreciation is shown in the Balance Sheet as a deduction from the asset.

Depreciation Methods

We will now use the following example to demonstrate both the straight line, the reducing balance and also the sum of the digits methods. The last of these is less common but you may encounter it.

Example

A vehicle bought for £20,000 with an estimated useful life of four years and an estimated residual value £2,592.

1. The Straight Line Method

The formula for calculating the annual depreciation provision under the straight line method is as follows:

$$\text{Annual Depreciation Provision} = \frac{(\text{Cost of Asset} - \text{Estimated Residual Value})}{\text{Expected Useful Life in years}}$$

$$= \frac{(£20,000 - £2,592)}{4}$$

$$= £4,352$$

The straight line method allocates the net cost equally against the profit and loss account, for each year of the estimated useful life of an asset. It is a simple method to apply and understand. However, it takes no account of the fact that an asset will tend to 'lose' a larger proportion of its value in the earlier years.

2. The Reducing Balance Method

With the reducing (or diminishing) balance method a fixed percentage is deducted from the annual balance that exists at the beginning of the accounting period (i.e. cost of asset less any accumulated depreciation). How this approach works can be readily seen using the above example where it is assumed that the relevant rate to apply is 40%. The depreciation for the first year would be £8,000, in the second year it would be (£20,000 – £8,000) x 40% = £4,800, and in the third year it would be (£20,000 – £8,000 – £4,800) x 40% = £2,880. This process would continue for one more year, that is until the end of the estimated useful life of the asset. In this fourth and final year, the depreciation charge would be £1,728 leaving a balance remaining of £2,592 which is the estimated residual value.

The formula used to calculate the percentage to be applied is as follows:

$$r = 1 - \sqrt[n]{\frac{s}{c}}$$

where

r = rate of depreciation

n = estimated useful life in years

s = estimated residual value

c = cost of asset

By applying the formula to the information relating to the example we can see how the rate of 40% is determined.

$$= \quad 1 \ - \ 0.6$$

$$= \quad 0.4 \quad \text{or} \quad 40\%$$

The reducing balance method allocates a higher proportion of the cost of an asset to the earlier years. In the above example, £8,000 was allocated for the first year while only £1,728 was allocated in the fourth and final year.

3. Sum of the Digits

This method is called the 'sum of the digits', or the 'sum of the years digits'. It can be compared to a reducing or diminishing balance method in that it allocates a higher proportion of the cost of an asset to the earlier years. Given the data in the above example, the annual depreciation charge is calculated as follows:

Table 3.2 Calculation of Sum of Digits Depreciation

Year 1	4	4/10	6,963
Year 2	3	3/10	5,222
Year 3	2	2/10	3,482
Year 4	1	1/10	1,741
	10	10/10	£17,408

The basis for determining the annual depreciation charge is found simply by reversing the order of the years, such that for year 1 the depreciation charge is determined from the last year (4 in this case) which is expressed as a fraction of the sum of the digits of the years (4+3+2+1 in this case). Thus, 4/10 of the net depreciation charge of £17,408 (i.e. £20,000 – £2,592), is charged against year 1, and so on for subsequent years.

Table 3.3   Comparison of Depreciation Methods – sum charged each year

	Straight Line £	Reducing Balance £	Sum of the Digits £
Year 1	4,352	8,000	6,963
Year 2	4,352	4,800	5,222
Year 3	4,352	2,880	3,482
Year 4	4,352	1,728	1,741
Total	17,408	17,408	17,408

UK companies are able to choose any method of depreciation, or even a range of methods for different categories of assets. While most use the straight line method, care needs to be exercised when making inter-firm comparisons since the use of different methods will affect the reported profits.

Accounting Treatment for Depreciation

Companies must state the method used to calculate depreciation for each major class of fixed asset. This can be found in the Accounting Principles section of the published accounts. The accounting treatment for depreciation of a fixed asset is as follows:

1. Calculate the depreciation provision for each asset. For example, Land and Buildings are normally depreciated over 50 years or for the estimated life of the building if less than 50 years. 'Other fixed assets are depreciated mainly at rates between 5% and 33% per year' (The Rank Group plc 1998 report).

2. The annual provision for depreciation is taken into the Profit and Loss account. This has the result of reducing both the taxable and retained profits for the year and ultimately the Profit and Loss account balance in the liabilities section of the Balance Sheet. (please note that the depreciation written into the Profit and Loss account and the depreciation 'allowed' for taxation purposes can be substantially different in amount).

3. The final adjustment is on the assets side of the Balance Sheet. Fixed assets are held at cost or realisable value with annual depreciation accumulating over the life of an asset. In published accounts you will typically find a single figure for tangible fixed assets; in a note to the accounts you will find a full page in tabular format providing all the information required i.e. opening balance, additions, disposals together with annual and accumulated depreciation by each major class of fixed asset.

Example – Depreciation of Fixed Assets

We will now show an example of the depreciation of a fixed asset. Assume that this example company has fixed assets of £300,000. They have been replaced at the beginning of the year and are due to be depreciated, straight line over five years i.e. £60,000 per year. On the liabilities side of the opening balance sheet, our example company has issued share capital of £100,000 and accumulated profits i.e. the profit and loss account opening balance of £200,000. For the purpose of this example, we will assume that the current assets equals the current liabilities at £600,000 each.

We will also assume that the company has a turnover (sales) of £2,000,000, cost of sales of £1,500,000, and administration and distribution costs of £300,000.

The opening balance sheet and profit and loss account and closing balance sheet for the first year are shown in *Table 3.4*.

Table 3.4   Opening Balance Sheet and Profit and Loss Account and Closing Balance Sheet

OPENING BALANCE SHEET

ASSETS	£	LIABILITIES	£
Fixed Assets	300,000	Issued Share Capital	100,000
less Depreciation	0	Other Reserves	0
Net Book Value (NBV)	300,000	Profit and Loss Account	200,000
			300,000
Current Assets	600,000	Current Liabilities	600,000
	900,000		900,000

Profit and Loss account

	£	
Turnover	2,000,000	
less Cost of Sales	1,500,000	(assume all cash items)
Operating Profit	500,000	
less Admin and Distribution	300,000	(assume all cash items)
Net Profit Before Taxation	200,000	

Closing Balance Sheet

Assets	£	Liabilities	£
Fixed Assets	300,000	Issued Share Capital	100,000
less Depreciation	0	Other Reserves	0
Net Book Value (NBV)	300,000	Profit and Loss Account	400,000
			500,000
Current Assets	800,000	Current Liabilities	600,000
	1,100,000		1,100,000

If we now assume that at the year end the company decides to provide for depreciation on its fixed assets over 5 years straight line. The annual depreciation provision would be £60,000.

In *Table 3.5* we now show the opening balance sheet the profit and loss account and closing balance sheet with depreciation included. (ignore taxation and dividend). You will notice that the annual charge for depreciation is added into the cost of sales (i.e. 1,500,000 + 60,000) which reduces the retained profit. This would result in the Liabilities side of the closing balance sheet being £60,000 less than the Assets side of the balance sheet. To correct this, we deduct the depreciation charge from the Fixed Asset (i.e. 300,000 − 60,000).

Table 3.5   *Opening Balance Sheet and Profit and Loss Account and Closing Balance Sheet*

Opening Balance Sheet

Assets	£	Liabilities	£
Fixed Assets	300,000	Issued Share Capital	100,000
less Depreciation	0	Other Reserves	0
Net Book Value (NBV)	300,000	Profit and Loss Account	200,000
			300,000
Current Assets	600,000	Current Liabilities	600,000
	900,000		900,000

PROFIT AND LOSS ACCOUNT

	£
Turnover	2,000,000
less Cost of Sales *	1,560,000
Operating Profit	440,000
less Admin and Distribution	300,000
Net Profit Before Taxation	140,000

* In Chapter 1, we gave a simplified view of cost of sales. In practice, it represents a large number of items including, for example, depreciation.

CLOSING BALANCE SHEET

ASSETS	£	LIABILITIES	£
Fixed Assets	300,000	Issued Share Capital	100,000
less Depreciation	60,000	Other Reserves	0
Net Book Value (NBV)	240,000	Profit and Loss Account	340,000
			440,000
Current Assets	800,000	Current Liabilities	600,000
	1,040,000		1,040,000

Finally, we will show the provision for depreciation for a second year. We will assume that the company has achieved the same turnover, and other costs from the previous year. The closing balance sheet (above), now becomes the opening balance sheet for this period; we will show the profit and loss account for the period and the closing balance sheet in *Table 3.6*.

Table 3.6   Profit and Loss Account and Closing Balance Sheet (end of second year)

PROFIT AND LOSS ACCOUNT

	£
Turnover	2,000,000
less Cost of Sales	1,560,000
Operating Profit	440,000
less Admin and Distribution	300,000
Net Profit Before Taxation	140,000

CLOSING BALANCE SHEET

ASSETS	£	LIABILITIES	£
Fixed Assets	300,000	Issued Share Capital	100,000
less Depreciation	120,000	Other Reserves	0
Net Book Value (NBV)	180,000	Profit and Loss Account	480,000
			580,000
Current Assets	1,000,000	Current Liabilities	600,000
	1,180,000		1,180,000

2.   Disposal of Assets

It is important to note that estimates of the rate of depreciation to be applied, the useful life of the asset and its disposal value may be nothing more than guesswork. The actual outcome may be very different from the estimates and how we deal with differences is explained below.

A company purchased a fixed asset on 1st January 1996 for £47,000. It had an estimated economic life of seven years and an expected disposal value of £5,000. The asset was sold on the 31st December 1999 for £15,000.

The company used the straight line method for depreciation such that the annual depreciation charge would be found as follows:

$$\text{Straight Line Depreciation} \quad = \quad \frac{(£47,000 \; - \; £5,000)}{7 \text{ years}}$$

$$= \quad £6,000 \text{ per annum}$$

Any loss on the disposal of the asset would be included in the profit and loss account and would result in a reduction of the profit for the period. (Similarly, any profit on the disposal of an asset would result in an increase in the profit for the period).

Had the company known that disposal would take place after four years rather than seven years, with proceeds of £15,000 its annual depreciation charge would have been:

$$\text{Straight Line Depreciation} \quad = \quad \frac{(£47,000 \; - \; £15,000)}{4 \text{ years}}$$

$$= \quad £8,000 \text{ per annum}$$

In other words, by depreciating the asset at £6,000 over four years, now, given perfect knowledge i.e. the life, 4 years and the disposal value £15,000 we can see that the company has undercharged depreciation over the actual life of the asset. 4 years at £2,000 per year has not been written off against profit which otherwise would have been. Upon the disposal, any profit or loss needs to be calculated as shown in *Table 3.7*.

Table 3.7   Profit or Loss on Disposal of Asset

	£	£
Sale Price		15,000
Cost of Asset at 1st January 1996	47,000	
less Accumulated Depreciation	24,000	
Net Book Value at 31st December 1999		23,000
Profit or Loss on Disposal of Asset		–8,000

Accounting Treatment for the Disposal of an Asset

The acquisition and disposal of assets becomes a regular activity within most companies. The acquisition of assets is straightforward since it only requires one transaction i.e. opening an account for the asset and reducing the cash/bank balance for the payment. The disposal of an asset requires additional transactions, the aim being to clear out from the accounts all evidence relating to that asset. A typical process would be to:

1. Transfer the cost of the asset being sold into an Asset Disposals account – which clears the asset out of the accounts.

2. Transfer the accumulated Depreciation into an Asset Disposals account – which clears the accumulated depreciation for the asset out of the accounts.

3. Post the remittance received from the sale of the asset. This has the effect of increasing the cash or bank balance. The other entry in the accounts would be in the Asset Disposals account

4. Transfer the balance (i.e. the difference) on the Asset Disposal Account to the Profit and Loss Account.

    ❏   If the net balance on the Disposal Account is greater than the remittance received there is a loss on the sale of the asset and this is taken into the Profit and Loss account as a cost.

    ❏   If the net balance on the Disposal Account is less than the remittance received there is a profit on the sale of the asset and this is taken into the Profit and Loss account as an income.

Example – Disposal of a Fixed Asset

We will continue with the example used in the previous section on depreciation i.e. *Table 3.6*. If we assume that at the end of the second year the company disposed of £100,000 of fixed assets and received a cheque for £50,000. The profit or loss on the disposal would be as follows:

Table 3.8   *Profit or loss on disposal of asset*

	£	£
Sale Price		50,000
Cost of Asset (at beginning of first year)	100,000	
less Accumulated Depreciation	40,000	
Net Book Value at (end of second year)		60,000
Profit or Loss on Disposal of Asset		–10,000

The profit or loss account and balance sheet after the disposal would be as shown in *Table 3.9* – (please note, this is *Table 3.6* adjusted for the disposal).

Table 3.9 *Profit and Loss Account and Closing Balance Sheet after Disposal (end of second year)*

Profit and Loss account

	£
Turnover	2,000,000
less Cost of Sales	1,560,000
Operating Profit	440,000
less Admin and Distribution	300,000
less Loss of Disposal of Asset	10,000
Net Profit Before Taxation	130,000

Closing Balance Sheet

Assets	£	Liabilities	£
Fixed Assets	200,000	Issued Share Capital	100,000
less Depreciation	80,000	Other Reserves	0
Net Book Value (NBV)	120,000	Profit and Loss Account	470,000
			570,000
Current Assets	1,050,000	Current Liabilities	600,000
	1,170,000		1,170,000

Notes to explain the movements following the disposal.

1. We have shown the loss on the disposal of the fixed asset as a separate item in the Profit and Loss account i.e. £10,000. This has the effect of reducing the profit before taxation by £10,000 to £130,000.

2. In the liabilities section of the Balance Sheet we show £130,000 being added to the profit and loss account (balance) to give £470,000.

3. In the fixed assets section of the Balance Sheet we deduct £100,000 from the (cost) of the fixed assets and £40,000 from the (accumulated) depreciation. This leaves a net book value for fixed assets of £120,000.

4. In the current assets section of the Balance Sheet we add the £50,000 received in payment for the fixed asset.

The Balance Sheet now balances at £1,170,000 total assets (i.e. fixed assets £120,000 plus current assets £1,050,000); £1,170,000 total liabilities (i.e. issued share capital £100,000 plus profit and loss account £470,000 plus current liabilities £600,000).

3. Revaluation of Assets

Not all assets are depreciated. Land, for example often increases in value and such revaluations are commonly seen in the balance sheets of UK companies.

Suppose a professional revaluation has been undertaken on the assets of our example company which has had the effect of increasing the total value from £200,000 to £500,000. This is shown in the balance sheet both as an increase in the fixed asset value from £200,000 to £500,000 and, at the same time, increasing the reserves (under the heading revaluation reserve) by £300,000; thus keeping the balance sheet in balance. Unlike depreciation, however, such revaluations have no impact either on the profit and loss account (since they do not involve an increase in profits from trading) or the cash flow statement (since they do not involve movements of cash).

Table 3.10 shows the impact of a revaluation of fixed assets on the Balance Sheet of our example company.

Table 3.10   Balance Sheet – Impact of Revaluation

BALANCE SHEET (without revaluation)

ASSETS	£	LIABILITIES	£
Fixed Assets	200,000	Issued Share Capital	100,000
less Depreciation	80,000	Other Reserves	0
Net Book Value (NBV)	120,000	Profit and Loss Account	470,000
			570,000
Current Assets	1,050,000	Current Liabilities	600,000
	1,170,000		1,170,000

CLOSING BALANCE SHEET (with revaluation)

ASSETS	£	LIABILITIES	£
Fixed Assets	500,000	Issued Share Capital	100,000
less Depreciation	80,000	Revaluation Reserve	300,000
Net Book Value (NBV)	420,000	Profit and Loss Account	470,000
			870,000
Current Assets	1,050,000	Current Liabilities	600,000
	1,470,000		1,470,000

Many companies now revalue their fixed assets on a regular basis. The outcome is a stronger balance sheet that reflects the current value of the assets and at the same time provides an increase in the equity of the business.

One potential advantage to the company of including current values of assets through revaluations on a regular basis is that it should make the cost of acquiring the company greater should a takeover be considered. The assumption for listed companies is that the revaluation will be incorporated by the market in the company's share price. Revaluations may also improve the ability of the company to borrow funds because the ability to borrow without recourse to the shareholders is usually limited to a percentage of assets. Anything that increases the assets should increase borrowing power.

Our discussion so far has focused upon accounting for tangible fixed assets. However, intangible fixed assets such as brands and goodwill have attracted a good deal of attention in the UK. We propose to deal briefly with the accounting issues associated with just these two categories of intangible asset in the next section.

4.   The treatment of goodwill (including brands)

Goodwill is the difference between the value of the business as a whole less the value of the assets less liabilities valued separately. In this case, goodwill can be positive or negative. If goodwill is positive this means that the value of the business as a whole is worth more than the value of the assets less liabilities valued separately. What elements might constitute goodwill? The most obvious is the value of brands, however, the development of a sound supply chain, access to research and development (or know-how), or access to a top class management team would all contribute to making the value of the business as a whole greater than the value of its assets less liabilities.

At this point it is important to introduce the distinction that is made between tangible fixed assets and intangible fixed assets.

❏   Tangible fixed assets are those physical assets that can be valued such as land and buildings, plant and machinery, equipment, vehicles, furniture and fittings.

❏   Intangible fixed assets are not physical, they are not located in a specific place and will include such items as goodwill and patents and trademarks.

Purchased and non-purchased goodwill

There is also a distinction to be made between purchased goodwill and non-purchased goodwill.

❏   Purchased goodwill is the excess between the amount paid for a company as a whole and the net worth of the tangible assets and liabilities acquired. Since the end of 1998, accounting standards in UK require companies to capitalise goodwill and write it off over a period not greater than 20 years. Where goodwill and intangible assets are regarded as having an indefinite useful economic life, they should not be amortised but be subject to an impairment review.

❏   Non-purchased goodwill relates to the decision by a company to include a value for internally developed brands, supply chain, know-how or human assets onto the balance sheet. *Rank Hovis McDougal* were the first company in the UK to include the value of brands into their balance sheet. They valued their brands at approximately £600 million – this had the effect of nearly doubling the asset value on their balance sheet. Recent accounting standards state that 'except when goodwill is evidenced by a purchase transaction, it is not an accepted practice to recognise it in financial statements'.

Prior to the end of 1998, the accepted practice was to write-off goodwill immediately on acquisition. This was consistent with the practice of not including non-purchased goodwill in the balance sheet. In other words, whether goodwill was purchased or internally developed it would not be included in the accounts.

Goodwill arising on acquisition

On the 30th April 200X, our example company acquired A Bunker for £350,000. The assets and liabilities acquired were as follows:

Fixed Assets	£100,000
Stock	£100,000
Debtors	£200,000
Creditors	£250,000

How much is the goodwill arising on acquisition?

Table 3.11 Calculation of Goodwill

	£'000	£'000
Purchase price		350
Fixed Assets	100	
Stock	100	
Debtors	200	
less Creditors	250	
Net Assets Acquired		150
Goodwill Arising on Acquisition		200

The effect on the balance sheet is shown in *Table 3.12*. We show the first balance sheet after the adjustment for revaluation but before any adjustment for purchased goodwill. We will then show the effect of the acquisition on the balance sheet while capitalising goodwill i.e. entering goodwill on the balance sheet.

Table 3.12   Balance Sheet – Effect of Purchased Goodwill Capitalised

---

CLOSING BALANCE SHEET (*after revaluation taken from Table 3.10*)

ASSETS	£	LIABILITIES	£
Fixed Assets	500,000	Issued Share Capital	100,000
less depreciation	80,000	Revaluation Reserve	300,000
Net Book Value (NBV)	420,000	Profit and Loss Account	470,000
			870,000
Current Assets	1,050,000	Current Liabilities	600,000
	1,470,000		1,470,000

REVISED CLOSING BALANCE SHEET (*with purchase and goodwill*)

ASSETS	£	LIABILITIES	£
Fixed Assets:		Issued Share Capital	100,000
Tangible	600,000	Revaluation Reserve	300,000
less depreciation	80,000	Profit and Loss Account	470,000
Net Book Value (NBV)	520,000		870,000
Intangible	200,000		
	720,000		
Current Assets	1,000,000	Current Liabilities	850,000
	1,720,000		1,720,000

Notes:

1. Fixed assets £500,000 + £100,000 = £600,000, therefore the net book value is £520,000.

2. Goodwill is included in the balance sheet (as an intangible asset) and will be written off over the period of its economic useful life. This means that the balance sheet looks stronger but there will be a charge against the profit and loss account each year until written–off.

3. Current assets. We take the opening £1,050,000 balance, add the acquired stock and debtors and deduct the purchase price for the acquisition (assuming that it was paid by cash or cheque) = (£1,050,000 + £100,000 + £200,000 – £350,000) = £1,000,000.

4. No change to the profit and loss account at the time of acquisition.

5. Current liabilities. We take the opening balance of £600,000 and add the acquired creditor balances of £250,000 to give £850,000.

3.3 Current Asset Adjustments

We will concentrate our discussion on two of the main elements which form part of the current assets section of the balance sheet. These are:

1. Stock, including methods of valuation and the effect on the profit and loss account.

2. Debtors, including debtor age analysis, the treatment of bad debts, provision for bad and doubtful debts and sundry debtors or prepayments.

1. Stock

The term stock is used to describe goods available for sale in the normal course of a business. In a manufacturing company it will also include work-in-progress and raw materials. A single value for stock is shown in the current assets section of the balance sheet with a breakdown (if necessary) shown in a note to the accounts. This value represents the closing stock of the business at the end of the accounting period. By default, the closing stock then becomes the opening stock for the next accounting period.

Perhaps the single most contentious issue with stock is the valuation. We will describe a number of the commonly used methods and show the impact a change in the valuation of stock has on the 'apparent' profits of a business. The following methods of valuation will be covered:

1. **First in first out (FIFO)**. Using this method stock is issued at the oldest price. This means that any closing stock will be valued at the latest prices.

2. **Last in first out (LIFO)**. Using this method stock is issued at the latest price. This means that any closing stock will be valued at the earliest prices.

3. **Average price**. Using this method stock is issued at an average price which will normally be recalculated each time a consignment of stock is received. Average price will tend to value closing stock at latest prices since the 'changing' average will 'drop' earliest prices.

Example – Stock Valuation Methods

A company is considering the method they will use for stock valuation. The following data has been collected:

Sales for the year £116,250,

Purchases in	January	2,000 units at £16.00 per unit
	June	2,600 units at £20.00 per unit
	November	1,200 units at £21.00 per unit

There was no opening stock

Closing stock 1,550 units

Table 3.13   Comparison of Stock Valuation Methods

	FIFO		Average		LIFO	
	£	£	£	£	£	£
Sales for Period		116,250		116,250		116,250
Opening Stock	0		0		0	
+ Purchases †	109,200		109,200		109,200	
	109,200		109,200		109,200	
– Closing Stock ‡	32,200		29,187		24,800	
= Cost of Sales		77,000		80,014		84,400
Gross Profit		39,250		36,237		31,850

† Purchases for the period are calculated as follows:

(2,000 x £16) + (2,600 x £20) + (1,200 x £21) = **£109,200**

‡ Closing Stock at the end of the period is calculated as follows:

FIFO	Latest purchase	1,200 x £21.00	=	£25,200		
	Next latest purchase	350 x £20.00	=	£7,000	=	**£32,200**

Average Cost £109,200 ÷ 5,800 units = £18.83 x 1,550 units = **£29,187**

LIFO	Opening Stock	0	0	0		
	Next latest purchase	1,550 x £16.00		£24,800	=	**£24,800**

2. Debtors

Trading with customers and allowing credit transactions will inevitably lead to a number of bad debts. However, an effective system of credit control will help to minimise bad debts. In this section we will cover the following:

1. Preparation of and Age Analysis of Debtor accounts.

2. The accounting treatment for writing off Bad Debts.

3. The accounting treatment for making a Provision for Doubtful Debts.

1. Age Analysis of Debtor Accounts

The assessment and control of bad and doubtful debts is an integral part of a credit control system. On a regular basis, and as a routine, debtor balances are assessed against the number of days outstanding. This means allocating part or the whole of the balance of a debtor's account into specific time periods. It is then possible to determine, for example, those accounts over a certain time period with a view to take immediate action. An example is shown in *Table 3.14*.

Table 3.14 Age Analysis of Debtors

	Total £	31 – 60 £	61 – 90 £	over 90 £	Action
A. Able	60,000				
Acorn Partnership	20,000		20,000		Review credit
B. Ball and Co.	150,000	20,000	40,000	30,000	Review credit
Bottle Ltd	10,000			10,000	Court action pending
Bunce Plc	350,000	100,000	100,000		
Calder and Sons	25,000				
Candy Stores Ltd	10,000				
Cookside B.C.	30,000		20,000		Review credit
....					
....					
Total	6,200,000	3,200,000	500,000	140,000	

From the totals above and the comments it might be thought prudent to make a provision of 2.25% of Debtors i.e. £140,000 ÷ £6,200,000 x 100.

2. Bad Debts Written Off

A debt is bad and will be written off when a company considers that it is unlikely to receive payment against the debt. The procedure is as follows:

1. Clear out any outstanding balance on individual debtor accounts into a Bad Debts account. This process will continue throughout the year as debtor accounts are closed and transferred into the Bad Debts account. Should the debt be recovered this process will be reversed.

2. At the end of the accounting period the balance on the Bad Debts account is transferred, as a cost, to the profit and loss account; the effect being to reduce the profit for the period.

3. Also at the year end it may be necessary to write off further Bad Debts. In this case we would have to increase the amount being written-off in the profit and loss account and deduct the additional bad debts from the debtor balance in the closing balance sheet.

3. Provision for Doubtful Debts

Throughout the year an assessment is made of each debtor account to consider the actions which must be taken to ensure prompt and timely payment on each account.

At the end of an accounting period an assessment is made of each debtor account to consider the collectability of the remaining balances. A provision for doubtful debts simply recognises the fact that not all debtor balances offer the same opportunity for payment. The provision takes a conservative view of all debtor balances and recognises the accounting principle of prudence.

The provision for doubtful debts will change each year depending on the collectability of the remaining balances and the economic environment, for example, if the economy is booming then there is less likelihood of default from payment of a debt.

Once the amount of the provision has been determined, the increase (or decrease) in the provision (from the previous year) will be taken into the Profit and Loss account, thereby reducing the profit for the period. The new provision will be deducted from the Debtor figure in the current assets section of the balance sheet.

3.   Prepayments (paid in advance)

Prepayments, i.e. amounts paid in advance, relate to expenditure incurred on goods or services for future benefit, which is to be charged to future operating periods.   Examples include; fire insurance, rent/rates, vehicle taxes paid in advance, payment for goods in advance.   At the end of the accounting period prepayments are in effect sundry debtors; they owe the company a product or service which will not be 'received' until (usually) the next account period.

Prepayments are deducted from the expense/cost in the Profit and Loss account and added into the Current Asset section of the balance sheet at the end of the period in which they are incurred.

Example

The Fire Insurance account shows an opening balance of £210, representing fire insurance paid in advance and covering the period 1st Jan 1999 to 31st March 1999.   Further payments were made for fire insurance in advance covering six monthly periods as follows, 1st April £480 and 1st October £500.

In this example we have an opening balance, i.e. at the end of the previous year £210 had been paid for a future period.   Similarly, at the end of this period £500 of fire insurance has been paid for the period 1st October 1999 to 31st March 2000.   Therefore, taking an equal amount, £250 relates to this period while the remaining £250 relates to a future period i.e. 1st January 2000 to 31st March 2000.

From the fire insurance account we would transfer (£210 + £480 + £500 − £250) £940 into the profit and loss account representing the fire insurance for the period. In the fire insurance account there would be a balance remaining of £250 i.e. at the end of the period, the fire insurance company was a sundry debtor to the company for three months of fire insurance.

The net result would mean that the cost of fire insurance would be reduced in the profit and loss account thereby increasing the retained profit. This would mean that the liabilities section of the balance sheet would be greater by the £250 reduction in the cost of fire insurance. We would have to include an item in the current assets section of the balance sheet as a sundry debtor to record the prepayment of fire insurance.

3.4   Long-Term Financing

Share Capital

Share capital relates to various classes of shares that can be offered by a company. Those subscribing to the shares, or buying them on the open market are referred to as shareholders. The various classes of shares can be described as follows:

Ordinary Shares

Ordinary shares are the most common method of shareholder financing. At any given time, a company will have a maximum limit of authorised share capital that the directors can issue. This can be increased following approval at a company's annual general meeting.

Issued share capital relates to the number of shares that have been issued; a monetary value is place on the share by multiplying the number of shares issued times their nominal or par value. Nominal value is the price at which shares were originally issued.

Preference Shares

Preference shares normally carry an entitlement to dividend at a fixed rate per annum. Cumulative preference shares relate to an entitlement to have the dividend cumulate until the company is able to pay out a dividend on the shares. Convertible preference shares relate to an entitlement to covert the shares into ordinary shares, usually within a given time period and at an agreed conversion. It is possible to have convertible cumulative preference shares. Preference shares may or may not have voting rights. At time of liquidation of a company the preference shareholders will receive payment before the ordinary shareholders.

Rights Issues

Rights issues are normally associated with companies who feel they can raise additional share capital from their existing shareholders. The terms of the issue might be that existing shareholders can apply for additional shares, say three shares for every eight held; the offer price will usually be attractive, set at a price that is less than the market price. A rights issue is not available to the general public.

Bonus, Script or Capitalisation Issues

Bonus, script or capitalisation issues are normally associated with a restructuring of the capital of a business. If a business has been successful and built up reserves through profitable trading, revaluation of assets or simply through acquiring an additional premium on shares the directors might be advised to restructure the share capital. A bonus/script/ capitalisation issue are free shares offered to existing shareholders, say one bonus share for every share held. An example might be that a company's shares are trading at £4.00. If a shareholder currently held 100 shares they would be worth £400. When a one to one bonus issue is made the shareholder will now have 200 shares but the value of the share will reduce to £2.00 per share, therefore, 200 shares at £2.00 per share – still worth £400. The reality is that the reduction in the share price might not be to £2.00, it might be £2.20; also, more trading tends to be carried out when share prices are lower, therefore, the £2.00 share price should increase at a faster rate than the previous £4.00 share price.

This not the only reason for bonus issues. Perhaps the more pressing reason is the restructuring of the shareholder's fund. By offering a bonus issue (free issue) to existing shareholders the company can transfer amounts from accumulated profits, share premium or revaluations into share capital.

Share Premium

Share premium is the difference between the amount paid for a share and its nominal value. If a company has been successful it will not issue new shares at the nominal (or par) value. It would expect to obtain a premium on the issue. Company law requires that issued share capital is shown at its nominal value and any excess is taken into a share premium account. The share premium account is a capital reserve that cannot be readily distributed to shareholders.

Please note, we are not referring here to cash. This side of the balance sheet is the source of funds not the funds themselves. For example, if a company wanted to issue further shares the following might be observed:

Issue 100,000 shares at £3.00; Market Value is £3.50; Nominal Value is £1.00.

The company would receive £300,000 cash (ignoring any issue expenses).

On the liabilities side of the balance sheet we would add 100,000 shares at £1.00 into the issued share capital and 100,000 shares at £2.00 (the premium) into the share premium account.

Revaluation Reserve

Please refer to our discussion on page 59 and 60.

Profit and Loss account

When we refer to the profit and loss account entry in the balance sheet we mean the accumulated profits of the business. Again, they do not represent cash; they only give an indication how some of the assets of the business are financed. It might be better to look at the other way. Instead of retaining and accumulating profits over a period of time a business was to distribute all its profits. The following might be observed see *Table 3.15* if we consider two example companies, say Company A that retains and accumulates profits and Company B who distributes all its profits.

Table 3.15 Comparison of Retaining or Distributing Profits

BALANCE SHEET (Company A – Retains all Profits)

ASSETS	£	LIABILITIES	£
Fixed Assets	300,000	Issued Share Capital	200,000
		Profit and Loss Account	300,000
		Shareholders' Funds	500,000
Current Assets	700,000	Current Liabilities	500,000
	1,000,000		1,000,000

CLOSING BALANCE SHEET (Company B – Distributes all Profits)

ASSETS	£	LIABILITIES	£
Fixed Assets	200,000	Issued Share Capital	200,000
		Profit and Loss Account	0
		Shareholders' Funds	200,000
Current Assets	500,000	Current Liabilities	500,000
	700,000		700,000

In *Table 3.15* it can be seen that Company B has £300,000 less in the profit and loss account and therefore £300,000 less shareholders' fund. This means that £300,000 less has been retained in the company. The balance sheet of Company A looks much healthier than Company B: it has spent an extra £100,000 on fixed assets while retaining an extra £200,000 in current assets.

Shareholders' Funds or Equity

Shareholders' funds or equity is simply the addition of issued share capital plus reserves. If the business were liquidated and received book values for all its assets, paid off all its debts, the remainder would equate to the shareholder's fund or equity.

3.5 Current Liabilities or Creditors: amounts owing within one year

One of the main problems the casual user of published accounts finds is in some of the terminology used. For decades, the accounts prepared in the UK have referred to current liabilities (one of the main sections of the balance sheet). This term is still used in other countries, for example in the US. The 4th EC Directive required harmonisation of accounts across the EC. This resulted in the term – Creditors: amounts owing within one year to be used as the preferred term for current liabilities.

In this section we are only going to discuss the term accruals, which is often one of the components of current liabilities.

Accruals (due, not yet paid)

An amount relating to a period which has not so far been taken into account because they have not yet been invoiced by the supplier, therefore, not included in the accounting system and not paid. Examples would be, wages (due not yet paid), interest (due not yet paid), electricity (due not yet paid). At the end of the accounting period accruals are in effect sundry creditors; the company owes the supplier for a product or service for which no invoice yet recorded, which will not be paid until the next account period.

These amounts are added to the expense/cost in the Profit and Loss account and added to the Current Liabilities section of the balance sheet at the end of the period in which they are incurred.

Example

Wages for October 200X have been paid for the weeks ending the 7th, 14th, 21st and 28th and amount to £36,000. At the end of the period, two days wages are due (30th and 31st October) amounting to £3,500.

In this example, wages paid during the month amount to £36,000. Using accruals and the matching principle the wages for the period are £36,000 plus £3,500 accrued giving £39,500.

❑ The effect on the profit and loss account would be to increase the expenses for the period thereby reducing the retained profit for the period.

❑ Given the adjustment in the profit and loss account, there would be an automatic reduction on the liabilities side of the balance sheet. To complete the accrual, a similar amount has to be added into the current liabilities (or Creditors: amounts owing within one year) section of the balance sheet. Therefore, at the end of the period the employees would be a sundry creditor of the company relating to £3,500 of wages which were due (not yet paid).

Appendix A

1. Depreciation

Motor Vehicle purchased on 1st January 1997 for £80,000, 4 year life, assume no residual value. Show transactions in the accounts to 1st January 2000.

Motor Vehicles

Dr.						Cr.
Jan 1	Balance b/d	80,000				

Provision for Depreciation – Motor Vehicles

Dr.						Cr.
1997			1997			
Dec 31	Balance c/d	20,000	Dec 31	Profit & Loss a/c	20,000	
1998			1998			
Dec 31	Balance c/d	40,000	Jan 1	Balance b/d	20,000	
			Dec 31	Profit & Loss a/c	20,000	
		40,000			40,000	
1999			1999			
Dec 31	Balance c/d	60,000	Jan 1	Balance b/d	40,000	
			Dec 31	Profit & Loss a/c	20,000	
		60,000			60,000	
2000			2000			
			Jan 1	Balance b/d	60,000	

Profit and Loss Account for the year ended 31st December

Dr.			Cr.
1997/1998/1999			
Depreciation Motor Vehicle	20,000		

Balance Sheet as at 31 December 1999

ASSETS		LIABILITIES	
Fixed Assets:			
Motor Vehicle at cost	80,000		
less Depreciation	60,000		
Net Book Value	20,000		

2. Bad Debts (written off)

Assume that the following debts were written off during the year:

3rd April   D. Danger Ltd   £400

16th July   U.N. Welcome Ltd   £1,200

9th Nov   U. Dunnit Ltd   £600

D. Danger Ltd

Dr.					Cr.
Apr 1	Balance b/d	400	Apr 3	Bad Debts a/c	400

U.N. Welcome Ltd

Dr.					Cr.
Jul 1	Balance b/d	1,200	Jul 16	Bad Debts a/c	1,200

U. Dunnit Ltd

Dr.					Cr.
Nov 1	Balance b/d	600	Nov 9	Bad Debts a/c	600

Bad Debts Account

Dr.					Cr.
Apr 3	D. Danger Ltd	400	Dec 31	Profit & Loss a/c	2,200
Jul 16	U.N. Welcome Ltd	1,200			
Nov 9	U. Dunnit Ltd	600			
		2,200			2,200

Profit and Loss Account for the year ended 31st December

Dr.			Cr.
Bad Debts Account	2,200		

3. Provision for Doubtful Debts

From the following notes the entries in the Provision for Bad Debts Account, the Profit and Loss Account and the Balance Sheet.

❑ Opening provision for bad debts at 1st January 1998 is £500.

❑ Year ended 31st December 1998, Debtor balances are £83,000; adjust provision for bad debts to £800.

❑ Year ended 31st December 1999, Debtor balances are £150,000; adjust provision for bad debts to £1,000.

Provision for Bad Debts Account

Dr.					Cr.
1998			1998		
Dec 31	Balance c/d	800	Jan 1	Balance b/d	500
			Dec 31	Profit & Loss a/c	300
		800			800
1999			1999		
Dec 31	Balance c/d	1,000	Jan 1	Balance b/d	800
			Dec 31	Profit & Loss a/c	200
		1,000			1,000
2000			2000		
			Jan 1	Balance b/d	1,000

Profit and Loss Account for the year ended 31st December

Dr.		Cr.
1998		
Provision for Bad Debts	300	
1999		
Provision for Bad Debts	200	

Balance Sheet as at 31 December 1999

ASSETS		*LIABILITIES*	
Current Assets:			
Debtors	150,000		
less Provision	1,000		
	149,000		

4. Accruals (due not yet paid)

From the following, show the entries in the Wages Account, the Profit and Loss Account and the Balance Sheet.

❐   Wages for October 200X have been paid for the weeks ending 7th, 14th, 21st and 28th and amount to £9,000 per week. At the end of the period, two days wages are due amounting to £3,500.

❐   Wages for November 200X have been paid for the weeks ending 4th, 11th, 18th and 25th and amount to £9,000 per week. At the end of the period, four days wages are due amounting to £6,500.

Wages Account

Dr.					Cr.
Oct 7	Cash	9,000	Oct 31	Profit & Loss a/c	39,500
Oct 14	Cash	9,000			
Oct 21	Cash	9,000			
Oct 28	Cash	9,000			
Oct 31	Balance c/d	3,500			
		39,500			39,500
Nov 4	Cash	9,000	Nov 1	Balance b/d	3,500
Nov 11	Cash	9,000	Nov 30	Profit & Loss a/c	39,000
Nov 18	Cash	9,000			
Nov 25	Cash	9,000			
Nov 30	Balance c/d	6,500			
		42,500			42,500
			Dec 1	Balance b/d	6,500

Profit and Loss Account for the period ended 31st October

Dr.			Cr.
Wages	39,500		

Balance Sheet as at 31st October

ASSETS		LIABILITIES	
		Current Liabilities:	
		Accruals (wages due)	3,500

5. Prepayments (paid in advance)

From the following, show the entries in the Insurance Account, the Profit and Loss Account and the Balance Sheet.

❐ The Fire Insurance account shows a debit balance of £210, representing an amount paid in advance and covering the period 1st Januanry to 31st March 200X. Further advance payments were made for fire insurance covering six monthly periods as follows; 1st April 200X £480 and 1st October 200X £500.

Fire Insurance Account

Dr.						Cr.
200X				200X		
Jan 1	Balance b/d	210		Dec 31	Profit & Loss a/c	940
Apr 1	Bank	480		Dec 31	Balance c/d	250
Oct 1	Bank	500				
		1,190				1,190
200X+1				200X+1		
Jan 1	Balance b/d	250				

Profit and Loss Account for the period ended 31st December 200X

Dr.			Cr.
Fire Insurance	940		

Balance Sheet as at 31st December 200X

ASSETS			LIABILITIES
Current Assets:			
Prepayments (fire insurance)	250		

3.1   Equipment was purchased in January 1997 for £500,000 with an estimated economic life of 4 years and a residual value of £40,000. The company adopts a straight line method of depreciation.

❒   Show the entries in the accounts for the years ended 31st December 1997 to 31st December 1999 and bring down the opening balance on the depreciation account for 1st January 2000.

3.2   Equipment was purchased in January 1997 for £500,000 with an estimated economic life of 4 years and a residual value of £40,000. The company adopts a 40% reducing balance method of depreciation.

❒   Show the entries in the accounts for the years ended 31st December 1997 to 31st December 1999 and bring down the opening balance on the depreciation account for 1st January 2000.

3.3   Assume that the following debts were written off during the year:

4th March	Albert Doe & Sons	£900
18th Aug	Barney Brothers	£3,500
7th Oct	Jim Cunning	£1,700

3.4   Assume that the following debts were written off during the year:

19th Feb	Blight & Co	£3,300
6th May	B. Dreadenough	£800
15th Sept	Harry Hardup Ltd	£6,000

3.5   From the following notes the entries in the Provision for Bad Debts Account, the Profit and Loss Account and the Balance Sheet.

❒   Opening provision for bad debts at 1st January 1998 is £8,000.

❒   Year ended 31st December 1998, Debtor balances are £750,000; adjust provision for bad debts to £9,500.

❒   Year ended 31st December 1999, Debtor balances are £1,150,000; adjust provision for bad debts to £11,500.

3.6   From the following notes the entries in the Provision for Bad Debts Account, the Profit and Loss Account and the Balance Sheet.

❐   Opening provision for bad debts at 1st January 1998 is £1,600.

❐   Year ended 31st December 1998, Debtor balances are £145,000; adjust provision for bad debts to £1,200.

❐   Year ended 31st December 1999, Debtor balances are £180,000; adjust provision for bad debts to £1,500.

3.7   From the following, show the entries in the Wages Account, the Profit and Loss Account and the Balance Sheet.

❐   Wages for October 200X have been paid for the weeks ending 7th, 14th, 21st and 28th and amount to £25,000 per week. At the end of the period, two days wages are due amounting to £9,500.

❐   Wages for November 200X have been paid for the weeks ending 4th, 11th, 18th and 25th and amount to £26,000 per week. At the end of the period, four days wages are due amounting to £22,500.

3.8   From the following, show the entries in the Rent Account, the Profit and Loss Account and the Balance Sheet.

❐   The Rent account shows a debit balance of £2,000, representing an amount paid in advance and covering the period 1st January to 31st March 200X. Further advance payments were made by cheque for rent covering six monthly periods as follows; 1st April 200X £4,200 and 1st October 200X £4,400.

CHAPTER FOUR

SOLE TRADER, PARTNERSHIP and CLUB ACCOUNTS

4.1   Introduction

In this chapter we will cover the preparation of final accounts unincorporated bodies such as:

1.   Sole Traders

2.   Partnerships

3.   Clubs/Societies.

Each have similarities such as the Balance Sheet but they all have unique differences.   For example, Sole Traders and Partnerships are conducting a business for the purpose of making profits.   They differ in they way in which capital is provided, salaries determined and profits and risks are shared.   While a Club or Society is formed for the purpose of pursuing an activity to which members pay annual subscriptions and any other fees due; it is not formed for the purpose of making a profit.

The basic accounting transactions are the same for all types of businesses / organisations, it is only how ownership differs and the effect on capital and profits/surpluses.

4.2   Rules (what is included in each of the accounts)

When a Trial Balance has been completed, the next stage is to check every item and identify which account it belongs to (i.e. Trading Account, Profit and Loss Account, or Balance Sheet).   You will find it helpful during your early attempts to refer to the rules which follow, when preparing final accounts.

Trading account

Which takes in the Sales for the accounting period, and deducts the Purchases (adjusted for the difference between opening and closing stock).   The output from the Trading Account is the gross profit/loss for the period.

Profit and Loss account

Takes the gross profit/loss and adds any other sources of income (e.g. interest received, rent received, income received), then deducts the expenses and provisions for the period.   Expenses will include such things as, wages, rent, rates, lighting and heating, administration, distribution, marketing, computing, interest paid, audit fee etc. etc. Provisions are for those items where the exact amount and the date at which a liability will occur are uncertain; the two main provisions are for depreciation of assets, and for doubtful debts.   The output from the Profit and Loss Account is the net profit/loss before taxation for the period.

Balance Sheet

Is a statement (not an account) of the financial position of a company at a given period of time. It records all the fixed assets and current assets (i.e. balances the company **OWNS)**, and all the current liabilities and long term financing from shareholders and other sources (i.e. balances the company **OWES)**. Examples of the main Balance Sheet items include:

Fixed Assets	**Long term financing**
Land and Buildings	Owners Capital
Plant and Machinery	Current Account (Partnerships)
Fixtures and Fittings	
Vehicles and others	Long term Loans
Current Assets	**Current Liabilities**
Stock	Creditors
Debtors	Bank Overdraft
Short term investments	Current Taxation
Cash and Bank balances	

4.3   Sole Trader

In this type of business/organisation, the ownership and control rest in one person. They are entitled to any profits/losses arising but are also liable to the full extent of their personal resources for their business debts and liabilities. It is the least formal of all businesses since all decisions are made by the single owner. No need for formal agreements on how profits should be made or the amount of salaries/holidays to be given.

With a sole trader it is normal to operate on a single capital account. To this account is added any profits or losses and drawings are deducted to give a closing balance on their capital account.

Apart from the above, the final accounts of the sole trader are similar in most respects to that of a limited company.

We will now produce two examples of the final accounts for sole traders. The first with adjustments covering closing stock and depreciation, while the second example will include other adjustments such as salaries due, insurance paid in advance and the provision for bad debts.

Example – Sole Trader 1

The following Trial Balance has been extracted from the books of Albert Smith as at 31st May 200X.

	Dr.	Cr.	Reference
Purchases	135,000		TA 2
Capital		93,750	BS 40
Drawings	15,000		BS 42
Premises	45,000		BS 31
Marketing and Selling	9,000		PL 11
Debtors	30,000		BS 37
Opening Stock at 1st June 200X-1	18,000		TA 1
Depreciation of Vehicles		7,500	BS 35
Bad Debts	1,500		PL 12
Office Equipment	7,500		BS 32
Sales		225,000	TA 6
Wages and Salaries	30,000		PL 13
Heating and Lighting	4,500		PL 14
Depreciation of Office Equipment		2,250	BS 33
Creditors		22,500	BS 44
Discount Allowed	2,250		PL 15
Cash	2,250		BS 39
Bank	7,500		BS 38
Discount Received		1,500	PL 21
Vehicles	45,000		BS 34
	352,500	352,500	

Adjustments:

Closing Stock	£27,900	TA 3 + BS 36
Depreciation of Office Equipment	£750	PL 16 + BS 33
Depreciation of Vehicles	£5,400	PL 17 + BS 35

Required:

Prepare Trading Account, Profit and Loss Account for the year ended 31st May 2000 and a Balance Sheet as at that date.

You will notice that each line in the Trial Balance has a reference at the end. If we select Opening Stock you will see that it refers to TA 1; i.e. Trading Account, Location 1. Notice that all the locations in the accounts are numbered and they correspond to a line in the Trial Balance.

We use this system for the initial exercise in Final Accounts, to show that each line in the Trial Balance has a single location, also to help with an 'audit' trail for the reader/ student to follow. We will also use the double entry bookkeeping principles applied to the trading account and the profit and loss account. In the next chapter we will use a vertical layout.

The Trading Account is similar one company/organisation to another, provided that they are involved in trading activity.

Albert Smith

Trading Account

for the year ended 31st May 200X

Dr.					Cr
1	Opening Stock	18,000	6	**Sales**	**225,000**
2	add Purchases	135,000			
3	less Closing Stock	27,900			
4	= Cost of Sales	125,100			
5	Gross Profit c/d	99,900			
		225,000			225,000

Note: Many accounts are 'built-up' during the year and their balances have to be transferred either to the Trading Account or the Profit and Loss Account. This completes the double entry exercise and clears the accounts ready for the start of a new period. Below, we can see the Sales Account with a credit balance of £225,000; then the transfer i.e. debit the Sales Account with £225,000 and credit the Trading Account with £225,000. All other entries for the Trading Account and Profit and Loss Account would follow the same procedure; with only the Balance Sheet items remaining as balances in the accounts.

Sales Account

Dr.				Cr
6	**Trading Account**	**225,000**	Balance c/d	225,000

The above transaction is shown only for completeness and would be carried out automatically given that a company/organisation was using accounting software. For the purpose of completing final accounts from a trial balance we will assume that all the accounts have been posted i.e. balances cleared.

A tip. When entering a posting into the final accounts, place a tick against the item in the trial balance. That way, you will be able to see what has been posted and what remains to be actioned.

Albert Smith

Profit and Loss Account

for the year ended 31st May 200X

Dr.					Cr
11	Marketing and Selling	9,000	20	Gross Profit b/d	99,900
12	Bad Debts	1,500	21	Discount Received	1,500
13	Wages and Salaries	30,000			
14	Heating and Lighting	4,500			
15	Discount Allowed	2,250			
16	Depreciation of Office Equip.	750			
17	Depreciation of Vehicles	5,400			
18		53,400			
19	Net Profit c/d	48,000			
		101,400			101,400

When completing the Profit and Loss Account, start at the top of the Trial Balance and post each item in turn; then action each of the adjustments.

You will notice that any postings into the credit side will increase the overall profit, while any postings into the debit side will reduce the overall profit.

All the postings, line 11 through to line 15 just go 'straight in' i.e. no adjustments. In line 16 we action the adjustment relating to the depreciation of office equipment. Here we are entering an amount of £750 which is the annual depreciation charge. The posting is debit the Profit and Loss Account and credit the Depreciation of Office Equipment Account. Unlike the items in the trial balance that close the accounts, adjustments to the trial balance result in an initial entry and automatically affect the balance sheet.

A similar posting is required at line 17, Depreciation of Vehicles.

Albert Smith
Balance Sheet
as at 31st May 200X

	ASSETS					*LIABILITIES*	
	Fixed Assets:					Owners Capital:	
31	Premises		45,000		40	Capital Account – Opening	93,750
32	Office Equip	7,500			41	add Profit for year	48,000
33	less Depn	3,000	4,500		42	less Drawings for year	15,000
34	Vehicles	45,000			43	Capital Account – Closing	126,750
35	less Depn.	12,900	32,100				
	Current Assets:					Current Liabilities:	
36	Stock	27,900			44	Creditors	22,500
37	Debtors	30,000					
38	Bank	7,500					
39	Cash	2,250					
			67,650				
			149,250				149,250

After carrying out postings to the trading account and the profit and loss account
we should only be left with balance sheet items. In this balance sheet we are
adopting the layout; assets on the left and liabilities on the right hand side.   It
can be seen that the total assets equals total liabilities, hence, the balance sheet or
the balance sheet equation.

For the purpose of learning there is no right or wrong way of laying out a balance
sheet i.e. as above, *or* with assets on the right hand side and liabilities on the left
hand side, *or* in some vertical layout.

There are two areas of the above balance sheet that need some explanation. The
fixed assets section. We take Office Equipment (at cost) from the trial balance i.e.
£7,500. From this we deduct the accumulated depreciation to the start of this
year, as shown in the trial balance plus the annual depreciation charge entered
into the profit and loss account i.e. £2,250 + £750 = £3,000. Deducted from the
office equipment at cost gives a net value of £4,500. A similar process is followed
for vehicles.

In the top right corner of the balance sheet we show the Capital Account (opening
balance) taken from the trial balance. To this we add the profit for the period
then deduct the drawings for the period to arrive at the Capital Account (closing
balance) i.e. £93,750 + £48,000 – £15,000 = £126,750.

Example – Sole Trader 2

The following Trial Balance has been extracted from the books of Aymi Soft Toys as at 29th February 200X.

	Dr.	Cr.	Reference
Capital		57,500	BS 41
Drawings	9,000		BS 43
Premises	25,000		BS 31
Debtors	15,000		BS 37
Creditors		9,500	BS 45
Sales		150,000	TA 9
Opening Stock 1st March 200X-1	12,000		TA 1
Advertising	800		PL 11
Bad Debts	600		PL 12
Office Equipment	5,000		BS 32
Purchases	115,000		TA 2
Rent Received		1,500	PL 21
Salaries	15,000		PL 13
Insurance	1,500		PL 14
Returns Inwards	1,500		TA 10
Returns Outwards		800	TA 4
Cash	1,500		BS 40
Bank Overdraft		5,000	BS 46
Depreciation of Office Equipment		1,500	BS 33
Depreciation of Shop Fixtures		5,000	BS 35
Carriage Inwards	3,000		TA 3
Carriage Outwards	1,500		PL 15
Provision for Doubtful Debts		600	Adj.
Shop Fixtures	25,000		BS 34
	231,400	231,400	

Notes:

Closing Stock	£15,000	TA 6 + BS 36
Depreciation of Office Equipment	£500	PL 16 + BS 33
Depreciation of Shop Fixtures	£3,000	PL 17 + BS 35
Provision for Doubtful Debts, adjust to	£750	PL 18 + BS 38
Insurance paid in advance	£800	PL 14 + BS 39
Salaries due	£800	PL 13 + BS 47

We are required to prepare a Trading and Profit and Loss account for the year ended 29th February 200X and a Balance Sheet as at that date.

In this example we follow the same procedures, but introduce a number of additional items that require some explanation.

Aymi's Soft Toys

Trading Account

for the year ended 29th February 200X

Dr.						Cr
1	Opening Stock		12,000	9	Sales	150,000
2	Purchases	115,000		10	less Returns Inwards	1,500
3	add Carriage Inwards	3,000				
4	less Returns Outwards	800				
5			117,200			
6	– Closing Stock		15,000			
7	= Cost of Sales		114,200			
8	Gross Profit c/d		34,300			
			148,500			148,500

There are three additional items in the trial balance that affect the trading account.

Two of these relate to Returns Inwards and Returns Outwards. As their name suggests, Returns Inwards relates to goods returned to a company by its customers while Returns Outwards relates to goods returned to a company's suppliers. The treatment in the trading account is to deduct returns outwards from purchases and returns inwards from sales.

The third items is Carriage Inwards. Normal practice requires that where carriage inwards is shown on an invoice it is posted separately. However, some invoices don't show carriage separately. In final accounts, carriage inwards is assumed to be part of the cost of purchases and is added to purchases. On the other hand, carriage outwards i.e. delivery costs to our customers is seen to be an expense of the business and therefore included in the profit and loss account.

Aymi's Soft Toys
Profit and Loss Account
for the year ended 29th February 200X

Dr.   Cr

11	Advertising	800	20	Gross Profit b/d	34,300
12	Bad Debts	600	21	Rent Received	1,500
13	Salaries	15,800			
14	Insurance	700			
15	Carriage Outwards	1,500			
16	Depreciation of Office Equip.	500			
17	Depreciation of Shop Fixtures	3,000			
18	Provision for Doubtful Debts	150			
		23,050			
19	Net Profit for year	12,750			
		35,800			35,800

In the Profit and Loss account above, there are four items that require some explanation.

The first is Bad Debts; in the previous chapter we saw that when a debtor is considered financially unable to pay the outstanding amount on their account, the balance is transferred to a Bad Debts account. This account builds up throughout the accounting period and is transferred to the Profit and Loss account as an expense associated with the business.

Salaries: In the trial balance salaries paid amount to £15,000. A note to the trial balance states that at the end of the accounting period there are salaries due of £800. Therefore, the total figure is included in the Profit and Loss account i.e. £15,000 + £800 being the salaries for the period. The £800 salaries due will also be shown in the Balance Sheet as an accrual in the current liabilities section.

Insurance: The trial balance shows that £1,500 has been paid for insurance. While a note to the trial balance states that £800 of insurance has been paid in advance. Therefore, the net figure is included in the Profit and Loss account i.e. £1,500 – £800 being the insurance for the period. The £800 of insurance paid in advance will also be shown in the Balance Sheet as a prepayment in the current assets section.

Finally, the provision for doubtful debts. (For a review of the provision for doubtful debts please refer to the previous chapter). In a note to the trial balance we are asked to make the provision for doubtful debts of £750. We must check the trial balance to see if there is an opening provision; in this case there is a balance of £600. Therefore, the net figure is included in the Profit and Loss account i.e. £750 – £600. In the Balance Sheet we deduct the total provision i.e. £750 from the Debtors figure in the current assets section.

Aymi's Soft Toys
Balance Sheet
as at 29th February 200X

	ASSETS					*LIABILITIES*	
	Fixed Assets:					Owners Capital Account:	
31	Premises		25,000		41	Capital Account – Opening	57,500
32	Office Equipment	5,000			42	add Profit for year	12,750
33	less Depreciation	2,000	3,000		43	less Drawings for year	9,000
34	Shop Fixtures	25,000			44	Capital Account – Closing	61,250
35	less Depreciation	8,000	17,000				
	Current Assets:					Current Liabilities:	
36	Stock		15,000		45	Creditors	9,500
37	Debtors	15,000			46	Bank Overdraft	5,000
38	less Provision	750	14,250		47	Salaries due	800
39	Insurance Prepaid		800				15,300
40	Cash		1,500				
			31,550				
			76,550				76,550

In the previous example we discussed the treatment of fixed assets and depreciation; also the opening capital account through profit for the year and drawings to arrive at the closing capital account balance.

In the above balance sheet our attention will focus on the adjustments required in the current assets and current liabilities sections. A tip to help understand the additional items that must be included is to work through all the notes to the trial balance; each note *must* be included in the closing balance sheet.

At line 37 in the current assets section we can see the figure for Debtors i.e. £15,000. At line 38 we show the Provision for Doubtful Debts i.e. £750 and to the right the net figure i.e. £14,250. At line 39 we include the Insurance paid in advance of £800.

Finally, at line 47 we include Salaries (due, not yet paid). At the balance sheet date, the salaried employees are sundry creditors of the business.

4.4 Partnerships

In the sole trader we saw that he/she was the single owner of the business. In a partnership there are two or more owners.

A Partnership is defined in Partnership Act 1890 as 'the relationship which exists between persons carrying on a business in common with a view to profit'.

❑ Therefore a partnership is a relationship in business. It could be compared to a relationship in a marriage. The common thing being that partners have to work to maintain the relationship. If/when the relationship ceases to work it is important to know how the partnership will be dissolved. This is one of the main benefits in preparing a partnership agreement at the outset. We will outline the main features of a partnership agreement below.

❑ It is also concerned with persons carrying on a business in common. This requires a clear definition of the boundaries of the business, the duties of the partners and a common goal or purpose. Business in this context means 'every trade, occupation or profession'.

❑ Finally, with a view to profit. An important element in a partnership; for example, a social club is a number of people undertaking some activity in common but without the view to profit.

For those contemplating forming a partnership we would strongly advise that you seek legal advice. Unlike a marriage, which is supposed to be 'till death do us part', a partnership often has a limited life. For example, if two partners formed a business, where Partner A contributed most of the capital while Partner B contributed most of the skill. When successful, and Partner B had managed to build up sufficient funds, Partner B might question the need for Partner A. One of our advisers refers to partnerships as 'sinking ships'.

Partnership agreement

The partnership agreement, like insurance, does not mean much until something goes wrong. The agreement should be prepared by a solicitor and should set out the rules governing how the partnership operates. Among other things it should cover the following:

❑ Who the partners are and how much capital each should contribute.

❑ How the profits/losses should be shared between the partners.

❑ If interest is payable on capital accounts, current account balances and interest charged on drawings.

❑ Any partners who are entitled to salaries, including how the amounts should be determined.

❑ The formulae to determine the amount of drawings each partner is allowed.

Example – Partnership Accounts

In this example we will concentrate on the additional elements concerned with partnership accounts i.e. the Partnership Appropriation Account and the Partners Capital Accounts.

The following Trial Balance has been extracted from the books of ASF Catering as at 31st January 200X.

	Dr.	Cr.
Creditors		36,000
Sales		270,000
Purchases	201,000	
Debtors	9,000	
Equipment	81,000	
Opening Stock at 1st February 200X-1	27,000	
Overheads	21,000	
Depreciation of Equipment		21,000
Capital – Alastair		36,000
Capital – Susan		21,000
Capital – Fiona		12,000
Drawings – Alastair	15,000	
Drawings – Susan	21,000	
Drawings – Fiona	12,000	
Bank	9,000	
	396,000	396,000

NOTES:

Closing Stock	£33,000
Depreciation of Equipment	£12,000
Interest on Capital at 15% per annum	
Salaries – Susan	£9,000
Salaries – Fiona	£6,000
Profits/Losses shared – Alastair	5
Profits/Losses shared – Susan	4
Profits/Losses shared – Fiona	3

ASF Catering
Trading Account
for the year ended 31st January 200X

Dr.			Cr
Opening Stock	27,000	Sales	270,000
Purchases	201,000		
	228,000		
– Closing Stock	33,000		
= Cost of Sales	195,000		
Gross Profit c/d	75,000		
	270,000		270,000

ASF Catering
Profit and Loss Account
for the year ended 31st January 200X

Dr.			Cr
Overheads	21,000	Gross Profit b/d	75,000
Depreciation of Equipment	12,000		
Net Profit	42,000		
	75,000		75,000

ASF Catering
Partnership Appropriation Accounts

	Alastair	Susan	Fiona	Total
Interest on Capital (1)	5,400	3,150	1,800	10,350
Salaries (2)		9,000	6,000	15,000
Balance (3)	6,938	5,550	4,162	16,650
	12,338	17,700	11,962	42,000

Tutorial notes:

1. Interest on capital. A note to the accounts indicates that partners are allowed 15% on the balance of their capital accounts:

	Alastair	Susan	Fiona
Opening Capital	*36,000*	*21,000*	*12,000*
Interest on Capital at 15%	5,400	3,150	1,800

2. Salaries. A note to the accounts gives the salaries payable to Susan £9,000 and Fiona £6,000.

3. Share of Profits/Losses. The profit for the period is £42,000. From this we deduct the interest on capital £10,350 and the total of the salaries £15,000 to give a net profit or balance of £16,650. A note to the accounts gives the proportion each partner is entitled to i.e. 5 : 4 : 3.

	Alastair	Susan	Fiona	Total
Profit Sharing Proportions	5	4	3	12
Net profit or balance				16,650
Alastair £16,650 ÷ 12 x 5	6,938			
Susan £16,650 ÷ 12 x 4		5,550		
Fiona £16,650 ÷ 12 x 3			4,162	

ASF Catering
Partnership Capital Accounts

	Alastair	Susan	Fiona
Opening Capital	36,000	21,000	12,000
add Profit appropriation	12,338	17,700	11,962
less Drawings	15,000	21,000	12,000
Closing Capital	33,338	17,700	11,962

The Partnership Capital Accounts are similar to the Sole Traders Capital Account. Simply, take the opening capital and add profits/loss and drawings to give the closing capital account balance.

ASF Catering
Balance Sheet
as at 31st January 200X

Fixed Assets:			Capital Accounts:	
Equipment	81,000		Alastair	33,338
less Depreciation	33,000	48,000	Susan	17,700
			Fiona	11,962
				63,000
Current Assets:			Current Liabilities:	
Stock	33,000		Creditors	36,000
Debtors	9,000			
Bank	9,000			
		51,000		
		99,000		99,000

In this example we show the partners capital accounts as a single entry. An alternative method is to keep the capital accounts intact and use partners current accounts to add profits/losses and drawings.

4.5   Club/Society accounts

We now turn our attention to club/society accounts. These are common in sports clubs, leisure clubs, social clubs, debating societies; the main difference from the previous accounts being that they are run on behalf of the members for the members, not with the view to profit.

In many cases clubs/societies do not maintain full accounting records. Instead, they maintain a receipts and payments account which is similar to a bank/cash account. Other differences include:

There might be a bar account which is similar to a combined trading and profit and loss account. Here the view is to make a surplus to help fund other activities enjoyed by the members. All clubs/societies are required to prepare an Income and Expenditure account and a Balance Sheet. The Income and Expenditure account is similar to the business Profit and Loss account.

Example – Club/Society Accounts

In the example that follows we have an opening balance sheet and a receipts and payments account, together with notes. These take the place of a trial balance.

We will produce a Bar Trading Account and Income and Expenditure Account for the year ended 30th September 200X and a Balance Sheet as at that date.

Fellow Accountants Golf Society
Opening Balance Sheet
as at 1st October 200X-1

Fixed Assets:			Accumulated Fund:		
Premises		256,000	Opening Capital Fund		282,800
Equipment	37,050		add Surplus for period		25,200
less Depreciation	1,850	35,200	Closing Capital Fund		308,000
Current Assets:			Current Liabilities:		
Stock – Bar	12,800		Creditors – Bar purchases	8,000	
Subs. in arrears	7,200		Subs. paid in advance	4,000	
Insurance in advance	2,400		Sundry bar expenses due	800	12,800
Cash	7,200	29,600			
		320,800			320,800

Fellow Accountants Golf Society
Receipts and Payments Account
for the year ended 30th September 200X

Dr.				Cr.
Balance b/f	7,200	Wages		192,000
Subscriptions	184,000	Sundry Bar Expenses		4,800
Bar Takings	220,800	Insurance		7,200
Locker Rents	3,200	Rates		5,600
		Printing and Stationery		3,200
		Bar Purchases		163,200
		Balance c/f		39,200
	415,200			415,200

NOTES:

Wages including bar attendant	£11,200
Insurance paid in advance	£3,040
Sundry bar expenses due	£480
Subscriptions due	£4,800
Subscriptions paid in advance	£2,400
Bar purchases due	£4,800
Bar Stock	£8,800

Depreciation of Furniture and Equipment, 5% on a reducing balance

Fellow Accountants Golf Society
Bar Trading Account
for the year ended 30th September 200X

Dr.				Cr.
Opening Stock (1)	12,800	Bar Takings		220,800
Purchases (2)	160,000			
	172,800			
− Closing Stock (3)	8,800			
= Cost of Sales	164,000			
Wages − Bar attendant (4)	11,200			
Sundry Bar Expenses (5)	4,480			
Profit from Bar	41,120			
	220,800			220,800

Tutorial notes:

1. Opening stock is taken from the opening balance sheet.

2. Purchases: £163,200 (Receipts and Payments) + £4,800 (Notes) − £8,000 (Opening Balance Sheet) = £160,000.

3. Closing stock is taken from the notes.

4. Wages − bar attendant is taken from the notes

5. Sundry bar expenses: £4,800 (Receipts and Payments) + £480 (Notes) − £800 (Opening Balance Sheet) = £4,480.

Fellow Accountants Golf Society
Income and Expenditure Account
for the year ended 30th September 200X

Dr.   Cr.

Wages (1)	180,800	Subscriptions (6)	183,200
Insurance (2)	6,560	Locker Rents (7)	3,200
Rates (3)	5,600	Profit from Bar (8)	41,120
Printing and Stationery (4)	3,200		
Depreciation of Equipment (5)	1,760		
Surplus to Capital a/c	29,600		
	227,520		227,520

Tutorial notes:

1. Wages: £192,000 (Receipts and Payments) – £11,200 (Notes) = £180,800.

2. Insurance: £7,200 (Receipts and Payments) + £2,400 (Opening Balance Sheet) – £3,040 (Notes) = £6,560.

3. Rates: £5,600 (Receipts and Payments).

4. Printing and Stationery: £3,200 (Receipts and Payments).

5. Depreciation: £35,200 (Opening Balance Sheet) x 5% (Notes) = £1,760.

6. Subscriptions: £184,000 (Receipts and Payments) + £4,000 (Opening Balance Sheet) – £7,200 (Opening Balance Sheet) + £4,800 (Notes) – £2,400 (Notes) = £183,200.

   This is a particularly difficult adjustment. The diagram below shows subscriptions due at the beginning of the year. These would be collected and included in the £184,000 therefore have to be deducted; similarly, the £2,400 paid in advance is also included in the £184,000 and has to be deducted.

£7,200	**£4,000**	**£184,000**	**£4,800**	£2,400

7. Locker rents: £3,200 (Receipts and Payments).

8. Profit from bar taken from the Bar Trading Account.

Fellow Accountants Golf Society
Balance Sheet
as at 30th September 200X

LIABILITIES			ASSETS		
Fixed Assets:			Accumulated Fund:		
Premises		256,000	Opening Capital Fund		308,000
Equipment	35,200		add Surplus for period		29,600
less Depreciation	1,760	33,440	Closing Capital Fund		337,600
Current Assets:			Current Liabilities:		
Stock – Bar	8,800		Creditors – Bar purchases	4,800	
Subs. in arrears (1)	4,800		Subs. paid in advance (2)	2,400	
Insurance in advance	3,040		Sundry bar expenses due	480	7,680
Cash	39,200	55,840			
		345,280			345,280

Tutorial notes:

The preparation of the Balance Sheet is similar to Sole Trader and Partnership accounts. A tip, when you are given an opening Balance Sheet use it as a template to produce your closing Balance Sheet. Below we will restrict our explanation to Subscriptions paid in arrears and in advance.

1. Subscriptions in arrears i.e. due. This can be confusing, but subscriptions due is similar to a sundry debtor therefore, it is included in the current assets section of the balance sheet.

2. Subscriptions paid in advance i.e. prepaid. Again, these can be confusing. Subscriptions paid in advance is similar to a sundry creditor therefore, it is included in the current liabilities section of the balance sheet.

Exercise 4.1

Trial Balance as at 31st August 200X

	£	£
General Expenses	4,200	
Rent	8,000	
Motor Expenses	14,700	
Salaries	71,200	
Insurance	7,800	
Opening Stock at 1st September 200X-1	67,700	
Purchases	300,000	
Sales		536,300
Motor Vehicle	56,000	
Creditors		103,200
Debtors	81,800	
Premises	400,000	
Bank	28,000	
Depreciation of Motor Vehicle		22,400
Capital		464,500
Drawings	87,000	
	1,126,400	1,126,400

Stock at 31st August 200X was £99,200.

Depreciation of Motor Vehicle, over 5 years straight line.

General Expense due £500.

Prepare a Trading, Profit and Loss Account for the year ending 31st August 200X and a Balance Sheet as at that date.

Exercise 4.2

The Trial Balance as at 31st December 200X was as follows:

	Dr.	Cr.
Creditors		40,000
Sales		300,000
Land and Buildings	100,000	
Administrative Overheads	60,000	
Purchases	200,000	
Debtors	30,000	
Vehicles	20,000	
Opening Stock at 1st January 200X-1	30,000	
Selling Overheads	19,000	
Provision for Doubtful Debts		700
Trade Investments (at cost)	20,000	
Audit Fee	1,000	
Income from Investments		2,000
Cash	5,000	
Drawings	15,000	
Owners Capital		138,300
Interest Paid	1,000	
Bank Overdraft		20,000
	501,000	501,000

Closing Stock at 31st December 200X	£40,000
Adjust Provision for Doubtful Debts to	£1,000
Administration costs due	£2,000

Prepare a Trading, Profit and Loss Account for the year ended 31st December 200X.

Exercise 4.3

Trial Balance as at 30th September 200X

	£	£
Rent	31,200	
Insurance	6,100	
Bank Overdraft		250,000
Lighting and Heating	10,320	
Motor Expenses	39,200	
Salaries and Wages	97,000	
Sales		712,000
Purchases	400,000	
Sundry Expenses	16,120	
Motor Vehicles	70,000	
Creditors		165,000
Debtors	136,200	
Furniture and Fittings	79,200	
Opening Stock at 1st October 200X-1	219,400	
Buildings	545,000	
Interest Payable	15,000	
Cash at Bank	22,680	
Drawings	125,560	
Capital		685,980
	1,812,980	1,812,980

Stock at 30th September 200X was £199,200

Insurance paid in advance £600

Bad Debt to be written off £6,000

Prepare a Trading, Profit and Loss Account for the year ending 30th September 200X and a Balance Sheet as at that date.

Exercise 4.4

The Trial Balance as at 31st October 200X was as follows:

	Dr.	Cr.
Land and Buildings	100,000	
Machinery	110,000	
Purchases	190,000	
Rates	4,000	
General Expenses	30,000	
Loan at 10%		100,000
Wages and Salaries	40,000	
Bad Debts Written Off	1,000	
Distribution Costs	25,000	
Debtors	25,000	
Depreciation of Machinery		33,000
Opening Stock at 1st November 200X-1	40,000	
Bank	20,000	
Owners Capital		86,000
Sales		350,000
Loan Interest	5,000	
Creditors		38,000
Drawings	17,000	
	607,000	607,000

Closing Stock at 31st October 200X, £20,000

Depreciation of Plant and Equipment, 10 years straight line.

Prepare a Trading, Profit and Loss Account for the year ended 31st October 200X and a Balance Sheet as at that date.

Exercise 4.5

Smith and Jones are in partnership on the following terms:

1. Interest at 5% per annum is to be allowed on opening capital account balances.

2. Jones is entitled to draw a salary of £3,000.

3. Profits/losses are shared two thirds Smith, one third Jones.

In addition, the following balances have been extracted from the accounts on 31st December 200X.

	Dr.	Cr.
Creditors		34,800
Sales		103,200
Discount Allowed	1,800	
Cash	900	
Fixtures and Fittings	5,400	
Purchases	86,400	
Debtors	37,200	
Freehold Premises	30,000	
Opening Stock at 1st January 200X-1	27,600	
Bad Debts	1,800	
General Expenses	5,400	
Depreciation of Equipment		900
Capital – Smith		12,000
Capital – Jones		5,400
Repairs to Premises	1,800	
Drawings – Smith	1,800	
Drawings – Jones	4,800	
Bank Overdraft		48,600
	204,900	204,900

NOTES:

Closing Stock   £31,200

Depreciation of Fixtures & Fittings, 10 years straight line

Insurance prepaid (in General Expenses)   £300

Prepare Trading, Profit and Loss Account, Parternship Appropriation Account, Partners Capital Accounts for the year ended 31st December 200X and a Balance Sheet as at that date.

Exercise 4.6

Jim, Dougal and Rosie are in partnership on the following terms:

1. Interest at 12% per annum is to be allowed on opening capital account balances.

2. Salaries to be paid, Dougal £24,000, Rosie £20,000.

3. Profits/losses are shared between Jim, Dougal and Rosie in the ratio 3 : 2 : 1

In addition, the following balances have been extracted from the accounts on 31st July 200X.

	Dr.	Cr.
Creditors		64,000
Sales		516,000
Purchases	268,000	
Debtors	48,000	
Equipment	220,000	
Opening Stock at 1st August 200X-1	56,000	
Overheads	60,000	
Depreciation of Equipment		36,000
Capital – Jim		60,000
Capital – Dougal		40,000
Capital – Rosie		32,000
Drawings – Jim	36,000	
Drawings – Dougal	28,000	
Drawings – Rosie	20,000	
Bank	12,000	
	748,000	748,000

NOTES:

Closing Stock	£44,000
Depreciation of Equipment	£46,000

Prepare Trading, Profit and Loss Account, Parternship Appropriation Account, Partners Capital Accounts for the year ended 31st July 200X and a Balance Sheet as at that date.

Exercise 4.7

The following particulars relate to the B One Fitness Club:

Opening Balance Sheet as at 31st March 200X-1

Fixed Assets:			Accumulated Fund		125,000
Club House at cost	75,000				
Furniture and Equipment	37,500				
	112,500				
Current Assets:			Current Liabilities:		
Subs in arrears	2,500		Creditors	2,500	
Cash	13,750		Subs paid in advance	1,250	
		16,250			3,750
		128,750			128,750

Receipts and Payments Account for the year ended 31st March 2000

Balance b/f	13,750	Wages		63,750
Subscriptions	75,000	General Expenses		3,750
Social Takings	23,750	Insurance		2,500
		Rates		3,750
		Printing and Stationery		2,500
		Balance c/f		36,250
	112,500			112,500

NOTES:

Subscriptions due	£1,250
Subscriptions paid in advance	£750

Depreciation of Furniture and Equipment at 25% on reducing balance.

You are required to prepare the club's Income and Expenditure Account for the year ended 31st March 200X and a Balance Sheet as at that date.

Exercise 4.8

From the following Opening Balance Sheet and Receipts and Payments Account you are required to prepare the club's Income and Expenditure Account for the year ended 31st October 200X and a Balance Sheet as at that date.

Opening Balance Sheet 1st November 200X-1

Fixed Assets:			Opening Capital Fund		82,600
Club House		108,000	add Surplus for period		45,500
Equipment	22,750		Closing Capital Fund		128,100
less Depreciation	5,950	16,800			
Current Assets:			Current Liabilities:		
Stock – bar	5,400		Creditors – bar purchases	4,200	
Subs. in arrears	2,100		Subs. paid in advance	3,300	
Insurance prepaid	1,500		Sundry bar expenses due	1,500	9,000
Cash	3,300	12,300			
		137,100			137,100

Receipts and Payments Account for the year ended 31st October 200X

Dr.			Cr.
Balance b/f	3,300	Wages	72,000
Subscriptions	90,000	Sundry Bar Expenses	1,800
Bar Takings	58,800	Insurance	2,700
Locker Rents	3,600	Rates	2,100
		Printing and Stationery	1,200
		Bar Purchases	49,200
		Balance c/f	26,700
	155,700		155,700

NOTES:
Wages include £3,000 for bar attendant

Insurance paid in advance	£1,320
Sundry bar expenses due	£420
Subscriptions due	£1,500
Subscriptions paid in advance	£2,100
Bar purchases due	£1,500
Closing Bar Stock	£3,600

Depreciation of Equipment over 20 years straight line.

CHAPTER FIVE

FINAL ACCOUNTS OF LIMITED COMPANIES

LEARNING OBJECTIVES

When you have finished studying this chapter and completed the exercises you should be able to:

❑ Understand the requirements for the preparation of the main financial statements of limited companies.

❑ Prepare, trading account, profit and loss account, profit and loss appropriation account and balance sheet in vertical formats.

❑ Describe the main components of published accounts.

❑ Have an appreciation of the formats for UK published accounts and the extent of UK accounting standards.

5.1   Introduction

The following example shows the preparation of the final accounts of limited companies. First we will provide a set of rules to determine which items go in which accounts i.e. trading account, profit and loss account, profit and loss appropriation account, balance sheet.

In the second part of the chapter we will describe the main components of published accounts including the chairperson's statement, the directors' report, the auditors' report, accounting policies, notes to the accounts and historical summaries. This is a section that you will often refer to when using published accounts for assignment purposes.

Appendices to the chapter provide alternative layouts for published accounts together with a listing of UK Accounting Standards.

Final Accounts of Limited Companies

These consist of:

> Trading Account;
>
> Profit and Loss Account;
>
> Profit and Loss Appropriation Account;
>
> Balance Sheet.

5.2   Rules (what is included in each of the accounts)

When a Trial Balance has been completed, the next stage is to check every item and identify which account it belongs to (i.e. Trading Account, Profit and Loss Account, Profit and Loss Appropriation Account or Balance Sheet). You will find it helpful during your early attempts to refer to the rules which follow, when preparing final accounts.

Trading account

Which takes in the Sales for the accounting period, and deducts the Purchases (adjusted for the difference between opening and closing stock). The output from the Trading Account is the gross profit/loss for the period.

Profit and Loss account

Takes the gross profit/loss and adds any other sources of income (e.g. interest received, rent received, income received), then deducts the expenses and provisions for the period. Expenses will include such things as, wages, rent, rates, lighting and heating, administration, distribution, marketing, computing, interest paid, audit fee etc. Provisions are for those items where the exact amount and the date at which a liability will occur are uncertain; the two main provisions are for depreciation of assets, and for bad and doubtful debts. The output from the Profit and Loss Account is the net profit/loss before taxation for the period.

Profit and Loss Appropriation account

Takes the net profit/loss before taxation and adds any accumulated profits from previous periods (these could be referred to as *Reserves: Revenue:* Profit and Loss account). This gives the amount of profit which can then be appropriated between taxation, shareholders (by way of dividend) and the amount retained in the business (which will be the closing figure for *Reserves: Revenue:* Profit and Loss account).

Balance Sheet

Is a statement (not an account) of the financial position of a company at a given period of time. It records all the fixed assets and current assets (i.e. balances the company OWNS), and all the current liabilities and long term financing from shareholders and other sources (i.e. balances the company OWES).

Examples of the main Balance Sheet items will include:

Fixed Assets
Land and Buildings
Plant and Machinery
Fixtures and Fittings
Vehicles and others

Share Capital and Reserves
Issued Share Capital
Share Premium
Revaluation
Profit and Loss account

Long term Loans/Debentures

Current Assets
Stock
Debtors
Prepayments
Short-Term Investments
Cash and Bank Balances

Creditors: amounts owing within one year
Creditors
Bank Overdraft
Accruals
Taxation Due
Dividends Proposed

5.3 Example – Oak Limited

The Trial Balance of OAK Ltd as at the 31st March 200X was as follows:–

		Dr.	Cr.
BS	Vehicles (at cost)	130,000	
TR	Purchases	720,000	
TR	Sales		1,000,000
BS	Depreciation of vehicles		26,000
TR	Stock at 1st April 1999	140,000	
BS	Debtors	85,000	
BS	Creditors		44,000
BS	Long Term Loans at 10%	60,000	
BS	Share Premium		25,000
BS	Profit and Loss Account		25,000
PL	Wages	35,000	
PL	Rates	2,500	
PL	Heating and Lighting	5,000	
PL	Salaries	20,000	
PL	Administration Expenses	65,000	
BS	Furniture and Fittings (at cost)	18,000	
BS	Depreciation of Furniture and Fittings		9,000
BS	Bank balance	50,000	
PL	Provision for Doubtful Debts		3,000
PL	Loan Interest Paid to 30th Sept 200X-1	3,000	
BS	Freehold Property	200,000	
BS	Issued Share Capital		300,000
PL	Bad Debts Written Off	3,500	
PL	Directors Fees	15,000	
		1,492,000	1,492,000

Prepare a Trading, Profit and Loss Account and Profit and Loss Appropriation account for the year ended 31st March 200X, and a Balance Sheet as at that date.

The following notes are to be taken into account:
1. Stock at 31st March 200X, £150,000
2. Wages outstanding at 31st March 200X, £1,500
3. Rates paid in advance amounting to £500
4. Depreciation of vehicles over 5 years (straight line)
5. Depreciation of furniture and fittings, 5% on cost
6. Provision for bad and doubtful debts, adjust to £3,500
7. Dividend proposed, 50% of profit attributable to shareholders

The notes to the Trial Balance are essentially adjustments which have not been recorded in the accounts. This means that each note affects the Trading Account, OR the Profit and Loss Account, OR the Profit and Loss Appropriation Account AND the Balance Sheet.

OAK Ltd

Trading Account for the year ended 31st March 200X

	£	£
Sales		1,000,000
Opening Stock	140,000	
+ Purchases	720,000	
	860,000	
− Closing stock	150,000	
= Cost of sales		710,000
Gross Profit c/d		290,000

Check the extraction of each item from the Trial Balance and note where they are recorded in the Trading Account. You will notice that the receipts are listed on the right hand side (credit), while the costs are listed on the left hand side (debit). In this example, the receipts are greater than the costs therefore the resulting balance is a gross profit. The double entry is effected by recording the gross profit on the credit side of the Profit and Loss Account.

OAK Ltd

Profit and Loss Account for the year ended 31st March 200X

	Note	£	£
Gross Profit b/d			290,000
Wages	2	36,500	
Rates	3	2,000	
Heating and Lighting		5,000	
Salaries		20,000	
Administrative Expenses		65,000	
Loan Interest	8	6,000	
Bad Debts Written Off		3,500	
Directors Fees		15,000	
Depreciation Vehicles	4	26,000	
Depreciation Furniture and Fittings	5	900	
Provision for Doubtful Debts	6	500	
			180,400
Net Profit Before Taxation c/d			109,600

The entries into the Profit and Loss Account follow a similar pattern to those in the Trading Account. Many of the costs / expenses can simply be recorded, however, those items which are included in the adjustments need special treatment. We will now discuss each adjustment that affects the Profit and Loss Account.

Notes to explain items in the Profit and Loss account

We have allocated an additional note for the interest due on the long-term loans. For an explanation see note 8 below.

2. Wages Outstanding £1,500

To obtain the total wages for the period, we take the wages shown in the Trial Balance and add any wages outstanding (£35,000 + £1,500). This occurs when there are a number of working days at the end of the accounting period where wages have been earned but not paid.

3. Rates Paid in Advance £500

To obtain the rates for the period, we take the rates shown in the Trial Balance and deduct any rates paid in advance i.e. (£2,500 − £500). This occurs when a company pays rates which includes a proportion that falls into the beginning of the next year.

4. Depreciation of Vehicles

The provision for depreciation of vehicles is calculated using the straight line method over five years. The provision for the year is £130,000 divided by 5 which equals £26,000.

5. Depreciation of Furniture and Fittings

The provision for the depreciation of furniture and fittings is calculated using 5% on cost. The provision for the year is £18,000 times 5 divided by 100 which equals £900.

6. Provision for Doubtful Debts

The entry for the Provision for Doubtful Debts is as follows:

	Closing provision required (note 6)	3,500
less	Opening provision (from the Trial Balance)	3,000
		500

The balance of £500 represents the additional provision required. The transaction would be; debit the Profit and Loss account and Credit the Provision for Doubtful Debts account. Should the closing provision be less than the opening provision the transaction would be reversed.

8. Long Term Loan: interest at 10%

The entry in the Trial Balance for interest paid represents only six months interest. Therefore the calculation for loan stock interest for the Profit and Loss Account must include interest for the complete accounting period: £60,000 times 10 divided by 100 which equals £6,000.

OAK Ltd

Profit and Loss Appropriation Account for the year ended 31st March 200X

	Note	£
Net Profit Before Taxation b/d		109,600
– Taxation		0
Profit After Taxation		109,600
– Dividend	7	54,800
Retained Profit		54,800

7. Provide for dividend

Dividend is calculated at 50% of profit attributable to shareholders; £109,600 times 50 divided by 100 which equals £54,800.

In published accounts the trading, profit and loss and profit and loss appropriation account would be shown in a single vertical layout with previous year figures also given. It is simply called a Profit and Loss account and requires less detail than shown in this example. However, some of the detail can often be found in the notes to the accounts.

Earnings per share is another figure that is required to be shown in published accounts together with an explanation how it has been calculated.

OAK Ltd

Balance Sheet as at 31st March 200X

FIXED ASSETS	Notes	COST	DEPN	N.B.V.
Freehold Property		200,000		200,000
Vehicles	1	130,000	52,000	78,000
Furniture and Fittings	2	18,000	9,900	8,100
		348,000	61,900	286,100

CURRENT ASSETS				
Stock			150,000	
Debtors		85,000		
less Doubtful Debts	3	3,500	81,500	
Prepaid	4		500	
Bank			50,000	
			282,000	

CREDITORS: amounts owing within one year				
Creditors		44,000		
Accruals	5	4,500		
Dividend Proposed	6	54,800		
			103,300	
				178,700

Total Assets less Current Liabilities	464,800
CREDITORS: amounts owing after one year	60,000
Net Assets	404,800

Financed as follows:
SHARE CAPITAL and RESERVES

	Notes	
Issued Share Capital		300,000
Share Premium		25,000
Profit and Loss Account	7	79,800
		404,800

A Balance Sheet is not an account, it is simply a statement which records a true and fair view of the financial position of a company. We will now discuss some of the points which often need clarification.

1. Accumulated Depreciation – Vehicles

Accumulated depreciation shown in the closing balance sheet is calculated by taking the depreciation provision shown in the Trial Balance and adding the depreciation provision for the current year (£26,000 + £26,000) which equals £52,000.

2. Accumulated Depreciation – Furniture and Fittings

Accumulated depreciation shown in the closing balance sheet is calculated by taking the depreciation provision shown in the Trial Balance and adding the depreciation provision for the current year (£9,000 + £900) which equals £9,900.

3. Debtors

Debtors are taken at the value shown in the Trial Balance less the provision for bad and doubtful debts i.e. (£85,000 – £3,500) = £81,500. In published accounts, it is normal just to show the net balance for debtors.

4. Prepayments

Prepayments represent the amounts that have been paid in advance of an accounting period. They could be listed under a heading 'sundry debtors'. The prepayment in this example is the deduction of £500 from the rates.

5. Accruals

Accruals represent the amounts due but not paid at the end of an accounting period. They could be listed under a heading 'sundry creditors'. The accruals in this example are the addition of loan interest due plus wages due: (£3,000 + £1,500) which equals £4,500.

6. Dividend Proposed

The dividend proposed was included in the Profit and Loss Appropriation Account and must be recorded in the Balance Sheet as a current liability. The dividend covers the accounting period under review, but will not be paid until it is approved at the shareholder's meeting which could be a number of months into the next accounting period.

7. Profit and Loss Account

This represents the retained profit for the year taken from the profit and loss appropriation account plus the retained profits from previous years taken from the trial balance i.e. £54,800 + £25,000 = £79,800.

5.4 Main Components of Published Accounts

Public Limited Companies plcs, are required to published reports and file them annually with the registrar of companies. Most annual reports contain more detail than is required either by company law or by the stock exchange. The readers of published accounts range from shareholders who have a financial interest in the company through suppliers and lenders through to employees whose interest is in the continuity of employment. Most annual reports will contain the following:

a. The Chairperson's Statement.

b. The Directors' Report.

c. The Auditors' Report.

d. Accounting Policies.

e. A Profit and Loss Account.

f. A Balance Sheet.

g. A Cash Flow Statement.

h. Notes to the Accounts.

i. Historical Summaries.

a. The Chairperson's (or opening) Statement

According to the Cadbury Report on 'The Financial Aspects of Corporate Governance' (1992), this statement is the most widely read part of company reports. It is generally a review of progress of the company and its business environment over the past year together with some indications of the proposed direction for the company in the forthcoming year. Remarks by the chairperson will generally not be convertible into a forecast of the results for the company for the next year, although usually much of value can be gleaned from the statement in terms, not only of what is included (and excluded), but also from the tone in which information is conveyed.

b. The Directors' Report

In contrast to the Chairperson's Statement, the content of the Directors' Report is laid down by statute and, to a lesser extent, by the requirements of the Stock Exchange for listed companies. Furthermore, the auditors are required to comment in their report if any information given in the Directors' Report is not, in their opinion, consistent with the company's accounts. The main requirements of the Directors' Report is provided in *Table 5.1.*

Table 5.1   Main Requirements of the Directors' Report

❏   Principal activities and business review.

❏   Results and dividends.

❏   Changes in fixed assets.

❏   Changes in share capital

❏   Names of directors, any movements, and details of their shareholdings.

❏   Research and development activities.

❏   A fair review of the year's business, and the end–of–year position.

❏   Likely future developments.

❏   Any important events since the year–end.

❏   Charitable and political contributions.

---

c. Auditors' Report

By law, every limited liability company is required to appoint at each annual general meeting an auditor (or auditors) to hold office from the conclusion of that meeting until the conclusion of the next AGM. The auditors are required to report to the shareholders on the accounts examined and laid before the company in a general meeting. It is important to understand that there is no responsibility as an auditor for the efficiency or otherwise of the business. Specifically, the auditors appointed by the shareholders have historically been required to report to them whether in their opinion:

❏   the balance sheet gives a true and fair view of the company's affairs;

❏   the profit and loss account gives a true and fair view of the profit or loss for the year, and;

❏   the accounts give the information required by the Companies Acts in the manner required.

d. Accounting Policies

As already discussed, SSAP 2 requires companies to include details of their chosen accounting policies in their statutory report. They will include details of their policies in relation to:

❏   basis of accounting and consolidation;

❏   fixed assets and depreciation;

❏   stocks;

❏   pension contributions;

❏   deferred taxation;

❏   foreign currencies;

❏   goodwill;

❏   leases.

e.   Published Profit and Loss Account

In the case of the published profit and loss account, companies do have an element of choice as the Act (by virtue of the 4th EC Directive) provides two horizontal and two vertical alternatives. The main difference between the alternatives concerns the way in which costs are analysed. The form frequently encountered is illustrated in the consolidated profit and loss account in *Table 5.2*.

The profit and loss account, in this case consolidated to show the effect on profit for the companies comprising the group, is characterised by 'layers' of profit, similar to those discussed in *Chapter 1*. The last item, the transfer to/(from) reserves is found by using the following 9 steps:

1   Add together all of the companies' revenue to obtain sales (turnover) for the group.

2   Add any other income to sales to obtain total revenue.

3   Add together the companies' costs of sales.

4   Add together the companies' distribution and selling and administrative costs.

5   Subtract the cost of sales and costs in 4. from total revenue to obtain operating profit for the group.

6   Subtract any interest payable by the group (from loans and overdrafts) from operating profit to obtain profit before taxation for the group.

7   Subtract the tax the group has to pay from profit before taxation to obtain group profit after taxation.

8   Subtract any extraordinary item to obtain the profit attributable to shareholders.

9   Subtract dividends to determine the retained profits to transfer to/(from) reserves.

Table 5.2 Published Consolidated Profit and Loss Account

CONSOLIDATED PROFIT AND LOSS ACCOUNT
for the year ended 31st December 200X

	200X £'000	200X-1 £'000
Sales	29,000	26,000
Cost of Sales	−21,000	−20,000
GROSS PROFIT	8,000	6,000
Distribution and Selling Cost	−2,700	−2,000
Administration Expenses	−3,000	−3,000
OPERATING PROFIT	2,300	1,000
Interest Payable	−300	−600
PROFIT/(LOSS) ON ORDINARY ACTIVITIES BEFORE TAX	2,000	400
Taxation	−700	−140
PROFIT/(LOSS) ON ORDINARY ACTIVITIES AFTER TAX	1,300	260
Dividends	−300	−100
TRANSFER TO/(FROM) RESERVES	1,000	160
EARNINGS PER SHARE:		
Undiluted	1.5p	−1.00p
Diluted	1.25p	

f.   Published Balance Sheet

Having considered the published profit and loss account, let us now consider the published balance sheet.

The balance sheet which is shown in *Table 5.3* consists of the following:

1.   The sum of all fixed assets within the group.

2.   The sum of all current assets within the group.

3.   The sum of all group liabilities falling due within one year, usually called current liabilities.

4.   Net current assets, which represent the difference between liabilities in 3 and current assets, often called working capital.

5.   Total assets less current liabilities, calculated from the sum of fixed assets and net current assets.

6.   Net assets, which represent the difference between total assets and all liabilities.

7.   Owners equity/shareholders' funds, which is the sum of the share capital and reserves of the group.

Table 5.3 *Published balance sheet*

CONSOLIDATED BALANCE SHEETS
as at 31st December 200X

	200X £'000	200X-1 £'000
FIXED ASSETS		
Tangible Assets	7,000	5,000
	7,000	5,000
CURRENT ASSETS		
Stocks	8,000	6,000
Debtors	7,000	6,000
Cash	7,000	3,000
	22,000	15,000
CREDITORS: amounts falling due within one year	10,000	6,000
NET CURRENT ASSETS (LIABILITIES)	12,000	9,000
TOTAL ASSETS LESS CURRENT LIABILITIES	19,000	14,000
CREDITORS: amounts falling due after more than one year	7,000	3,000
NET ASSETS	£12,000	£11,000
CAPITAL and RESERVES		
Called up Share Capital	6,000	5,900
Share Premium Account	4,500	3,900
Profit and Loss Account	1,500	1,200
SHAREHOLDERS' FUNDS	£12,000	£11,000

Please note that the contents illustrated in the consolidated balance sheets *Table 5.3*, may differ from some you will encounter in practice. Apart from differences in the nature of the business, which will affect mix and even types of assets and/or liabilities, there are other reasons, for example, where subsidiaries are not wholly owned, thereby giving rise to what are known as 'minority interests' (external shareholdings outside the group).

You will observe areas of similarity between published and internal balance sheets discussed earlier. However, one key point to note is that whilst the liabilities in published balance sheets are also separated with reference to the length of time of the obligation incurred, the following labels are normally used:

❏ Creditors: amounts falling due within one year;

❏ Creditors: amounts falling due after more than one year.

As indicated in the illustration in *Table 5.3*, the total in the top part of the balance sheet is calculated as follows:

FIXED ASSETS + CURRENT ASSETS – ALL CREDITORS = NET ASSETS

and that

NET ASSETS = OWNERS' EQUITY (SHAREHOLDERS' FUNDS)

The owners' equity/shareholders' funds comprises the sum of capital and reserves and is sometimes also referred to as net worth. This section includes all of the called up share capital of a company. In some company accounts, and indeed in our example company, you will find an item in the reserves called the 'share premium account'. This arises where new shares are offered at an issue price which is more than their nominal or face value. The nominal value of the new shares will be included in Issued Share Capital. The difference between the nominal value and the issue price is the share premium and will be credited to that account.

g. Cash Flow Statement

This statement is required to be produced by a UK accounting standard (FRS 1) and is also a US reporting requirement. The purpose of the statement is to provide an explanation of the sources from which cash has been generated during the year and how it has been used. The UK approach requires cash flows to be reported using the following standard headings:

❏ Operating activities.

❏ Returns on investment and servicing of finance.

❏ Taxation.

❏ Investing activities.

❏ Financing.

h. Notes to the Accounts

In its published form the profit and loss account is a summarised statement which can only provide a limited indication of how well a business has performed. In working with such a statement you will often want more information to form a more complete view, some of which will be found in supporting notes to the accounts. You will rarely find all of the information you wish because for competitive reasons companies are often reluctant to provide more than the minimum required of them.

Greater detail on all items contained within a profit and loss account are available from the notes to published accounts, the relevant note usually being cross referenced in a separate column in the profit and loss account. What form do such notes take? The following is an illustration of a note that might be found for earnings per share:

> *The Earnings per Ordinary Share are based on the profits after taxation and preference dividend of £1,800,000 (1998, loss £500,000) and 120,000,000 Ordinary Shares (1998, 100,000,000) being the weighted average number of shares in issue during the year.*

Other notes to accounts would typically include:

❐ Turnover and profit or loss for each different type of business.

❐ Turnover for different geographical markets.

❐ Details of net operating costs, including raw materials and consumables, depreciation, staff costs and auditors fees.

❐ Interest payable and receivable.

❐ Details of directors' remuneration, and employees with emoluments over £30,000.

❐ The average number of employees, total wages, social security and pension costs.

❐ Details of tax.

❐ Details of preference and ordinary dividends.

i. Historical Summaries

Historical Summaries are not a legal requirement, but have been provided by the vast majority of large companies since asked for by the Chairman of the Stock Exchange some 25 years ago. The usual period covered is five years and the more usual items included are:

❐ Turnover.

❐ Profit.

❐ Dividends.

❐ Capital employed.

❐ Various ratios such as earnings per share, return on capital, profit on turnover and assets per share. These have to be interpreted guardedly because, with the exception of earnings per share, there is no commonly accepted standard for any ratio.

5.5 Interim Reporting

Although the information provided in an annual report may be valuable, it becomes limited with the passage of time. More up-to-date information can be obtained from interim reports.

In addition to a requirement to produce annual reports, the Stock Exchange's Yellow Book, Admission of Securities to Listing, requires as a minimum the following to be provided on an interim basis:

❐ Net turnover.

❐ Profit before tax and extraordinary items.

❐ The taxation charge.

❐ Minority interests.

❐ Ordinary profit attributable to shareholders.

❐ Extraordinary items.

❐ Dividends.

❐ Earnings per share.

❐ Comparative figures.

❐ An explanatory statement to include information on any events and trends during the period as well as details about future prospects.

The whole interim report must be sent to all shareholders, or alternatively, it must appear in two national newspapers. Such reports are not usually audited and thus lack the authority and accuracy which annual reports appear to possess. There are no guidelines on the preparation of interim reports in company law or accounting standards.

APPENDIX A – Formats for UK Published Accounts

PROFIT AND LOSS ACCOUNT (Format 1)

Turnover
Cost of Sales
Gross Profit
Distribution Costs
Administration Expenses
Other Operating Income
Interest Receivable
Interest Payable and Similar Charges
Profit on Ordinary Activities before Taxation
Tax on Profit on Ordinary Activities
Profit on Ordinary Activities after Taxation
Dividends
Profit Retained for the Year
Earnings per Ordinary Share

PROFIT AND LOSS ACCOUNT (Format 2)

Turnover
Change in Stocks of Finished Goods and Work in Progress
Raw Materials and Consumables
Own Work Capitalised
Other External Charges
Staff Costs
Depreciation
Other Operating Charges
Interest Receivable
Interest Payable and Similar Charges
Profit on Ordinary Activities before Taxation
Tax on Profit on Ordinary Activities
Profit on Ordinary Activities after Taxation
Dividends
Profit Retained for the year
Earnings per Ordinary Share

CONSOLIDATED BALANCE SHEET (Format 1)

Fixed Assets

Intangible Assets

Tangible Assets

Investments

Current Assets

Stocks

Debtors

Investments

Cash at Bank and in Hand

Creditors: amounts falling due within one year

Net Current Assets

Total Assets less Current Liabilities

Creditors: amounts falling due after more than one year

Provisions for Liabilities and Charges

Net Assets

Capital and Reserves

Called up Share Capital

Share Premium Account

Revaluation Reserve

Appendix B – Accounting Standards

Standard Statement of Accounting Practice (SSAP)

SSAP 1   Accounting for associated companies

SSAP 2   Disclosure of accounting policies

SSAP 3   Earnings per share

SSAP 4   Accounting for government grants

SSAP 5   Accounting for value added tax

SSAP 8   The treatment of taxation under the imputation system in the accounts of companies

SSAP 9   Stocks and long-term contracts

SSAP 12   Accounting for depreciation

SSAP 13   Accounting for research and development

SSAP 15   Accounting for deferred tax

SSAP 17   Accounting for post balance sheet events

SSAP 18   Accounting for contingencies

SSAP 19   Accounting for investment properties

SSAP 20   Foreign currency translation

SSAP 21   Accounting for leases and hire purchase contracts

SSAP 22   Accounting for goodwill

SSAP 24   Accounting for pension costs

SSAP 25   Segmental reporting

Financial Reporting Statement (FRS)

FRS 1   Cash Flow Statements

FRS 2   Accounting for Subsidiary Undertakings

FRS 3   Reporting Financial Performance

FRS 4   Capital Instruments

FRS 5   Reporting the Substance of Transactions

FRS 6   Acquisitions and Mergers

FRS 7   Fair Values in Acquisition Accounting

FRS 8   Related Party Disclosures

FRS 9   Associates and Joint Ventures

FRS 10   Goodwill and Intangible Assets

FRS 11   Impairment of Fixed Assets and Goodwill

FRS 12   Provisions, Contingent Liabilities and Contingent Assets

FRS 13   Derivatives and Other Financial Instruments: Disclosures

FRS 14   Earnings Per Share

FRS 15   Tangible Fixed Assets (supersedes SSAP 12)

5.1   The Trial Balance of Aero Engineers Ltd as at 30th April 200X was as follows:

	Dr.	Cr.
Creditors		72,000
Sales		540,000
Land and Buildings	234,000	
Administrative costs	108,000	
Purchases	360,000	
Debtors	54,000	
Rent Received		2,000
Vehicles	36,000	
Opening Stock at 1st May 200X-1	54,000	
Selling costs	34,200	
Trade Investments	36,000	
Provision for Doubtful Debts		800
Audit Fee	1,800	
Income from Investments		3,600
Cash	9,000	
Profit and Loss Account		94,400
Issued Share Capital		180,000
Interest Paid	1,800	
Bank Overdraft		36,000
	928,800	928,800

Closing Stock at 30th April 200X, £72,000

Depreciation of vehicles, straight line over six years, residual value £6,000.

Interest due at 30th April 200X, £360.

Adjust provision for doubtful debts to £500.

Required

Prepare a Trading, Profit and Loss Account for the year ended 30th April 200X and a Balance Sheet as at that date.

5.2   The Trial Balance of Tru Systems Ltd as at 31st March 200X was as follows:

	Dr.	Cr.
Sales		1,890,000
Land and Buildings	819,000	
Interest Paid	6,300	
Purchases	1,260,000	
Issued Share Capital		630,000
Creditors		252,000
Discount Allowed	12,200	
Vehicles	126,000	
Opening Stock at 1st April 200X-1	189,000	
Selling costs	119,700	
Audit Fee	6,100	
Income from Investments		12,600
Cash	31,500	
Bad Debts written off	3,600	
Profit and Loss Account		318,000
Administrative costs	378,000	
Trade Investments	114,000	
Discount Received		22,200
Debtors	185,400	
Bank Overdraft		126,000
	3,250,800	3,250,800

Closing Stock at 31st March 200X, £252,000.
Further bad debt write off, £800.
Administration costs due, £2,900.

Required

Prepare a Trading, Profit and Loss Account for the year ended 31st March 200X and a Balance Sheet as at that date.

5.3   The following Trial Balance has been extracted from the books of Icandoit Ltd as at 30th June 200X.

	Dr.	Cr.
Creditors		144,900
Long Term Loans at 10%		147,000
Purchases	2,604,000	
Rent and Rates	157,500	
Sales		4,410,000
Trade Debtors	630,000	
Directors' Remuneration	115,500	
Income from Investments		8,400
Equipment at cost	882,000	
Accumulated Depreciation of Equipment		319,200
Office Expenses	102,900	
Issued Share Capital		420,000
Preference Share Capital at 8%		105,000
Dividend – Preference Shares	8,400	
Heating and Lighting	58,800	
Sales Expenses	114,800	
Bank	14,700	
Insurance	35,700	
Investments – Quoted	58,800	
Profit and Loss Account		277,200
Provision for Doubtful Debts		16,800
Stock at 1st July 200X-1	281,400	
Vehicles at Cost	168,000	
Accumulated Depreciation of Vehicles		84,000
Wages and Salaries	675,000	
Auditor's Remuneration	25,000	
	5,932,500	5,932,500

Further Information:
1.   Stock at 30th June 200X amounted to £325,500
2.   Depreciation is to be provided on equipment and vehicles at a rate of 20% and 25% respectively on cost
3.   Provision is to be made for Wages, due not yet paid, amounting to £25,200
4.   Rates paid in advance at 30th June 200X amounted to £6,300
5.   The provision for doubtful debts is to be made equal to 5% of outstanding trade debtors as at 30th June 200X.
6.   Corporation tax based on the profit for the year of £126,000 is to be provided
7.   An ordinary dividend of £40,000 is proposed

Prepare Icandoit Limited's Trading, Profit and Loss account and Profit and Loss Appropriation account for the year ended 30th June 200X, and a Balance Sheet as at that date.

5.4 The following Trial Balance has been extracted from the books of Rusty and Dusty Musty Limited as at 31st October 200X.

	Dr.	Cr.
Administrative Expenses	441,000	
Bad Debts written off	72,000	
Bank	63,000	
Creditors		621,000
Debtors	2,700,000	
Depreciation of Equipment		1,368,000
Depreciation of Vehicles		360,000
Directors' Remuneration	495,000	
Heating and Lighting	252,000	
Income from Investments		36,000
Insurance	153,000	
Interim Dividend	36,000	
Investments – Quoted	252,000	
Issued Share Capital (2,250,000 shares at £1.00)		2,250,000
Long Term Loan at 12%		630,000
Equipment at cost	3,780,000	
Marketing and Selling Expenses	270,000	
Profit and Loss Account		1,188,000
Provision for Doubtful Debts		72,000
Purchases	11,160,000	
Rent and Rates	675,000	
Sales		18,900,000
Stock at 1st November 200X-1	1,206,000	
Vehicles at Cost	720,000	
Wages and Salaries	3,150,000	
	25,425,000	25,425,000

Further Information:

1. Stock at 31st October 200X amounted to £1,395,000
2. A further bad debts write off amounting to £26,000.
3. Adjust provision for doubtful debts to 5% of outstanding trade debtors as at 31st October 200X.
4. Insurance paid in advance at 31st October 200X amounted to £27,000
5. Depreciation is to be provided on equipment and vehicles at a rate of 20% and 25% respectively on cost
6. Make provision for corporation tax of £540,000.
7. A final dividend of 6p per share is proposed

Prepare Trading, Profit and Loss account and Profit and Loss Appropriation account for the year ended 31st October 200X, and a Balance Sheet as at that date.

5.5   The following Trial Balance has been extracted from the books of Uaddit Limited as at 30th September 200X.

	Dr.	Cr.
Creditors		360,000
Sales		2,700,000
Land and Buildings	1,080,000	
Marketing and Selling Costs	540,000	
Purchases	1,710,000	
Debtors	270,000	
Equipment	360,000	
Opening Stock at 1st October 200X-1	270,000	
Administration Costs	171,000	
Depreciation of Equipment		36,000
Vehicles	180,000	
Audit Fee	9,000	
Rent Received		18,000
Cash	45,000	
Profit and Loss Account		387,000
Issued Share Capital		855,000
Depreciation of Vehicles		90,000
Provision for Bad Debts		18,000
Rates	9,000	
Bank Overdraft		180,000
	4,644,000	4,644,000

Further Information:

Closing Stock at 30th September 200X	360,000
Depreciation of Equipment	36,000
Depreciation of Vehicles	18,000
Bad Debts write off	9,000
Provision for Bad Debts	19,800
Administration costs due	32,400
Provision for Corporation Tax	58,500
Dividend 8% of Net Profit before tax	

Prepare Uaddit Limited's Trading, Profit and Loss account and Profit and Loss Appropriation account for the year ended 30th September 200X, and a Balance Sheet as at that date.

5.6 The following Trial Balance has been extracted from the books of Horace and Doris Morris Limited as at 28th February 200X.

	Dr.	Cr.
Advertising	90,000	
Bank	21,000	
Creditors		207,000
Long Term Loan at 10%		210,000
Trade Debtors	900,000	
Directors' Remuneration	165,000	
Electricity	84,000	
Insurance	51,000	
Investments – Quoted	84,000	
Income from Investments		12,000
Equipment at cost	1,260,000	
Accumulated Depreciation of Equipment		456,000
Office Expenses	147,000	
Issued Share Capital (750,000 shares at £1.00)		750,000
Interim Dividend	12,000	
Profit and Loss Account		396,000
Provision for Doubtful Debts		24,000
Purchases	3,720,000	
Rent and Rates	225,000	
Sales		6,300,000
Stock at 1st March 200X-1	402,000	
Vehicles at Cost	240,000	
Accumulated Depreciation of Vehicles		120,000
Wages and Salaries	1,074,000	
	8,475,000	8,475,000

Further Information:
1. Stock at 28th February 200X amounted to £465,000.
2. Depreciation is to be provided on equipment and vehicles at a rate of 20% and 25% respectively on cost.
3. Provision is to be made for auditors' remuneration of £36,000.
4. Insurance paid in advance at 28th February 200X amounted to £9,000.
5. The provision for doubtful debts is to be made equal to 5% of outstanding trade debtors as at 28th February 200X.
6. Corporation tax based on the profit for the year of £180,000 is to be provided
7. An final dividend of 10p per share is proposed.

Prepare Horace and Doris Morris Limited's Trading, Profit and Loss account and Profit and Loss Appropriation account for the year ended 28th February 200X, and a Balance Sheet as at that date.

BASIC FINANCIAL RATIOS

CHAPTER SIX

LEARNING OBJECTIVES

When you have finished studying this chapter you should be able to:

❏ Describe, calculate and interpret:

- Profitability ratios including return on total assets (ROTA), profit margin% and sales generation.

- Working capital or liquidity ratios, including current ratio and acid test.

- Gearing ratios, including borrowing ratio and income gearing ratio.

- Employee ratios, including sales per employee and profit per employee.

❏ Describe certain weaknesses in traditional ratios including profitability and liquidity.

6.1   Introduction

Performance measurement is a key issue for all organisations. Management needs to measure the results of its actions, not only in comparison to competitor organisations, but in relation to its past performance too. This is a difficult area since the amount, complexity and interpretations placed on data, both published and unpublished, have an infinite variability.

This chapter attempts to show a simplified route through this maze. By explaining the development and use of the most important ratios and the form which they are likely to be presented, you will be equipped with the skill necessary to take a critical view of an important area of company performance measurement.

One major challenge you will have to face as your career progresses, is to understand and make sense of internally generated and externally published financial information. In this chapter we will show how the sense of financial information can be achieved using ratio analysis, whereby one piece of financial data (e.g. profit) is expressed in terms of another (e.g. total assets), then the result of which is compared with the same ratio for another time period or another company.

It is possible to calculate any number of ratios and great care has to be exercised to ensure that an approach is adopted whereby only those which are relevant and essential are selected. This can be achieved in assessing profitability by adopting a hierarchical approach involving the calculation of a 'key' ratio and further related ratios. As we will show, the 'key' ratio relates to profit information from the profit and loss account and to the capital employed in the business in terms of assets to be found in the balance sheet. The rationale for its calculation is much the same as that for undertaking personal investment – you need to know how much return or profit will be generated in absolute terms but also how it relates to the amount of money to be tied up.

It is important to apply agreed rules regarding the specification of the various components of any ratio in a consistent manner and to interpret changes in the resulting ratios against previous levels, industry averages or simple benchmarks.

Our discussion of ratio analysis is not restricted to analysing profitability. We will consider other important areas of ratio analysis such as liquidity, financial structure (gearing) and employee based ratios.

We will reinforce the ratios to be discussed by using examples based upon figures taken from the profit and loss account and balance sheet illustrated in *Table 6.1*, together with some additional information.

Table 6.1 Balance sheet, and profit and loss account

Balance Sheet as at 31st May 200X

	£m	£m	£m
FIXED ASSETS (Net Book Value)			400
CURRENT ASSETS			
Stock		950	
Debtors		500	
Cash		50	
		1,500	
CURRENT LIABILITIES			
Creditors	425		
Bank Overdraft	675		
		1,100	
NET WORKING CAPITAL			400
TOTAL ASSETS less CURRENT LIABILITIES			800
LONG-TERM LOAN			120
NET ASSETS			£680
CAPITAL and RESERVES			
Issued Share Capital (at £0.25 per share)			130
Profit and Loss Account			550
			680

Profit and Loss Account for the year ended 31st May 200X

	£m
SALES	5,500
Cost of Sales	–2,850
Administrative Costs	–1,800
Selling and Distribution Costs	–600
Interest Payable	–140
NET PROFIT BEFORE TAXATION	110
Taxation	–40
PROFIT ATTRIBUTABLE TO SHAREHOLDERS	70
Dividend	–20
RETAINED PROFIT	50

Notes: *Number of Employees*   *35,000*

6.2   Profitability Ratios

In this section we will illustrate how the key financial ratio, Return on Total Assets (ROTA)% may be used as an analytical tool for gauging profitability performance at the business-level. Providing the necessary financial data is available it can be further subdivided so that more detailed analysis of a number of interrelated ratios can be calculated.

The data required for its calculation is shown in *Table 6.2*, which has been extracted from *Table 6.1*.

Table 6.2   *Basic Data for Calculation of Profitability Ratios*

	Latest year £'m	Extracted from
Fixed Assets	400	Balance Sheet
Current Assets	1,500	
Profit Before Taxation	110	Profit and Loss Account
Interest Payable	140	
Sales	5,500	

1.   Return On Total Assets (ROTA%) – The Key Ratio

Return on total assets ROTA% seeks to provide the answer to a very simple question 'What profit is generated as a percentage of total assets'? It is calculated by expressing Profit Before Interest payable and Taxation (PBIT) as a percentage of total assets. As a general rule, the higher the ratio the better.

For the example company, profit is taken before interest payable and taxation is £250 million (£110m + £140m). Total assets is the sum of fixed assets (excluding intangibles) plus current assets i.e. £400m + £1,500m which gives £1,900 million.

Using this information we can calculate ROTA% to give an indication of the return which a company achieves on its capital employed, sometimes referred to as return on capital employed, or ROCE.

Operating ROTA% $=$ $$\frac{\text{Profit Before Interest Payable and Tax}}{\text{Total Assets (excluding Intangibles)}} \quad \text{x} \quad 100$$

$$= \quad \frac{\text{£250 m}}{\text{£1,900 m}} \quad \text{x} \quad 100$$

$$= \quad 13.2\%$$

ROTA% may fall because of a decrease in profits and/or a increase in total assets. ROTA% can be affected by the accounting principles or policies adopted which affect both the profit calculation and total assets. You may recall that we demonstrated the effect upon profit of using different methods for depreciating assets in *Chapter 3*. ROTA% can also be used to show whether or not a company is likely to produce a higher or lower level profit per £ of total assets than it has in the past or relative to their competitors' or industry performance.

But what happens if the ROTA% calculated is lower than that generated in the previous year or by competitors? Is there any way of identifying possible reasons? The answer is yes. ROTA% is the 'key' ratio at the top of a business level ratio hierarchy which can be analysed in more detail by the introduction of sales from the profit and loss account. Introducing sales for the period of £5,500 million enables another level of interrelated ratios within the hierarchy to be calculated which is shown in *Figure 6.1*.

Figure 6.1   Hierarchy of business level profitability ratios

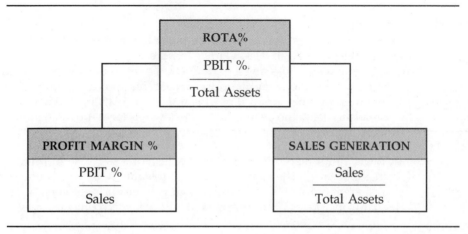

By expanding the key ratio we can see how the level of profitability is being achieved, which could be from a higher or lower PBIT as a percentage of sales, known as the 'profit margin' ratio, from a higher or lower level of sales to total assets, known as the sales generation ratio, or from a combination of the two.

2.   Profit Margin

The profit margin ratio gives an indication of the average profit margin achieved by a company. It is calculated by expressing profit before interest payable and taxation as a percentage of sales revenue.

Again profit is taken before interest payable and taxation (PBIT) which for the example company we have already calculated as £250 million. Sales revenue is taken from the profit and loss account in common with PBIT and is £5,500 million.

Using this information we can calculate the ratio to find the profit margin percentage.

Operating   Profit Margin % $= \dfrac{\text{Profit Before Interest Payable and Tax}}{\text{Sales}} \times 100$

$$= \frac{£250 \text{ m}}{£5,500 \text{ m}} \times 100$$

$$= 4.5\%$$

The ratio of 4.5% shows that the average profit margin across all the lines or products is 4.5% or that 4.5 pence of profit before interest payable and taxation is generated per £ of sales. However, the ratio can hide both high and low margins, and even loss making products. For example, the profit before interest payable and taxation may comprise a profit from product group A of £400m and a loss from product group B of £150m (£400m – £150m = £250m). Clearly, it is desirable to break the profit margin % down as far as possible to reflect the real underlying position, although this may often be difficult.

A lower profit margin% may arise because of a decrease in profits and/or an increase in sales. The expected value of this ratio will differ quite considerably for different types of businesses. A high volume business, such as a retailer, will tend to operate on low margins while a low volume business, such as a contractor, will tend to require much greater margins.

When comparing a profit margin ratio with previous years or against competitors, any significant differences in the profit margin% can be further analysed with a view to identifying likely problem areas. The following headings represent a checklist of areas for further analysis:

❑ Percentage growth in sales.

❑ Product mix from various activities.

❑ Market mix for profit and sales by division and geographical area.

❑ Expansion of activities by merger or acquisition.

❑ Changes in selling prices (usually only available from management accounts and not from published accounts).

❑ Changes in costs (major cost items are shown in published accounts).

The UK accounting standard, *SSAP 25* requires companies to provide an analysis of turnover and contribution to operating profit by principal activities. This information is found in the notes to the accounts as illustrated in *Table 6.3*.

Table 6.3   Analysis of Turnover and Operating Profit

Division (or Principal Activity)	Turnover (Sales)		Profit Before Interest Payable and Tax	
	£'000	%	£'000	%
A	2,200	40	75	30
B	1,320	24	85	34
C	880	16	30	12
D	880	16	40	16
E	220	4	20	8
Total	£5,500	100	£250	100

This table provides useful interpretive information. The overall profit margin we calculated as being 4.5%, and with this information we can readily calculate the PBIT margin made by each division. For a complete interpretive analysis you should obtain figures for previous years and industry averages, in this way you will be able to determine trends in turnover and/or PBIT by division (and/or geographic area).

Profit Margin: Analysis by Cost

The main categories of cost from the profit and loss account can be expressed as a percentage of sales, with a view to identifying those costs which require further investigation. The logic behind such investigation is that any cost reduction should, other things being equal, feed through to the profit margin% and therefore improve ROTA%. Do bear in mind that the profit margin% and associated ratios will vary from industry to industry. Low volume businesses are often reliant upon higher margins than high volume businesses such as retailing (e.g. a petrol station), which often operate on low margins such that cost control can be absolutely critical to their success.

In *Figure 6.2* we show how the profit margin% ratio can be broken down into subsidiary ratios such as cost of sales, administration costs and other costs. In practice, these subsidiary ratios would be those appropriate to the analysis being performed.

Figure 6.2   Profit Margin % – Analysis by Cost

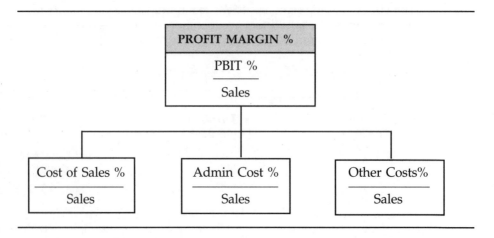

3.   Sales Generation ratio

The sales generation ratio shows the value of sales generated from each £ of total assets. It is calculated by dividing sales revenue by total assets.

$$\text{Sales Generation Ratio} \quad = \quad \frac{\text{Sales}}{\text{Total Assets}}$$

$$= \frac{£5,500 \text{ m}}{£1,900 \text{ m}}$$

$$= \quad 2.89 \text{ to } 1$$

The above ratio indicates that the company has generated £2.89 of sales for each £1.00 of total assets, and can also be calculated by division/principal activity if the information is available.

A low ratio could be due to a decrease in sales and/or a increase in total assets. As a general rule, the higher the ratio the better.

The sales generation ratio can be affected by increases or decreases in fixed assets, current assets and changes in the mix of assets. Increases in this ratio, can be achieved by an increase in sales and/or decrease of the level of total assets.

Sales Generation: Analysis by Asset

Figure 6.3   Sales Generation: Analysis by Asset

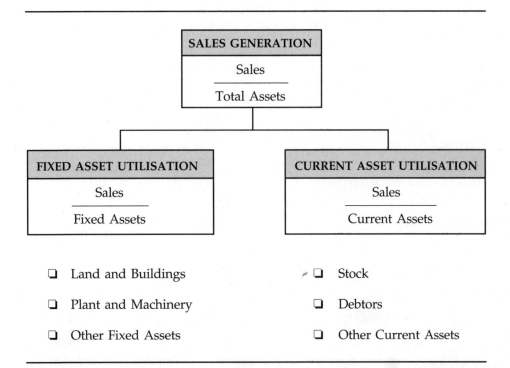

4. Profitability Ratios, Summary

A summary of the three profitability ratios is given below:

1	Return on Total Assets	13.2%
2	Profit Margin	4.5%
3	Sales Generation ratio	2.89 to 1

Changes in the profit margin % and the sales generation ratio will have direct impact upon ROTA%. Any improvement in either ratio should, other things equal, cause an improvement in the ROTA%

The importance of (Tests)

6.3 Liquidity (or Working Capital) Ratios

An analysis of profitability ratios alone is totally inadequate for obtaining a well balanced view of the performance of a company. While profitability is undeniably important, the need to achieve a satisfactory liquidity position is vital for survival. It is a fact that many companies which have failed were profitable but unable to maintain a satisfactory level of liquidity.

The data required for the calculation of liquidity ratios is shown in *Table 6.4*, which has been extracted from *Table 6.1*.

Table 6.4   Basic data for calculation of liquidity ratios

	Latest year £'m	Extracted from
Current Assets	1,500	
Stock	950	
Debtors	500	Balance Sheet
Current Liabilities	1,100	
Cost of Sales	2,850	Profit and Loss
Sales	5,500	Account

In this section we will describe four ratios designed to measure different components of liquidity within the working capital cycle. These are:

1   Current Ratio.

2   Liquid (or Acid Test) Ratio.

3   Stock Turn.

4   Debtor Weeks.

Figure 6.4   Working Capital Cycle

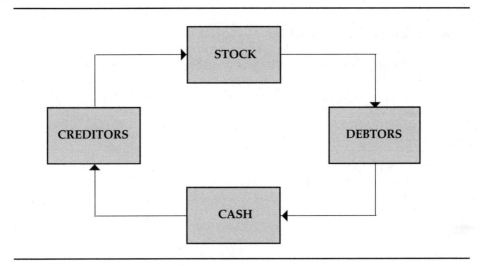

1.   The Current Ratio

The current ratio attempts to measure the ability of a company to meet its financial obligations falling due within one year. It is calculated by dividing current assets by current liabilities.

$$\text{Current Ratio} = \frac{\text{Current Assets}}{\text{Current Liabilities}}$$

$$= \frac{\text{£}1,500 \text{ m}}{\text{£}1,100 \text{ m}}$$

$$= 1.36 \text{ to } 1$$

For decades, the interpretation of the current ratio has suffered against the unrealistic rule of thumb that current assets should be double that of current liabilities for all companies. This implies that the proportions of current assets and current liabilities should be the same for a fast food company with small stocks and virtually no debtors through to the company undertaking a long term contract with high stocks, high debtors, creditors and bank overdraft.

A very low current ratio indicates potential difficulties, the determination of low varying by the type of business. A high current ratio is not necessarily a good sign; it could mean that a company had idle resources. For example, the current ratio would increase if a company were to increase its stocks or increase its debtors. Similarly, the current ratio would decrease if a company took actions to decrease its stocks or decrease its debtors. We cannot say whether these actions are necessarily good or bad, and care should be taken when attempting to interpret both the size of the current ratio, and the movements year on year.

2.   Liquid (or Acid Test) Ratio

The liquid ratio or acid test ratio attempts to measure a company's ability to pay its way in the short-term without having to liquidate stock. Simply it is the 'acid test' – can we pay our way? It is calculated by deducting stock from current assets then dividing the result by current liabilities.

$$\text{Liquid Ratio} = \frac{(\text{Current Assets} - \text{Stock})}{\text{Current Liabilities}}$$

$$= \frac{(£1{,}500 \text{ m} - £950 \text{ m})}{£1{,}100 \text{ m}}$$

$$= \quad 0.50 \text{ to } 1$$

What do we mean by paying our way in the short-term? For purposes of this ratio, the short-term is considered to be up to 13 weeks, and paying our way to mean that we can pay our debts as and when they fall due. It does not mean that every business needs to maintain the same level to cover all current liabilities.

In common with the current ratio, different liquid ratios apply to different industries. For example, in retailing it has become normal to find a level of around 0.25 to 1 cover for current liabilities. This is possible through cash trading, a high level of commitment from their suppliers and the fact that stock could be liquidated in time to meet maturing debts. Similar to the current ratio, if these companies maintained a higher level of cover for current liabilities there would be idle resources.

3.   Stock Turn

The stock turn ratio is a measure showing the number of times stock is 'turned over' on average in a given period (usually one year). It is calculated by dividing the cost of sales by stock.

In published accounts it maybe impossible to obtain a reliable figure for cost of sales. To maintain consistency we suggest that you take sales and deduct profit before tax, interest payable, selling and distribution costs and administration costs. In this example (£5,500m – £110m – £140m – £600m – £1,800m) which gives £2,850 million. Stock is taken from the current assets section of the balance sheet and will include raw materials, work in progress and finished goods. In this example it is £950 million.

Using this information we can calculate the stock turn:

$$\text{Stock Turn} \quad = \quad \frac{\text{Cost of Sales}}{\text{Stock}}$$

$$= \quad \frac{\text{£2,850 m}}{\text{£950 m}}$$

$$= \quad 3.0 \;\; \text{times}$$

A low stock turn ratio indicates that a company may be holding too much stock. The actual size of the ratio will depend upon the mix of stock held and the average holding in the industry. As a general rule, the higher the ratio the better.

If a company holds too much stock then there are potential disadvantages arising from the cost of holding stock, the possibility of obsolescence, and the cost associated with tying up additional working capital, to the detriment of other components within the working capital cycle.

4.   Debtor Weeks

The debtor weeks ratio shows the number of weeks on average that debtors take to pay their invoices. It is calculated by multiplying debtors by the number of weeks in the period, then dividing the result by sales revenue for the period.

If we consider calculation of the ratio for our example company, debtors is taken from the current assets section of the balance sheet, i.e. £500 million. Sales revenue is taken from the profit and loss account, i.e. £5,500 million. Using this information we can calculate the debtor weeks as follows:

$$\text{Debtor Weeks} \quad = \quad \frac{\text{Debtors} \ \times \ \text{Number of Weeks in the period}}{\text{Sales for the period}}$$

$$= \quad \frac{\text{£500 m} \quad \times \quad 52}{\text{£5,500 m}}$$

$$= \quad 4.7 \ \text{weeks}$$

The lower the debtor weeks ratio the more effective is the system of credit control and as a general rule, the lower the ratio the better. The actual size of the ratio will depend upon the mix of debtors between large, medium and small customers and the average holding in the industry.

A high debtor weeks ratio means that a company is allowing customers too much time to pay their debts. Other customers might follow by extending the time taken to pay. Furthermore, the cost of financing additional debtors, the possibility of increased bad debts, and tying up additional working capital often lead to detrimental effects on other components within the working capital cycle, e.g. a shortage of funds to finance stock requirements.

In addition to monitoring debtors weeks in aggregate, it is desirable where possible to undertake debtor age analysis to distinguish long outstanding debts from those that are more recent. For example, of the £500m debtors the following breakdown by age may be the case:

Less than 4 weeks,	£200m	40%
More than 4 weeks and less than 8 weeks	£250m	50%
More than 8 weeks	£50m	10%

It is recognised that the longer a debt is outstanding the less likelihood there is that payment will be made at all. For this reason most organisations will aim to decrease the proportion of long term debts outstanding as far as possible.

5. Working Capital Ratios, Summary

A summary of the four working capital ratios is given below:

1	Current Ratio	1.36 to 1
2	Liquid (or Acid Test) Ratio	0.50 to 1
3	Stock Turn	3.0 times
4	Debtor Weeks	4.7 weeks

6.4   Gearing Ratios

Businesses can secure finances from many sources, ranging from shareholders who are owners of the company to those who lend money to the business. One of the key distinctions between these two sources of financing is that, the interest payable on borrowed funds is deductible as an expense in calculating the tax payable. This is known as the 'tax shield'. Imagine a company with a £10m loan on which it is paying interest at 10%. The company's marginal rate of tax, is 25% and because of the deductability of the interest as an expense, the company will pay £750,000 that is 7.5% rather than 10%. The same does not apply, however, for funding from the issues of shares. In that case dividends are paid from after tax income and there is no tax shield.

From this you might be conclude that there is a distinct advantage for a company raising debt as opposed to equity. Depending upon relative rates of interest, this can be the case. By combining debt and equity, it can be shown that a company can lower the cost of its capital. However, there will come a point where increasing the proportion of debt to equity will be perceived as being a risk, first to new borrowers who might doubt the company's potential to service the interest and, second to shareholders who might be concerned at the very high level of debt relative to equity. As a consequence, beyond a certain level, it is generally thought that a company's cost of capital from taking on more debt will actually increase.

Thus, while there is an advantage in holding both equity and debt the relative proportions of each need to be carefully assessed for the risks involved. Hence we calculate 'gearing' ratios to measure the proportion of debt to equity and other measures to assess the firm's ability to service its debts from current profits.

As with other ratios there are different definitions of gearing depending on the interests of the users. In the following section we describe the two most popular measures of gearing: the borrowing ratio and the income gearing ratio.

1. Borrowing Ratio

The borrowing ratio is a very conservative measure showing the number of times total borrowings exceed equity. It is calculated by dividing total borrowings by equity (shareholders' funds).

Total borrowings is the sum of short-term loans (including bank overdraft) and long-term loans, in this example, £795m (£675m + £120m). Equity is the sum of issued share capital plus reserves, £680m (£130m + £550m). Reserves will include such items as share premium, revaluation reserve and profit and loss account.

Using this information we can calculate the borrowings ratio:

$$\text{Borrowing Ratio} \quad = \quad \frac{\text{Total Borrowings}}{\text{Equity}}$$

$$= \quad \frac{£795\text{ m}}{£680\text{ m}}$$

$$= \quad 1.17 \text{ to } 1$$

A high borrowing ratio simply indicates that a company has placed a greater reliance upon borrowing than equity to finance its operations. The higher the ratio the more highly geared the company is said to be. Although it should provide a higher return to its shareholders when the economy is experiencing boom conditions, during periods of increased interest rates, economic recession or simply loss of customers the opposite will apply. A company which has high gearing is particularly vulnerable and might find that it cannot continue to finance its borrowings.

2. Income Gearing

The income gearing ratio measures the extent to which interest payable is covered from pre-tax profits plus interest payable. It is calculated by dividing interest payable by profit before interest payable and taxation and expressing the result as a percentage.

Interest payable is taken from the profit and loss account, which for the example company is £140m. Profit before interest payable and taxation (PBIT) is the sum of profit before taxation plus interest payable, £250m (£110m + £140m). Using this information we can calculate the income gearing ratio as follows:

$$\text{Income Gearing} = \frac{\text{Interest Payable}}{\text{Profit Before Interest Payable and Tax}} \times 100$$

$$= \frac{\pounds140\ m}{\pounds250\ m} \times 100$$

$$= 56\ \%$$

The higher the income gearing ratio the greater the amount of available profit a company is liable to pay as interest. The income gearing ratio shows the effect of a company's gearing policy. For example, if a company increased its borrowings this would tend to increase the income gearing ratio. The income gearing ratio also shows the effect on a company of changes in economic circumstances. If interest rates rise or consumer demand fall, other things remaining equal, the income gearing ratio will worsen.

The income gearing ratio provides an indication of the ability to service debt commitments from profit. In the case of the example company, it can 'cover' interest payable just over one and three quarter times, that is the profit before interest payable and tax is 1.79 the size of the interest payable (£250m divided by £140m). When expressed in this form, the ratio is known as the interest cover ratio and is calculated as follows:

$$\text{Interest Cover} = \frac{\text{Profit Before Interest Payable and Tax}}{\text{Interest Payable}}$$

3. Gearing Ratios, Summary

A summary of the two gearing ratios is given below:

1. Borrowing Ratio   1.17 to 1

2. Income Gearing   56%

6.5   Employee Ratios

Organisations of all types try to ensure that they derive as much value as possible from the resources used. In many cases one of the most valuable, but also the most expensive of resources, is that associated with employees.

We illustrate four popular employee ratios used by a number of commercial organisations:

1.   Profit per employee.

2.   Sales per employee.

3.   Fixed assets per employee.

4.   Borrowings per employee.

1.   Profit Per Employee

The profit per employee ratio shows the £ value of profit before taxation (PBT) generated by each employee. It is calculated by dividing profit before taxation by the average number of employees.

In the case of the example company, profit before taxation is £110 million. The average number of employees is usually found in the Report of the Directors or in the notes to the accounts, in this example the figure is given, i.e. 35,000. Using this information we can calculate the profit per employee ratio.

$$\text{Profit Per Employee} \quad = \quad \frac{\text{Profit Before Taxation}}{\text{Number of Employees}}$$

$$= \quad \frac{£110 \text{ m}}{35,000}$$

$$= \quad £3,143$$

It is important to ensure that the average number of employees used as the denominator are stated in full time equivalents. In some companies, the average number of employees will include part-time employees working between say 8 and 30 hours per week. If this is the case then you should substitute aggregate remuneration for the denominator and express the result per £1,000 of employee remuneration. With employee remuneration given at £600 million the calculation would be:

Profit Per £1,000 $\quad=\quad \dfrac{\text{Profit Before Taxation}}{\text{Employee Remuneration}} \quad \times \quad 1{,}000$

$\quad\quad\quad\quad\quad = \quad \dfrac{£110\text{ m}}{£600\text{ m}} \times 1{,}000$

$\quad\quad\quad\quad\quad = \quad £183$

In the above example, the result is stated as £183 profit per £1,000 remuneration.

2. Sales Per Employee

The sales per employee ratio shows the £ value of sales generated by each employee. It is calculated by dividing sales, taken from the profit and loss account, by the average number of employees.

Sales Per Employee $\quad=\quad \dfrac{\text{Sales (Turnover)}}{\text{Number of Employees}}$

$\quad\quad\quad\quad\quad = \quad \dfrac{£5{,}500\text{ m}}{35{,}000}$

$\quad\quad\quad\quad\quad = \quad £157{,}143$

3. Fixed Assets Per Employee

The fixed assets per employee ratio shows the £ value of fixed assets per employee. It is calculated by dividing fixed assets, taken from the balance sheet, by the average number of employees.

Fixed Assets Per Employee $\quad=\quad \dfrac{\text{Fixed Assets}}{\text{Number of Employees}}$

$\quad\quad\quad\quad\quad = \quad \dfrac{£400\text{ m}}{35{,}000}$

$\quad\quad\quad\quad\quad = \quad £11{,}429$

4. Borrowings Per Employee

The borrowings per employee ratio shows the £ value of borrowings attributable to each employee. It is calculated by dividing total borrowings by the average number of employees. Borrowings is the sum of short-term loans including bank overdraft and long term loans of £795 million.

$$\text{Borrowings Per Employee} \quad = \quad \frac{\text{Total Borrowings}}{\text{Number of Employees}}$$

$$= \quad \frac{£795 \text{ m}}{35,000}$$

$$= \quad £22,714$$

Total borrowing per employee ratios should be compared against trends year-on-year or against competitors/industry figures. A low comparative ratio would indicate that a company was not utilising sufficient financing through debts and/or it was overstaffed.

5. Employee Ratios, Summary

The strength and popularity of employee ratios is in their simplicity both in calculation and interpretation. A summary of all four ratios is given below.

1.	Profit per employee	£3,143
2.	Sales per employee	£157,143
3.	Fixed assets per employee	£11,429
4.	Borrowings per employee	£22,714

Appendix A: Total Assets or Net Assets

Bliss (1924) provides a useful definition of profitability when he writes 'The real measure of the earning power of a business is the operating profits earned on the total capacity used in such operations shown by the asset footing of the balance sheet'. Here it is not clear what he means by operating profits and these can be defined in a number of ways. What is clear, however, is the statement regarding the asset base – he means total assets.

Horngren (1970) confirms this when he states 'The measurement of operating performance (i.e. how profitably assets are employed) should not be influenced by the management's financial decisions (i.e. how assets are obtained). Operating performance is best measured by the rate of return on total assets'. Here again there is no precise definition given for profit, which it is assumed that he means 'rate of return'. While there is some debate regarding profit the use of total assets seems to be widely supported, with *Dobson (1967)* being one of the earliest writers in the UK to agree with and suggest the use of total assets.

The UK position of using net assets can be traced back to a report in *Accountancy* in 1956, on the findings of a BIM study group that stated 'It should be understood that capital employed is here regarded in terms of a statement of net operating assets, i.e. gross assets excluding intangible assets such as goodwill, less current liabilities, and this approach is necessary if further examination is to be made into the component parts of employed capital'. This statement has been the basis for the denominator of profitability ratios in the UK since that date.

Parker (1975) gives a fuller definition of the profitability ratio when he states the basis for profit and the basis for what he terms net tangible assets: "Profit is taken before interest and tax in order to separate managerial performance from the effects of different financial structures and from changes in tax rates" and 'Net tangible assets, (defined in his glossary as) Assets except for intangible assets, (goodwill, patents and trademarks), less current liabilities'.

Return On Net Assets (RONA) %

In this chapter we have outlined the calculation for the key profitability using total assets as the denominator i.e. ROTA%. We also showed the breakdown of ROTA% into the profit margin and the sales generation ratio.

In the UK, the ratio most commonly used is return on net assets (RONA)% i.e. profit before taxation and interest payable expressed as a percentage of net assets. Net assets is the sum of total assets minus current liabilities (or fixed assets plus net working capital).

It is important that we offer a word of caution about net assets. If you extract the figures from a published balance sheet you should be able to identify a description "total assets less current liabilities" which is the same as net assets for the purpose of financial ratio analysis. However, we often find the practitioner extracting 'net current assets' which is another name for net working capital and does not include fixed assets, and those described as net assets which, in published accounts, are after the deduction of long-term loans.

In what follows we will compare RONA% with ROTA% discussed earlier in this chapter.

Table 4.6 Basic Data

		Col. 1	Col.2	Col.3
Fixed Assets		5,000	15,000	15,000
+ Current Assets		45,000	45,000	45,000
Total Assets	(A)	50,000	60,000	60,000
Current Liabilities		30,000	40,000	30,000
Net Assets	(B)	20,000	20,000	30,000
PBIT	(C)	6,000	6,000	6,000

Table 4.6 Column 1, contains data extracted from a balance sheet. Column 2 and 3 both show the purchase of a fixed asset for £10,000, but in Column 2, the purchase is financed through short-term borrowings (included in the £40,000) whilst in Column 3 the purchase is financed using a long-term loan therefore, not included in current liabilities.

From the basic data in *Table 4.6*, the RONA% and ROTA% are:

	Col. 1	Col.2	Col.3
RONA% ((C) B (B) x 100	30%	30%	20%
ROTA% ((C) (A) x 100	12%	10%	10%

The most noticeable difference is in the absolute size of the ratios. Is it better to claim that the company is making a return on net assets of 30% or a return on total assets of only 12%.

On closer inspection we find with RONA% that the purchase of the fixed asset when financed through short-term borrowings has produced no increase in the profitability of the company, while with ROTA% there is a slight decrease. However, when long-term borrowings are used (i.e. Column 3) there is a significant reduction in RONA% (i.e. 30% to 20%) while ROTA% shows no movement.

This example serves to illustrate that RONA% can be affected significantly by the method of finance used. A company which uses short-term finance to purchase fixed assets and generate the same profits as in the preceeding period, RONA% will remain the same (the increase in fixed assets being off-set by the increase in short-term borrowings).

Consider the position of a company in poor financial health that uses short-term finance (just to keep things going). Its fixed and current assets are also declining. During the early stages, this company could produce an increase in profitability when using RONA%.

ROTA%, which is the method we recommend, is unaffected by the method of financing assets. This is evident from our example where the same percentage results irrespective of the method of finance used i.e. 10% in column 2 and in column 3.

6.1 Given a gearing ratio (total borrowing/equity) of 0.72 to 1 and the following Balance Sheet values:

Closing Stock	£210,000	Profit and Loss Account	£140,000
Cash	£45,000	Bank Overdraft	£70,000
Issued Share Capital	£110,000	Debtors	£105,000
Trade Creditors	£170,000		

a. What is the value of Long Term Loans?

b. What is the value of Fixed Assets?

c. Calculate the Current Ratio.

d. Given a profit before tax and interest payable of £48,000 calculate the return on net assets (RONA).

6.2 The following figures have been extracted from the accounts of BacDor Limited for the year ended 31st July 200X:

	£'000		£'000
Sales	25,500	Cost of Sales	20,000
Profit before Taxation	500	Interest Payable	3,500
Issued Share Capital	1,000	Profit and Loss Account	9,000
Long Term Loan	9,000	Trade Creditors	16,000
Bank Overdraft	6,000	Premises	9,000
Vehicles	6,000	Stock	16,000
Debtors	9,000	Cash	1,000

Required:

a. Calculate ratios covering profitability, liquidity and gearing.

b. Interpret the ratios calculated (in a. above) with reference to industry average figures for the same period (shown below). Make suitable assumptions to assist with your interpretation.

1.	Profit / Net Assets	18%
2.	Profit / Sales	6%
3.	Sales / Net Assets	3.00 to 1
4.	Current Ratio	1.50 to 1
5.	Liquid Ratio (or Acid Test)	0.70 to 1
6.	Stock Turn	4 times
7.	Debtor Ratio	12 weeks
8.	Borrowings / Equity	0.80 to 1
9.	Interest Payable / Profit before Tax plus Interest Payable	30%

6.3   From the following data, calculate three profitability ratios, two liquidity ratios and two gearing ratios:

Profit before taxation	£22,000	Interest payable	£8,000
Stock	£50,000	Issued Share Capital	£50,000
Long Term Loans	£50,000	Fixed Assets	£90,000
Debtors	£30,000	Bank Overdraft	£20,000
Profit & Loss Account	£20,000	Cash	£10,000
Creditors	£40,000	Cost of Sales	£480,000
Sales	£700,000		

6.4   The following figures have been extracted from the accounts of I Dilly & U. Dally Ltd for the year ended 31st January 200X:

	£'000		£'000
Sales	8,000	Cost of Sales	6,300
Profit before Taxation	200	Interest Payable	700
Issued Share Capital	200	Profit and Loss Account	2,800
Long Term Loan	1,800	Trade Creditors	5,000
Bank Overdraft	2,000	Premises	3,000
Vehicles	1,500	Stock	4,500
Debtors	2,500	Cash	300

Required:

a.   Calculate ratios covering profitability, liquidity and gearing.

b.   Interpret the ratios calculated (in a. above) with reference to the previous years figures shown below. Make suitable assumptions to assist with your interpretation.

1.	Profit / Net Assets	15%
2.	Profit / Sales	8.3%
3.	Sales / Net Assets	1.81 to 1
4.	Current Ratio	1.25 to 1
5.	Liquid Ratio (or Acid Test)	0.60 to 1
6.	Stock Turn	2.1 times
7.	Debtor Ratio	10 weeks
8.	Borrowings / Equity	0.70 to 1
9.	Profit Before Tax / Profit before Tax plus Interest Payable	45%

6.5   Given the following Balance Sheet values:

Issued Share Capital	100,000	Wages accrued	20,000
Debtors	250,000	Profit and Loss Account	50,000
Cash	20,000	Bank Overdraft	80,000
Equipment	110,000	Closing Stock	150,000
Long Term Loans	160,000	Trade Creditors	220,000

a   Calculate the (balancing) figure for Land and Buildings.

b   Calculate the Gearing ratio (Borrowings to Equity).

c   Calculate the Current ratio.

d   Assume that the Return on Net Assets is 15%, calculate the value of Profit (for the period).

6.6   The following ratios have been calculated from the accounts of N.O. Bother plc

N.O. Bother	1995	1996	1997	1998	1999
PROFITABILITY RATIOS:					
Profit Before Tax / Net Assets %	30.9	19.8	8.9	–1.5	–7.1
Profit Before Tax / Sales %	12.5	10	2.3	–0.6	–3.1
Sales / Net Assets	2.47	1.98	3.80	2.43	2.32
WORKING CAPITAL RATIOS:					
Current Assets / Current Liabilities	1.15	1.87	0.99	2.40	2.06
Liquid Assets / Current Liabilities	0.28	0.46	0.21	1.02	0.90
Cost of Sales / Stock	1.2	1.4	1.3	2.4	2.1
Debtors / Average Weekly Sales	3.9	4.4	4.7	5.3	4.2
GEARING RATIOS:					
Borrowing / Equity	0.54	0.63	1.22	0.43	0.32
Interest Payable / P.B.I.T. %	8.0	20.0	128.6	–500	–25.0

The above profitability, working capital and gearing ratios have been calculated for the period 1995 to 1999. You are required to provide an interpretation of the movements in each ratio making any assumptions which you feel are necessary.

6.7   The following figures have been extracted from the accounts of RR Limited for the year ended 31st March 200X:

	£000
Sales	3,500
Premises	300
Interest Payable	100
Share Capital	400
Cost of Sales	2,000
Creditors	2,000
Cash	200
Bank Overdraft	800
Vehicles	200
Stock	2,100
Profit Before Taxation	200
Debtors	1,200
Profit and Loss Account	800

Required

1.   You are required to calculate profitability, liquidity and working capital ratios for RR Limited.

2.   Given the following ratios which reflect the averages for the same industrial sector, comment on the differences between the ratios calculated in above and the industry averages below.

Profit / Net Assets	32%
Profit / Sales	4%
Sales / Net Assets	8.00 to 1
Current Ratio	1.60 to 1
Liquid Ratio (or Acid Test)	0.60 to 1
Stock Turn	3 times
Debtor Weeks	12 weeks

6.8   The following Balance Sheet and Profit and Loss Account data should be used with question 3, and other questions which refer to its use.

CONSOLIDATED BALANCE SHEET DATA FOR FIVE YEARS (£000)

	1995	1996	1997	1998	1999
Fixed Assets	26,000	70,000	80,000	96,000	135,000
Stock	50,000	50,000	51,000	52,000	58,000
Debtors	24,000	25,000	26,000	28,000	24,000
Current Assets	76,000	77,000	80,000	83,000	90,000
Creditors	52,000	50,000	52,000	55,000	65,000
Bank Overdraft	11,000	12,000	12,000	12,000	32,000
Current Liabilities	65,000	64,000	67,000	70,000	100,000
Share Capital	8,000	8,000	16,000	16,000	16,000
Profit and Loss Account	10,000	49,000	51,000	64,000	376,000
Long Term Loans	19,000	26,000	26,000	29,000	33,000

CONSOLIDATED PROFIT AND LOSS ACCOUNT DATA FOR FIVE YEARS (£000)

	1995	1996	1997	1998	1999
Sales	90,000	118,000	124,000	140,000	170,000
Cost of Sales	78,000	103,000	104,500	111,400	135,000
Interest Payable	3,000	3,000	3,500	3,600	10,000
Profit Before Tax	9,000	12,000	16,000	25,000	25,000

Required

1.   Calculate profitability ratios for the five years and provide a brief overview of what they reveal about the performance of the company.

2.   Calculate liquidity ratios for the five years and provide a brief overview of what they reveal about the performance of the company.

3.   Calculate gearing ratios for the five years and provide a brief overview of what they reveal about the performance of the company.

6.9   The chairman of H.O. Ratio Limited has obtained figures from a comparison of a competitor.

Total Assets	£258,750
Current Liabilities	£125,000
Administration Expenses	£33,250
Current ratio	1.75 1
Quick ratio	1.05 1
Average age of outstanding customer debts (based on a 52 week year)	12 weeks
Net Profit/Net Current Assets %	20%
Gross Profit/Sales %	20%

Required

1.   From the information above, prepare in as much detail as possible, a Profit and Loss account for the year ended 31st October 200X and a Balance Sheet as at that date.

2.   Comment on the limitations in using ratio analysis as a means of measuring the financial performance of a company.

C O S T
A C C O U N T I N G

When you have finished studying this chapter you should be able to:

❏ Describe the main elements of costs and the various classifications of costs.

❏ Calculate overhead recovery rates and prepare product costs using absorption costing techniques.

❏ Prepare product costs with materials and labour and absorption of variable and fixed overheads.

❏ Describe and calculate costs using Activity Based Costing.

7.1   Introduction

Costs may often represent a significant proportion of an organisation's income and, therefore, are a very important area to be able to manage. For example, from an examination of the 1997 Report and Accounts of the *Standard Chartered Bank* it can be seen that 82% of the Group's net revenue is accounted for by operating expenses (in 1998, 94% of *Tesco's* revenue is accounted for by operating expenses).

Cost management is a declared priority of the Group, a point made in repeated Chairman's Statements. It is particularly important because profit depends upon knowing the cost of doing business. However, there is a major problem in knowing whether the costs incurred are really warranted. Are they really necessary? Could they be avoided? How can we tell?

Cost management is associated with cost accounting. The management of costs within an organisation may well be influenced by the way in which they have been accounted for. At its simplest the concern with cost accounting is to determine what it costs to produce a good or provide a service. This can be very straightforward in a one product or one service organisation where all costs can be clearly identified with the product/service being provided. However, very few such organisations exist and in a multi-product or multi-service environment procedures have to be found and used if costs are to be identified with that which is produced or provided.

If you refer to most cost accounting texts you will discover that procedures have been developed primarily in manufacturing organisations to deal with the cost accounting problems of different types of operation. Thus, you will encounter descriptions and discussions about cost accounting techniques and approaches for organisations producing bespoke one-off products, and those dealing with batch operations, process operations and long-term contracts. These techniques will focus upon the various elements of cost like labour and materials and the problems of accounting for raw materials, work in progress and finished goods.

What is important for you to understand about cost accounting is that it is not a science, and that considerable judgement is typically employed. In accounting for costs, particularly overheads, considerable judgement is employed in allocating and apportioning them to products and/or services. How such judgement based allocation and apportionment is applied we review in the next section. Thereafter, we will consider one important development in cost accounting, and more importantly cost management known as Activity Based Costing, or ABC. This approach has a claimed advantage over traditional methods because it attempts to relate the costs of an organisation to those activities responsible for generating them.

Whilst ABC provides one means of encouraging cost control, there are some costs in very large organisations that are notoriously difficult to control. This is because they are incurred centrally and distributed throughout the organisation. Management informations systems costs are a good example of such internally transferred costs. How these can be managed using what are known as service level agreements we consider in the last section.

7.2   Elements of Cost

Originally cost accounting methods were developed to provide ways of accumulating costs and charging these to units of product or service in order to establish stock valuations. These were principally related to historical calculations, but the advantages of using these methods for planning were soon realised and cost accounting was extended to the areas of budgeting and decision analysis.

Almost every decision made by management has an affect on cost, and a good understanding of the types of costs and how they are used for cost control and cost management is important for sound financial management.

Total costs of a product or service comprise three main elements:

1.   materials – the cost of materials consumed in making the product or providing the service;

2.   labour – the cost of wages and salaries of employees, who are involved in producing the product or providing the service;

3.   expenses – the cost of other expenses; which will include occupancy costs, power, depreciation, interest charges, telecoms. etc.

As we shall see later in this chapter there are different possible treatments of these three basic elements, arising from differing views of how they should be analysed and reported, which allow for alternative views of the 'cost' of a product or service.

7.3   Classifications of Cost

This expression covers the way in which costs can be grouped, or classified, for analysis and reporting. A very common usage is the grouping of costs by function, e.g. splitting the costs of the organisation into production, selling, distribution, administration. These can be further subdivided into, say, departmental costs within each function, and is a system commonly used in the budgeting process.

Two other important classifications of cost are:

1.   Direct/indirect costs,

2.   Variable/fixed costs,

and an understanding of these is important as they are linked to two methods of costing, absorption costing and marginal costing, which you will meet later in this chapter.

1   Direct/Indirect Costs

A direct cost is a cost that can be traced in full to the product, service or function etc. that is being costed, whereas an indirect cost is a cost that has been incurred in the making of a product, providing a service, etc., but that cannot be traced in full to the product, service or function.

As an illustration, if a management consultant is currently working for three clients, the actual time spent on each client can be identified and charged directly to the individual client's account, but the cost of the administrative facilities, such as, say, occupancy costs cannot be traced directly to each client, These are indirect costs, which have to be shared on some basis between the clients to arrive at a total client cost.

Materials costs, labour costs and expenses can be classified as a direct cost or an indirect cost. When the three basic elements of cost are classified in this way the total of the direct costs is known as prime cost and the total of the indirect costs is known as overhead. Total cost is the sum of prime cost and overhead.

2   Variable/Fixed Costs

This classification is based on a basic principle of cost behaviour, which assumes that as activity increases so usually will cost. It will usually cost more to send 10 faxes than to send 5. It will usually cost more to produce 150 cars than to produce 120. However, not all costs will increase in the same way or by the same amount. A definition of cost behaviour is:

"The way in which costs of output are affected by fluctuations in the level of activity". (CIMA Official Terminology)

Costs which tend to vary directly with the volume of output are variable costs. The most obvious of these is direct materials, and the relationship between cost and volume can be shown graphically as follows:

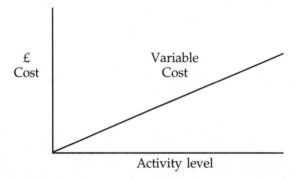

Costs which tend to be unaffected by increases or decreases in volume of output, and as such will be incurred regardless of output volume, are fixed costs. Examples of these would be rent and salaries. Of course in the long term all costs are likely to change – the rent of the premises and employees' salaries would inevitably rise, but they do not alter as a direct result of making one more item. Graphically, a fixed cost would look like this:

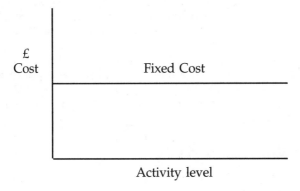

However, many items of a fixed cost nature are fixed within a particular activity level. For example, it could be that a number of administrators could handle a certain level of purchase orders, but beyond that certain level another administrator would have to be employed. This type of situation gives rise to what are called stepped fixed costs, and also introduces the concept of the 'relevant range', that is the activity level over which the cost is fixed. A stepped fixed cost situation such as that described would appear graphically as follows:

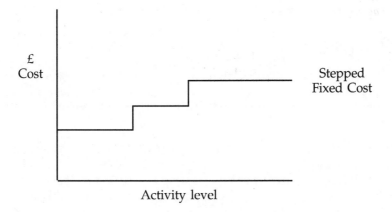

Some costs include parts that are variable and fixed. Such costs are usually called mixed, semi-variable or semi-fixed costs. Common examples are telephone and electricity charges, where there is a fixed rental element and a variable portion depending upon usage.

7.4   Techniques of Costing

Costing is undertaken in organisations with the purpose of providing management with the information they need to be able to plan, control and make the necessary decisions. As such it has evolved, and continues to evolve, providing a 'toolkit' of methods and techniques that can be selected by management to suit their analytical and reporting purposes. There is no 'regulatory framework' requiring companies to produce costing statements etc., but some requirements of the accounting standards do demand that organisations prepare figures for their statutory accounts using particular techniques. For example, organisations are required to value their stocks at 'full production cost' which means that for their annual accounts they must use absorption costing techniques. However, internally, they are free to choose the most relevant and valuable for their type of operation. In the following section we will review the main costing techniques.

1. Overhead Absorption Costing

Overhead absorption costing is concerned with the process of charging indirect costs i.e. overheads to products or services. It is concerned principally with the charging of indirect production costs, i.e. not non-production costs such as selling, distribution and administration overhead. In determining the cost of a product or service it is not usually the direct costs which are difficult to charge to products or services. It is finding an equitable way of apportioning overheads to products or services to enable an understanding of product/service cost and profitability which poses the challenge. The following section looks at the process of allocation and apportionment of overhead, and the ways in which overhead can be 'absorbed' into product/service cost.

Overheads, Allocation and Apportionment

Organisations of all types incur overhead costs in the form of those costs that cannot readily be identified with individual products or services. Given that such costs may well be a very significant proportion of total costs, some means has to be found for distributing them across products and services if the full cost of products and services is to be determined. 'Cost plus' pricing remains a common method of pricing products and services, of course bearing in mind key market considerations.

The way that costs are distributed traditionally is by a process known as 'allocation and apportionment' whereby, for example, an overhead like rent would be apportioned typically according to area occupied and allocated to parts of the business on that basis. This process can be most readily understood from the following example.

1. Example

The PVY Company has two production departments and a raw material and finished goods store.

The budgeted costs for the last quarter of 200X are as follows:

	£
Rent	12,000
Maintenance to Plant	4,000
Depreciation of Plant	12,000
Lighting and Heating	4,000
Supervision	9,500
Fire Insurance	500
Power	10,000
Personnel Services	12,000
General Expenses	8,000

Additional information has been collected for use in allocating and/or apportioning the budgeted costs to departments.

	Dept. A	Dept. B	Store	Total
Number of Employees	10	7	2	19
Area (square metres)	1,700	300	400	2,400
Machine Hours (for quarter)	1,750	370	0	2,120
Direct Labour Hours (weekly)	460	308	87	855
Plant Value	£564,000	£100,000	0	£664,000
Value of Stock Used	£10,200	£1,800	0	£12,000
kW Hours, metered	160,000	25,600	0	185,600

allocating *or*

The Factory Manager has given an estimate for supervision costs being the time spent in the two departments.

Apportionment

Department A   £7,500
Department B   £2,000

Complete an overhead analysis sheet showing clearly the basis used for apportionment. (Round all figures to the nearest hundred)

Table 7.1   Overhead Analysis Sheet

Budgeted costs	Basis of Apportionment	Total £	Dept A £	Dept B £	Store £
Rent	Floor Area	12,000	8,500	1,500	2,000
Maintenance to Plant	Mach. Hours	4,000	3,300	700	0
Depreciation of Plant	Plant Value	12,000	10,200	1,800	0
Lighting and Heating	Floor Area	4,000	2,800	500	800
Supervision	Tech.Estimate	9,500	7,500	2,000	0
Fire Insurance	Floor Area	500	300	100	100
Power	kW Hours	10,000	8,600	1,400	0
Personnel Services	No. Employees	12,000	6,300	4,400	1,300
General Expenses	Labour Hours	8,000	4,300	2,900	800
		72,000	51,800	15,300	4,900
Service Dept (Store)	Stock Value	0	4,200	700	–4,900
		72,000	56,000	16,000	0

Example for the apportionment of rent to Department A:

$$\text{Department A} = \frac{£12,000}{2,400} \times 1,700$$

$$= £8,500$$

The bases for apportionment shown in *Table 7.1* are used simply to illustrate the process. Apportionment is an art. It is possible to question the use of floor area as a means for apportioning the costs of items such as rent, lighting, heating and fire insurance, in fact it is possible to present a good case against any apportionment base.

Consider the case of using floor area for lighting and heating, clearly, there is a requirement for different forms of lighting and heating in a variety of work situations few of which would correspond to floor area.

Similarly, consider the case of using machine hours to apportion the maintenance of plant. This suggests that the more a machine is used the more maintenance will be required and vice versa. Therefore, if we use a machine infrequently it will not require much maintenance! It also assumes that all machines cost the same and are of similar age.

2.   Overheads, Absorption Rates

Once the overhead allocation and apportionment process has been completed the total overhead cost for a part of the business can be calculated by simple addition. For example, the total overhead for Department B we calculated as being £16,000. We can now use this figure to determine a future unit charge out rate by absorbing it over a number of bases. One common base is labour hours, such that if labour hours were 2,000 we would have an overhead absorption rate of £8 per labour hour (£16,000 ÷ 2,000). In costing future products we would charge overhead to them according to the number of labour hours. Therefore, if a product required two hours of labour, a charge of £16 for overhead (£8 x 2) would be made.

How this approach can be applied using different bases and the effect of different methods of absorption we illustrate in the following example:

The PVY Company has prepared a Production Cost Budget for the last quarter of 200X as follows:

		£	£
Direct Materials			24,000
Direct Labour – Department A		32,000	
– Department B		16,000	
			48,000
Prime Cost			72,000
Overheads – Department A		56,000	
– Department B		16,000	
			72,000
Production Cost			144,000

Department A is a machine based department with a total of 1,750 machine hours budgeted during the quarter. The labour rate in the department has been set at £6.00 per hour.

Department B is a labour based department with a total of 4,000 labour hours budgeted during the quarter. The labour rate in the department has been set at £4.00 per hour.

We will calculate an overhead absorption rate using each of the following bases:

a.   Percentage on Direct Materials.

b.   Percentage on Direct Labour   –   Whole Company

c.   Percentage on Direct Labour   –   Department A

d.   Percentage on Direct Labour   –   Department B

e.   Machine Hour Rate   –   Department A

f.   Labour Hour Rate   –   Department B

The calculation of absorption rates (also known as overhead recovery rates) requires that an overhead cost is divided by an agreed absorption base. We will now show the calculations for the most popular methods and comment on each one.

a. Percentage on Direct Materials

$$\frac{\text{Overheads}}{\text{Material Costs}} \times 100 = \frac{£72,000}{£24,000} \times 100 = 300\%$$

The percentage on direct materials is a simple method. However, it is difficult to find a situation in which to use the method. The problem is that it can only be used in a single (including single quality) material environment. If it were used in a mixed material environment, products would absorb overheads on the basis of their material cost.

b. Percentage on Direct Labour – Whole Company

$$\frac{\text{Overheads}}{\text{Labour Costs}} \times 100 = \frac{£72,000}{£48,000} \times 100 = 150\%$$

The percentage on direct labour is also a simple method but unlike materials is widely used. In this example, overheads would be absorbed at 150% of the total labour cost for each product or service. The major problem with this method arises when there are different levels of labour costs in different departments or cost centres. In order to address this problem most companies calculate separate absorption rates for each department or cost centre.

An example is shown in c, and d below. It can be seen that instead of using 150% for the whole company, we would now use 175% absorption rate to recover overheads in Department A and 100% absorption rate to recover overheads in Department B.

c. Percentage on Direct Labour – Department A

$$\frac{\text{Overheads}}{\text{Labour Costs}} \times 100 = \frac{£56,000}{£32,000} \times 100 = 175\%$$

d. Percentage on Direct Labour – Department B

$$\frac{\text{Overheads}}{\text{Labour Costs}} \times 100 = \frac{£16,000}{£16,000} \times 100 = 100\%$$

One of the most popular methods to absorb overheads is using the hourly rate. This method also requires that separate absorption rates are calculated for each department or cost centre. In this example, we would absorb overheads for Department A based on the number of machine hours required times the rate of £32 per machine hour. Similarly, if the product used labour hours in Department B, there would be an absorption of overheads based on the number of labour hours required times the rate of £4 per machine hour. See calculations below.

e. Machine Hour Rate – Department A

$$\frac{\text{Overheads}}{\text{Machine Hours}} = \frac{£56,000}{1,750} = £32.00 \text{ per machine hour}$$

f. Labour Hour Rate – Department B

$$\frac{\text{Overheads}}{\text{Labour Hours}} = \frac{£16,000}{4,000} = £4.00 \text{ per labour hour}$$

3. Overheads, Comparison of Absorption Methods

We have described the calculation of absorption rates and commented on each. However, there still remains the question 'What absorption method should we use'? We will complete this example by showing the effect of using each of the absorption methods on the production costs of two products. Each product comprises different proportions of materials and labour. The example will use the following data:

❏ The executives of the PVY Company are trying to agree the method to be used for absorbing overheads to products.

❏ The following information is available to calculate the prime costs for Products 101 and 102.

	Product 101 per unit	Product 102 per unit
Direct Material Cost	£14	£28
Direct Labour Hours – Department A	4 hours	1 hour
– Department B	3 hours	4 hours

For convenience, we now restate the direct labour rate which was used in the previous section.

Direct Labour Rate	– Department A	£6.00 per hour
	– Department B	£4.00 per hour

An estimate of machine hours for both products is as follows:

Machine Hours (per 100 units)	Product 101	47 hours
	Product 102	15 hours

Using the information for Products 101 and 102, we will prepare a table to show the effect of using absorption methods based on materials, direct labour and hourly rates. Costs will be calculated, per 100 units.

In *Table 7.2* we have taken the direct material cost for Product 101 and multiplied it by 100 (£14 x 100) to give £1,400. The direct labour cost is found by multiplying the direct labour hours per unit for Product 101 spent in Department A by 100 (4 hours x 100) to give 400 hours, then multiplying the hours by the direct labour hourly rate (400 hours x £6) to give £2,400. A similar calculation is performed for Department B. Finally, the direct material costs and the direct labour costs are added (£1,400 + £3,600) to give the prime cost for Product 101. Now check the calculations for Product 102.

Table 7.2   Comparison of Absorption Methods

		Cost per 100 units			
	Product 101			Product 102	
		£	£		£	£
Direct Material			1,400			2,800
Direct Labour:						
Dept. A (£6 p.h.)	400 hrs	2,400		100 hrs	600	
Dept. B (£4 p.h.)	300 hrs	1,200		400 hrs	1,600	
			3,600			2,200
Prime Cost			5,000			5,000

1. 300 % on Direct Materials	4,200	8,400
	9,200	13,400

In this first example we have multiplied the direct materials for each product by 300%. For Product 101 (£1,400 x 300%) to give the overheads of £4,200. Finally, we added the overhead to the prime cost (£4,200 + £5,000) to give the total production cost of £9,200. Similar calculations for Product 102 gives a total production cost of £13,400. Both costs are arithmetically accurate, but they are heavily influenced by the material cost and subsequent overhead absorption using materials.

2. 150% on Total Labour	5,400	3,300
	10,400	8,300

When using a percentage on total labour the calculations are similar. In this case we use the total labour cost for Product 101, £3,600 x 150% to give the overheads of £5,400 and £3,300 for Product 102. You will notice the difference between the two methods, with Product 102 now lower, due to the direct labour costs.

3. 175% on Labour Dept. A	4,200		1,050	
4. 100% on Labour Dept. B	1,200		1,600	
		5,400		2,650
		10,400		7,650

When using individual absorption rates we take the rate and multiply it by the direct labour cost for a department. For example for Product 101 we take the direct labour cost of £2,400 x 175% to give £4,200 of overheads for Department A, then add the direct labour cost of £1,200 x 100% to give £1,200 of overheads for Department B. Total absorbed overheads for both departments amounting to £5,400. Similar calculations for Product 102 produce total absorbed overheads of £2,650. We discussed the problem of using a percentage on total labour in the previous section. We can now see the effect of using individual absorption rates for each department or cost centre.

5.	£32 M.Hour Dept. A	47 hrs	1,504	15 hrs	480	
6.	£4 L.Hour Dept. B	300 hrs	1,200	400 hrs	1,600	
			2,704		2,080	
			7,704		7,080	

In the final section we have used the hourly rate method. If Product 101 requires 47 machine hours in Department A, the absorbed overhead is (47 hours x £32) which gives £1,504. Overheads are absorbed in Department B using direct labour hours, the overhead is (300 hours x £4) which gives £1,200. To complete the calculations we add the two overhead figures to give £2,704, then add in the prime cost of £5,000 to give £7,704.

The purpose of the above example is to demonstrate the differing ways in which the overhead could be attributed to products. The method applied should be that which most closely aligns overhead and product. Most commonly used are time-based methods, (i.e. labour hour, machine hour) although there is growing interest in using 'an activity base'. This is discussed in more detail in *Section 7.5*.

Before moving on to consider other techniques of costing, we will now look at the construction of a quotation for an order, which is based on absorption costing principles.

7.5 Example – Quotation for an Order

Mouldit Ltd makes a range of products in expanded polystyrene (cups, trays, DIY materials etc.). The budget for the six months to 31st October 200X is as follows:

	£	£	£
Sales			780,000
Polystyrene (5,000 kg)	200,000		
Direct Labour (10,000 hours)	50,000		
Variable Overhead	150,000		
Total Variable Costs		400,000	
Fixed Overhead		250,000	
Total Cost			650,000
Budgeted Profit			130,000

You have been asked to quote for an order which is estimated to require 100 kg of polystyrene and 240 hours of direct labour.

The order is from a regular customer. The company applies normal absorption costing principles. Variable overhead is assumed to be related to direct labour hours, and fixed overhead and profit are based on a loading of total variable cost and total cost respectively.

Table 7.3   Calculation of Quote Price

		£
Materials	100kg at £40 per kg	4,000
Labour	240 hours at £5.00 per hour	1,200
Variable Overhead	240 hours at £15.00 per hour	3,600
Total Variable Costs		8,800
Fixed Overhead	£8,800 x 62.5 ÷ 100	5,500
Total Cost		14,300
Budgeted Profit	£14,300 x 20 ÷ 100	2,860
Quote Price		17,160

The steps to be taken in the calculation of the product cost/quote price are shown below:

1. Materials: Calculate the price per kilogram, i.e. £200,000 ÷ 5,000 kg = £40.00 per kg.

2. Labour: Calculate the labour hour rate, i.e. £50,000 ÷ 10,000 hours = £5.00 per labour hour.

3. Variable Overhead: Calculate the variable overheads on a labour hour basis i.e. variable overheads divided by labour hours = £150,000 ÷ 10,000 hours = £15.00 per labour hour.

    Please note, in 2. above we have found that the labour hour rate is £5.00 per labour hour, while in 3. above we have found that the variable overhead rate is £15.00 per labour hour. Therefore for each hour worked we have to recover £5.00 to pay the wages plus £15.00 to cover our variable overheads.

4. Total variable cost is the sum of materials + labour + variable overheads i.e. £4,000 + £1,200 + £3,600 = £8,800.

5. Fixed Overhead: We are told that this will be recovered as a percentage of total variable cost, therefore we have to calculate this percentage i.e. £250,000 ÷ £400,000 x 100 = 62.5%.

6. Total cost is the sum of total variable cost plus fixed overhead i.e. £8,800 + £5,500 = £14,300.

7. Budgeted Profit: We are told that budgeted profit will be added as a percentage of total cost, therefore we have to calculate this percentage. Budgeted profit is £130,000 and total cost is (£250,000 + £400,000) £650,000. Therefore the percentage is £130,000 ÷ £650,000 x 100 = 20%.

8. The price to quote is the total cost plus the budgeted profit i.e. £14,300 + £2,860 = £17.160.

In summary, in determining the cost of a product or service it is not usually the direct costs that are difficult. It is the apportionment of overheads that provides the challenge. Overhead absorption costing is a mechanism to enable the total production cost, including overheads, to be identified with a product or service to enable management to more fully understand and appreciate the determinants of product/service cost and profitability. However, it does have its opponents. Concern about the 'traditional' methods of apportioning and absorbing overhead accurately led to the original development of activity based costing (which is reviewed later in this chapter). Concern about the validity of apportioning fixed costs over products/services and including fixed costs in stock valuations led to the development of an alternative method of costing. This is marginal costing and will be reviewed in the next section.

7.5   Activity based (costing) analysis

1. Introduction

Traditionally the costing of products was associated with manufacturing organisations. Costing systems decades ago were required by companies which manufactured a narrow range of products where direct labour and materials were the dominant factory costs. For such organisations overhead costs were relatively small and the distortions arising from overhead allocations were not significant.

We have illustrated how costs are allocated to cost centres by applying judgement, for example rent and rates on the basis of floor space occupied. Once all such overheads have been allocated, they could then be apportioned to products or services on the basis of labour hours.

Although such cost allocation and apportionment methods have been developed in manufacturing organisations they are not readily transferrable to the growing service sector. In services the relationship between costs and the activities from which costs arise is more problematic. It is this background which has led to the development of Activity Based Costing (ABC).

For financial service providers, like banks, activity-based costing has particular attractions because such organisations operate in highly competitive environment and they incur a large amount of support overhead costs that cannot be directly assigned to specific cost objects. Furthermore, their products and customers differ significantly in terms of consuming overhead resources.

ABC systems assume that activities cause costs to be incurred and that products (or other selected cost objects, such as customers and branches in the case of a bank) consume activities in varying amounts. A link is made between activities and products by assigning the cost of activities to products based on an individual product's demand for each activity.

The development of an ABC system will involve the following:

❏ The identification of the key activities that take place in the organisation.

❏ The creation of a cost pool for each major activity.

❏ The assignment of costs to activity cost pools.

❏ The determination of the cost driver for each activity cost pool.

❏ The determination of the unit cost for each activity.

❏ The assignment of the costs of activities to selected cost objects (for example, products) according to the cost object's demand for each activity.

Stage 1 identifies the major activities performed in the enterprise. Activities are simply the tasks that people or machines perform in order to provide a product or service. For example, in retail banking this would correspond with processing a deposit, issuing a credit card, processing a cheque, setting up a loan, opening an account or processing monthly statements, and so on. In a support activity like a personnel department, activities would be recruitment, remuneration, training, union negotiation, personnel administration, and staff welfare.

Stage 2 creates a cost pool for each activity.

Stage 3 costs are analysed and assigned to the appropriate activity pool. For example, the total cost of processing a deposit might constitute one activity cost pool in a retail bank for all deposit processing related costs, with separate cost pools being created for each type of deposit account if different types of deposits consume resources differently. In a personnel department, recruitment may constitute an activity pool for recruitment related costs like advertising, interviewing, contracts, and induction.

Stage 4 then identifies the factors that influence the cost of a particular activity. The term 'cost driver' is used to describe the events or forces that are the significant determinants of the cost of the activities. For example, if the cost of processing deposits is generated by the number of deposits processed then the number of deposits processed would represent the cost driver for deposit processing activities. In the case of a personnel department the cost drivers would be staff recruited, staff retired, staff on roll.

The cost driver selected for each cost pool should be the one that, as closely as possible, mirrors the consumption of the activities represented by the cost centre. Examples of cost drivers that might be appropriate for other retail banking activities include:

❏ Number of applications processed for setting up a loan;

❏ Number of statements mailed for processing monthly statements;

❏ Number of mortgage payments past due date for processing activities relating to mortgage arrears.

The next stage divides the cost traced to each activity cost pool by the total number of driver units in order to calculate a cost per unit of activity.

Finally, the cost of specific activities is traced to products (or services) according to their demand for the activities by multiplying unit activity costs by the quantity of each activity that a product consumes.

The total cost of a product or service is then found by adding the individual costs of the activities that are required to deliver the product or service. In other words, a product or service can be viewed as a bundle of activities. ABC focuses on the costing of these activities and the bundling of them into products, customers or any other cost objects.

ABC seeks to measure as accurately as possible those resources consumed by products or services, whereas traditional costing systems just allocate and apportion costs to products or services. The ABC approach seems to offer considerable advantages as can be seen if we reconsider our retail banking example. The traditional approach might allocate deposit transaction processing costs to customers, or different types of deposit accounts, on the basis of the number of customer accounts. This would distort product costs if deposit processing costs are driven by the number of transactions processed. Allocating cost according to the number of customers will lead to low value deposit accounts that involve numerous 'over-the-counter' transactions being under-costed, whereas high value long term savings accounts requiring very few transactions will be over-costed. In contrast, an ABC system would establish a separate cost centre for deposit processing activities, ascertain what causes the costs (that is, determine the appropriate cost driver, such as the number of transactions processed) and assign costs to products on the basis of a product's demand for the activity.

2. How is ABC applied?

Activity-based profitability analysis is best thought of in hierarchical terms. First, the costs of undertaking the various activities should be listed, and those that can be analysed by products should be deducted from revenues, so that a contribution to profits can be derived for each product. Products in our retail banking example are deposit accounts and loans and an example of a specific cost would be an advertising campaign aimed at one specific type of loan.

The next level is the product line or product group. For example, deposit accounts and loans may represent some of the individual products within the product line. Although some expenses can be traced to them individually, some of those incurred are common to all products within the product line and are not identifiable with individual products. These expenses are function, or product-line-sustaining expenses and are traced to product lines but not to individual products within the line.

Not all costs can be readily assigned to products. Some costs are common and joint to all products. These costs are called business or facility-sustaining expenses and include such items as top management salaries. When deducted as a lump sum from the total of all the profit margins from all the individual products lines yield the overall profit of the enterprise or a particular strategic business unit.

3. Example

The following example is set in a manufacturing environment and will trace the factory overhead costs through two components. First we will calculate the factory overhead costs allocated using traditional costing techniques then using ABC cost drivers. Typically, these examples are 'prepared' in order to show that the ABC technique is 'more comprehensive in that it apportions each element of overhead relative to its consumption for each activity and will provide a more realistic basis for determining the overhead for each line of business'. To conclude this example, we will question the overheads used in the example and rework using a more balanced set of overheads while still retaining machine hours as the absorption rate.

In this example we have two components RUF and TUF that are similar in appearance and use the same processes and machinery. The following data has been gathered:

	RUF	TUF
Budget Volume (components)	3,000	24,000
Machine Hours per component	3	3
Number of Purchase Orders	100	300
Number of Setups	50	80
Total Machine Hours	9,000	72,000

Fixed Factory Overheads:

Volume related	£160,000
Purchasing related	£130,000
Setup related	£250,000
	£540,000

First we apportion Factory fixed overheads using traditional overhead apportionment techniques.

Table 7.4   Traditional Overhead Apportionment

Fixed Factory Overheads ÷ Total Machine Hours
£540,000 ÷ 81,000 hours = £6.667 per machine hour

		RUF		TUF
Cost per component (£6,667 x 3hrs)		£20.00	(£6.667 x 3hrs)	£20.00
Overhead costs absorbed				
	(3,000 x £20)	**£60,000**	(24,000 x £20)	**£480,000**

In *Table 7.4* we calculated a machine hour rate of £6.667. We then calculated the cost per unit for each component; since the machine hours are the same for both components it follows that the cost per unit will also be the same i.e. £20.00 per unit. The last section shows the total overheads absorbed by RUF and TUF i.e. £60,000 and £480,000.

We will now show the ABC method of apportionment that calculates absorption rates based on costs traced to activities divided by the consumption of these activities. In this example we have to calculate three rates as follows:

Volume related rate:

£160,000 ÷ 81,000 machine hours = £1.9753 per machine hour

Purchasing related rate:

£130,000 ÷ 400 purchase orders = £325 per purchase order

Setup related rate:

£250,000 ÷ 130 setups = £1,923.08 per setup

Table 7.5   ABC method of apportionment

		RUF		TUF
Volume costs	(9,000 x £1.9753)	17,778	(72,000 x £1.9753)	142,222
Purchasing costs	(100 x £325)	32,500	(300 x £325)	97,500
Setup costs	(50 x £1923.08)	96,154	(80 x £1923.08)	153,846
		146,432		**393,568**

It is clear that the two methods give widely different results. The traditional method apportions only £60,000 to RUF while the ABC method apportions £146,432. The assumption here is that the traditional method favours the lower volume component because it does not take into account the high costs on the non-volume related activities i.e. purchasing and setups. This indeed would be worrying, if it were the case. However, there does seem to be an imbalance between the breakdown of the Fixed Factory Overheads. Let us consider the components that might be found in Fixed Factory Overheads and recalculate.

Fixed Factory Overheads

Rent	75,000
Heating and Lighting	35,000
Maintenance	50,000
Depreciation of Machinery	170,000
Insurance	10,000
Supervision	35,000
Purchasing/Receiving	75,000
Setup costs	90,000
	540,000

From the above figures it can be seen that Depreciation of Machinery is the largest item. Purchasing costs and setup costs have been reduced. In this case purchase orders per unit would be £75,000 ÷ 400 = £187.50. It is considered unlikely that setup costs would exceed depreciation, else there should be a case for a capital project to reduce setup costs.

Table 7.6   *Traditional method of apportionment – Alternative*

	Total	RUF	TUF
Rent	75,000	10,000	65,000
Heating and Light	35,000	5,000	30,000
Maintenance	50,000	10,000	40,000
Depn of Machinery	170,000	20,000	150,000
Insurance	10,000	3,000	7,000
Supervision	35,000	5,000	30,000
Purchase orders	75,000	20,000	55,000
Setup costs	90,000	35,000	55,000
	540,000	**108,000**	**432,000**

In the above example we have left out the bases of apportionment, these might be floor area, machine hours, labour hours, plant value, number of employees, technical estimate.   Using the traditional method of apportionment and spreadsheets it is possible to construct complex bases that will compare favourably against other methods e.g. ABC.

However, in order to compare like with like we have recalculated the apportionment using an ABC technique and the Fixed Factory Overheads in *Table 7.6*.

Table 7.7   *ABC method of apportionment – Alternative*

		RUF		TUF
Volume costs	(9,000 x £4.62963)	41,667	(72,000 x £4.62963)	333,333
Purchasing costs	(100 x £187.5)	18,750	(300 x £187.5)	56,250
Setup costs	(50 x £692.31)	34,616	(80 x £692.31)	55,384
		95,033		**444,967**

From this brief review of the traditional compared to the ABC techniques it is clear that the whole activity of attempting to apportion overhead costs is open to question.

7.1   a. From the following information calculate the production cost for Job Numbers A1127 and A1131.

  b. Discuss the problems associated with the use of floor area and plant value as a basis for apportionment.

JOBS

Direct Costs:	A1127	A1131
Direct Materials	£184.00	£262.00
Direct Labour Shop 1 at £5.00 per hour	18 hrs	22hrs
Direct Labour Shop 2 at £7.00 per hour	nil	14 hrs
Outwork	£99.00	£55.00

The following information is contained in the annual budget for 200X:

Direct Labour	Shop 1	12,000 hours
Direct Labour	Shop 2	18,000 hours

Works Overhead:	£
Indirect Labour	8,400
Salaries	42,000
Depreciation	18,900
Maintenance	19,600
Rent and Rates	32,200
	121,100

Additional Information:	Shop 1	Shop 2
Plant Value	£75,600	£113,400
Floor Area (square metres)	3,000	3,000
Maintenance (estimate)	£12,000	£7,600

The direct labour hour is to be used for the calculation of overhead absorption rates.

7.2   a.   From the following information calculate the production cost for Job Numbers E102 and E110.

      b.   Discuss the problems associated with the use of floor area and plant value as a basis for apportionment.

JOBS

Direct Costs:	E102	E110
Direct Materials	£71.80	£228.04
Direct Labour Shop 1 at £7.50 per hour	16 hrs	12hrs
Direct Labour Shop 2 at £10.50 per hour	nil	8 hrs
Outwork	£65.00	£40.00

The following information is contained in the annual budget for 200X:

Direct Labour	Shop 1	5,000 hours
Direct Labour	Shop 2	15,000 hours

Works Overhead:	£
Indirect Labour	12,000
Salaries	30,000
Depreciation	16,600
Maintenance	14,000
Rent and Rates	20,000
	92,600

Additional Information:	Shop 1	Shop 2
Plant Value	£62,000	£104,000
Floor Area (square metres)	2,000	4,000
Maintenance (estimate)	£4,400	£9,600

The direct labour hour is to be used for the calculation of overhead absorption rates.

7.3   You are asked to prepare a quote for an order which is estimated to require 544 kg of materials and 220 hours of direct labour. The order is from a regular customer. The company applies normal absorption costing principles. Variable overhead is assumed to be related to direct labour hours, and fixed overhead and profit are based on a percentage of total variable cost and total cost respectively.

The budget for the six months to 31st December 200X is as follows:

Sales		£468,000
Direct Materials 24,000 kg	£120,000	
Direct Labour 5,000 hours	£30,000	
Variable Overhead	£90,000	
Total Variable Cost		£240,000
Fixed Overhead		£120,000
Total Cost		360,000
Budgeted Profit		£108,000

The price you would quote is

7.4   The overhead recovery rate for Shop 1 is £12.00 per machine hour, and the overhead recovery rate for Shop 2 is £10.00 per labour hour. The labour rates for Shop 1 and Shop 2 are £7.00 per hour and £5.00 per hour respectively. Administrative costs are charged at 30% of manufacturing costs and profit is added at 20% of total costs.

You are asked to prepare a quote given the following:

Direct Materials	£200.00
Direct Labour – Shop 1	5 hours
Direct Labour – Shop 2	3 hours
Machine Hours – Shop 1	10 hours

The price to quote is

7.5   The apportionment and absorption of overheads can often cause concern. List four basis of apportionment and four methods of absorption.

7.6   You are asked to prepare a quote for an order which is estimated to require 550 kg of materials and 220 hours of direct labour. The company has a shortage of direct labour with 5,000 hours being the maximum available for the period.

The budget for the six months to 31 December 200X is as follows:

Sales			£650,000
Direct Materials 26,000 kg	£104,000		
Direct Labour 5,000 hours	£45,000		
Variable Cost	£151,000		
Total Variable Cost		£300,000	
Fixed Costs		£200,000	
Total Cost			£500,000
Budgeted Profit			£150,000

The price you would quote is

7.7   The budget for L. Driver Ltd provide the following estimates for the current year ending 31st October 200X.

	Machine	Assembly
Machine Hours	48,000	6,000
Direct Labour Hours	18,000	15,000
Hourly Wage Rate	£6.00	£5.00
Production Overhead	£120,000	£60,000

In response to a request for a quotation from Fairway Ltd, the estimating department have provided the following costs and timings:

Direct Materials	£144.00
Direct Labour – Machine Shop	1 hour
Direct Labour – Assembly	2 hours
Machine Hours – Machine Shop	4 hours
Delivery Charge – External Carrier	£30.00

REQUIRED

1. Calculate the predetermined overhead absorption rates that need to be applied to jobs passing through the factory for the current year.

2. Calculate the price to quote to Fairway Ltd, given that administrative costs are charged at 25% of manufacturing costs, and profit is added at 15% of total costs.

7.8   Company produces two components A1123 and A1139 that are similar in appearance and use the same processes and machinery. The following data has been gathered:

	A1123	A1139
Budget Volume (components)	5,000	25,000
Machine Hours per component	4	4
Number of Purchase Orders	150	350
Number of Setups	70	120
Total Machine Hours	20,000	100,000

Fixed Factory Overheads:

Volume related	£250,000
Purchasing related	£125,000
Setup related	£150,000
	£525,000

REQUIRED

a. Prepare statements showing the apportionment of Fixed Factory overheads using:

   i   Traditional apportionment techniques.

   ii   Activity Based Costing techniques.

b. Comment on the results.

COST-VOLUME -PROFIT ANALYSIS

When you have finished studying this chapter you should be able to:

❏ Describe the main differences between fixed and variable costs, relevant and irrelevant costs.

❏ Calculate and interpret break even in units, minimum selling price and volume required to meet a target profit.

❏ Prepare and interpret break even charts.

❏ Understand the limitations of cost, volume and profit (CVP) analysis.

❏ Prepare and interpret statements using relevant costs.

8.1   Introduction

Not all managerial action can be preplanned and handled within a budgetary context. The reality of management is that periodically events will arise on a non-routine or adhoc basis which require a decision to be taken. What tends to make such events difficult to deal with is that rarely are they the same. However, there are some guidelines that are generally applicable which can be summarised as:

❐   Establish the exact nature of the issues requiring a decision to be taken.

❐   Identify the alternative courses of action.

❐   Identify the most appropriate data, irrespective of its source.

❐   Measure data correctly and logically analyse it.

❐   Ensure that financial and non financial data is presented well to facilitate information sharing and its correct interpretation.

In this chapter we are primarily concerned with decisions directed towards the short-term, which is frequently defined as one year or less, and the accounting information required to make these decisions. Decisions with implications greater than one year are discussed in the next chapter, however, it must be emphasised that much of the discussion about organising and analysing short-term decisions is relevant to dealing with long-term decisions.

As we will illustrate, dealing with short-term decisions requires a sound understanding of the economic issues of each situation to ensure an appropriate action is taken. In particular, use of the right data in the right way for each decision is critical for making good decisions. Unfortunately, there can often be confusion concerning the correct data to use because of a temptation to rely upon systems developed and currently operating to provide data for routine accounting purposes, such as budgetary control. Such systems will often have been developed for specific purposes relating to the control of activities and the information provided by it is often inadequate for answering the key question for managing decisions which is:

> *'How do costs and revenues differ if one*
>
> *course of action is adopted rather than another?'*

Answering this key question requires the ability to identify costs and revenues which are likely to change as a consequence of the decision, irrespective of their source. For example, in a decision whether to discontinue an operation or not, the historical cost of the stock from the accounting system may often be irrelevant. The crucial question is what alternative uses are there for the stock. If the only alternative is to sell the stock, the relevant information is its resale value which may be totally different from its historical cost. It also should not be ignored that there will often be non-financial information to be taken into consideration which may have a significant impact upon a particular situation, such as the effect on labour relations in the case of discontinuing an operation. Once all relevant points have been considered, it is critical that the resulting information is presented in the most appropriate form to ensure it is interpreted and correctly acted upon by the parties involved.

In this chapter we will consider the evaluation of non-routine decisions with the aid of a number of illustrations which represent the subtle differences in emphasis as to the type of data required. We first focus upon those decisions which require the analysis of cost behaviour and its application in what is now popularly called *cost-volume-profit* analysis. This type of approach can be useful for studying such issues as what is the effect on profit when a new product range is introduced. It is also relevant to managers in not-for-profit organisations, mainly because knowledge of how costs fluctuate in response to changes in volume is valuable regardless of whether profit is an objective. No organisation ever has unlimited resources!

8.2   Cost-Volume-Profit Relationships

A good understanding of how cost, volume and profit relate to one another can be invaluable in dealing with certain types of short-term decisions. Consider for example a request by a customer to provide a large consignment of standard product at a substantial discount. In order to establish the viability of such a request one issue likely to be of importance is the profitability that will result. We will illustrate how using Cost-Volume-Profit (CVP) analysis such a request can be readily evaluated but before then, it is important to be aware of some basic terminology associated with its use.

1.   Fixed and Variable Costs

At its simplest, cost-volume-profit analysis is reliant upon a classification of costs in which fixed and variable costs are separated from one another. Fixed costs are those which are generally time related and are not influenced by the level of activity. For example, the rent payable by a manufacturer for factory space will not be related to the number of items produced. Whether times are good or bad the cost will have to be incurred and the same will apply to any other costs which are contractually incurred. Of course if activity is to be increased beyond the capacity of the premises additional rent would have to be incurred, but within what is known as the 'relevant range' of activity the cost is fixed. Variable costs on the other hand are directly related to the level of activity; if activity increases variable costs will increase and vice versa if activity decreases.

Fixed and variable costs can be readily understood when portrayed graphically as illustrated in *Figure 8.1.*

Figure 8.1 Illustration of Fixed and Variable Costs

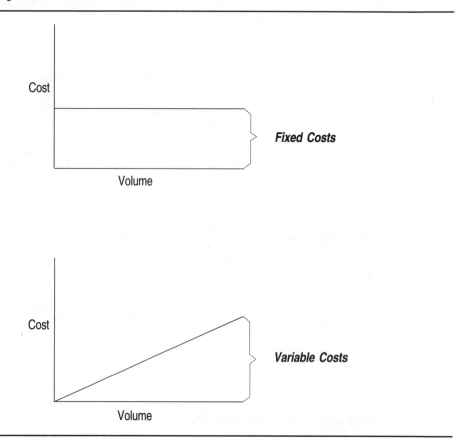

Fixed costs are shown to be constant for all levels of activity within the relevant range, whilst variable costs can be seen to increase in proportion to the level of activity. The sum of the fixed and the variable costs equals the total costs to be incurred over the level of activity within the relevant range.

In considering cost-volume-profit relationships it is usual to consider cost behaviour within the context of a model comprising only straight lines. This assumption can, of course, be relaxed to accommodate non-linear relationships, but it does make the analysis more difficult and in considering whether so to do, it is important to determine whether the benefit derived from greater accuracy of the input data will warrant the effort required to be expended.

Finally, you should not ignore the fact that costs may be simultaneously affected by more than one activity base. For example, labour costs associated with road haulage may be affected by both the weight and the number of units handled.

2. Uses of Cost-Volume-Profit Analysis

The ability to analyse and use cost-volume-profit relationships is an important management tool. The knowledge of patterns of cost behaviour offers insights valuable in planning and controlling short and long run operations. The example of increasing capacity is a good illustration of the power of the technique in planning. The implications of making changes upon profit can be determined as well as the requirements to achieve a given level of profit. The technique can be used to work forwards or backwards and, as should be only too obvious, it is ideal for spreadsheet analysis, whereby the effects of all sorts of modifications and assumptions can be evaluated.

The technique is also useful within the context of control. The implications of changes in the level of activity can be measured by flexing a budget using knowledge of cost behaviour, thereby permitting comparison to be made of actual and budgeted performance for any of activity.

8.3 An Example of Cost-Volume-Profit Analysis

The following data relates to a new product due to be launched on the 1st May:

Selling Price	£20.00 per unit
Forecast Volume	120,000 units
Variable Costs	£16.00 per unit
Fixed Costs	£300,000

In the following we will apply the principles to CVP analysis to the following five situations in which each has been treated as being independent of the other

1   Break even point in units.

2   Break even point in units if variable costs per unit increase to £17.00.

3   Break even point in £ sterling if the fixed costs increase to £336,000.

4   Minimum selling price to meet a profit target of £120,000.

5   Volume of sales required at a selling price of £19.00 per unit.

Finally, we will prepare a breakeven chart using the original data.

The first step in tackling such a problem is to calculate the total contribution and the contribution per unit.

	£	£ per unit
Sales	2,400,000	20.00
less Variable Costs	1,920,000	16.00
CONTRIBUTION	480,000	4.00
less Fixed Costs	300,000	
Profit	180,000	

1. Using this information we calculate the breakeven point by dividing the costs to be incurred irrespective of the level of activity (i.e. fixed costs) by the contribution each unit will generate.

$$\text{Break Even Point (units)} = \frac{\text{Fixed Costs}}{\text{Contribution Per Unit}}$$

$$= \frac{£300,000}{£4.00}$$

$$= 75,000 \text{ units}$$

2. Where the variable costs per unit change, so too will the contribution per unit:

	£ per unit
Sales	20.00
Variable Costs	17.00
Contribution	3.00

With an unchanged £20.00 selling price and a revised variable cost of £17.00 a contribution per unit of £3.00 will result. Assuming that the fixed costs remain unchanged at £300,000, the break even point in units is 100,000 (£300,000 ÷ £3).

3. Break even always arises where total cost equals total revenue. To find the break even point in value rather than volume, we first calculate the break even point in units and then multiply it by the selling price.

    In this case where fixed costs are £336,000 (with no other changes), the break even point in units will be £336,000 divided by £4.00, which equals 84,000 units. Break even in value can be found by multiplying 84,000 by £20.00, which equals £1,680,000.

4. The minimum selling price to meet a target profit is found from the sum of the contribution per unit plus the variable cost per unit. The contribution per unit in this situation can be found by dividing the required units into the sum of the fixed costs and the profit target. For example, we are told that the profit target is £120,000 which added to the fixed costs of £300,000 gives £420,000 (i.e. the contribution in value). The contribution per unit can now be found by dividing £420,000 by 120,000 units to give £3.50. Therefore, the minimum selling price is £3.50 plus the unit variable cost of £16.00 which equals £19.50.

5. The calculation of total volume to cover fixed costs and meet the target profit is similar to the approach used to determine the break even volume. The only difference is that the profit target is added to the fixed costs in order to calculate the number of units (volume) required to cover fixed costs and to cover the profit target from a given contribution per unit.

    In this case the requirement is to identify the volume to cover fixed costs and profit assuming that the selling price per unit is decreased to £19.00. Where the selling price is £19.00, the unit contribution falls to £3.00, i.e.

	£ per unit
Sales	19.00
Variable Costs	16.00
Contribution	3.00

The volume of sales under those circumstances is found by adding the fixed costs of £300,000 to the profit target of £180,000 and then dividing the result by £3.00, to give 160,000 units.

Breakeven analysis can also be plotted on a graph. The basic data required is total forecast volume, total sales revenue, total fixed costs and total variable costs. A breakeven graph, using the original data from the previous example is shown in *Figure 8.2*.

Figure 8.2   Break-Even Graph

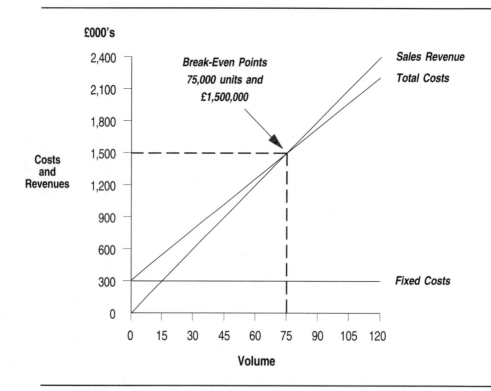

One of the most difficult tasks when preparing a breakeven chart is to determine the intervals between the values (e.g. units of 15 for the volume). You must also consider the overall size of the graph, its position on the page and give it a suitable heading.

In the above graph,

1. First, plot the total fixed costs i.e. £300,000, a straight line across the page.

2. Next, plot the total variable costs i.e. £1,920,000, from £300,000 at zero units to £2,220,000 (£1,920,000 + £300,000) at 120,000 units.

3. Finally, plot the total sales revenue i.e. £2,400,000, from £0 at zero units to £2,400,000 at 120,000 units.

Breakeven is the point where total costs equal total revenues. Also at this point, the total cost per unit equals the selling price per unit. To the left of the breakeven point the total costs exceed the total revenues and represents the loss segment, while to the right of the breakeven point the total revenues exceed the total costs and represents the profit segment.

Breakeven is shown to be 75,000 units in terms of volume and £1,500,000 costs and revenues. It can be seen that the only values to affect break even are any change in:

1. Total fixed cost. For example, should total fixed costs increase then break even will also increase.

2. Variable costs which in turn will affect total costs. For example, an increase in variable costs will increase the break even volume.

3. Selling prices which in turn will affect the total sales revenue line. For example a decrease in selling prices will increase the break even volume.

8.4 Contribution Margin and Gross Margin

We have shown the contribution margin to be the excess of sales over all variable costs. It can be expressed as a total amount, a unit amount, and a percentage.

You should be aware of the potential for confusion about the difference between contribution and gross profit. Gross profit is a widely used concept, particularly in the retailing industry and is the excess of sales over the cost of goods sold. However, the cost of goods sold will usually be very different in nature and amount from the contribution. The cost of goods sold relates solely to the direct costs associated with those items sold and any attributed overhead. It, therefore, usually contains elements of both fixed and variable costs unlike the contribution margin which is calculated with sole reference to variable costs.

Wagner plc manufactures an instrument which has a variable cost structure as follows:

	£
Materials	54.00
Labour	13.50
Variable Costs	5.40
	72.90

The instrument sells at £121.50 each and the company expects a sales revenue from this product in the current year of £1,822,500 and fixed overhead expense attributable to this product is budgeted at £189,000. A wage agreement with the employees states that a 10% increase will be paid to labour in the forthcoming year, whilst the managing director believes that from the beginning of the new financial year material prices will rise by 7.5%, variable overhead by 5% and fixed overheads by 3%.

Required

1. Calculate the new selling price if the contribution/sales ratio is to be maintained.

2. Calculate the sales volume required in the forthcoming year if the price remains the same and the profit level is to be maintained. (The selling price is to remain at £121.50 in spite of the increase in costs).

	Existing Variable cost		Revised Variable cost
	£	%	£
Materials	54.00	7.5	58.05
Labour	13.50	10.0	14.85
Variable Costs	5.40	5.0	5.67
	72.90		78.57

1. Revised selling price

$$\text{Contribution to Sales Ratio} \quad = \quad \frac{(121.50 - 72.90) \times 100}{121.50}$$

$$= \quad 40\%$$

Thus, to maintain the current contribution to sales ratio, the revised variable cost must equal 60% of the selling price.

$$\text{Revised Selling Price} \quad = \quad \frac{£78.57 \times 100}{60}$$

$$= \quad £130.95$$

2. Alternative sales volume required:

$$\text{Existing Sales Volume} \quad = \quad \frac{£1,822,500}{£121.50}$$

$$= \quad 15,000$$

Existing profit level:

Contribution (15,000 x £48.60)	729,000
less Fixed Costs	189,000
	540,000

$$\text{Revised Fixed Costs} \quad = \quad \frac{£189,000 \times 103}{100}$$

$$= \quad £194,670$$

Existing Profit Level	540,000
Revised Fixed Costs	194,670
Contribution Required	734,670

$$\text{Sales Volume Required} \quad = \quad \frac{£734,670}{(£121.50 - £78.57)}$$

$$= \quad 17,113$$

8.5. Limitations of Cost-Volume-Profit (CVP) Analysis

A major limitation of conventional CVP analysis that we have already identified is the assumption and use of linear relationships. Yet another limitation relates to the difficulty of dividing fixed costs among many products and/or services. Whilst variable costs can usually be identified with production services, most fixed costs usually can only be divided by allocation and apportionment methods reliant upon a good deal of judgement (covered in *Chapter 7*). However, perhaps the major limitation of the technique relates to the initial separation of fixed and variable costs. This can often be difficult to achieve with any sort of precision because many costs do not fall neatly into one or other of the two categories, and methods for separating fixed and variable costs may be required for the technique to be used. If this is the case, then you should be particularly mindful about applying a great deal of sophistication to any analysis because this may serve to cloud the key topic which is the quality of the data input.

The quality of input data is an important point and one you will find we often emphasise. In our opinion too much emphasis has been placed upon how to make techniques more sophisticated without sufficient consideration of the quality of the data to which such sophisticated techniques will be applied. With this in mind let us consider briefly how fixed and variable costs can be separated.

First, judgement can be applied to the data in an attempt to separate those costs which can be considered as being wholly fixed or wholly variable. Bearing in mind that we are considering a defined range of activity, examples of fixed costs would be salaried staff and occupancy costs, such as rents and rates, whilst materials costs and sales commissions are illustrative of typical variable costs to a commercial oriented manufacturing operation.

Of course, the likelihood of separating a substantial proportion of total costs in this way is often very low and the remainder will fall somewhere between the two extremes of wholly fixed and wholly variable costs. This remainder, known as semi-fixed, or semi-variable costs, need to be separated in order to make cost-volume-profit analysis operable.

A number of methods are available to make such a separation possible ranging from comparing costs at high and low levels of activity, to regression analysis, whereby using statistical analysis a line of best fit is found from available cost data. Irrespective of the method applied, the result will only be an approximation! Yes, it is possible to minimise the approximation but you should weigh the cost of so doing against the relative likely benefit that will be achieved.

8.6   Relevant Costs

The application of the principles of CVP analysis does suffer one major limitation for many decisions, other than those discussed earlier. In situations where there are different potential courses of action, relevant data for evaluating the alternatives is required and the cost behaviour information used in CVP analysis is unlikely to meet all of its requirements. What must be identified in such circumstances is the amount by which costs will change if one course of action is taken rather than another.

Surely, you must be thinking, this is simply an extension of cost-volume-profit analysis, but this need not be so. In discussing and applying cost-volume-profit analysis we did not question the relevance of the input data used to the decision in question. Questioning cost relevance is an important part of choosing between alternative courses of action.

As a manager, you must avoid using irrelevant information for evaluating alternatives no matter how impressive it may appear to be. The problem is, how do you avoid the use of irrelevant information and identify that which is relevant?

First, the accounting information used in any decision must relate to the future, not the past. It is essential that only costs and revenues yet to be incurred are used for purposes of decision making. This is because they alone will be incurred as a result of taking the decision in question. Past costs and revenues, which are often referred to as 'sunk' costs and revenues, are irrelevant to decision making, apart from their use in helping to forecast the future.

Second, where you are faced with a decision, the only relevant costs or revenues are those which are different under the alternative courses of action. Such costs are often referred to as *differential or incremental* costs. An understanding of how to use differential costs is important because most decisions will require at least two courses of action to be considered, given that one course of action may merely be to confirm current practice!

1.   Cost Relevance in Action

E. Tee, an aspiring manager, recently hit by the increase in interest rates upon his newly acquired mortgage, has a problem with the financial arrangements for his golf. He can either pay £9.00 every time he plays or £140.00 for a non-refundable season ticket plus £2.00 for every round played. Which should he choose? This you should immediately recognise as being similar in principle to the earlier discussion of cost-volume-profit analysis. In order to make a decision between these two alternatives we can work out how many times E. Tee would have to play so that he is indifferent between either of the two. This point of indifference where he is no better or worse off is like the breakeven point discussed earlier. It is found by taking the cost of the annual season ticket and dividing it by the savings (the differential cost/benefit) achieved each time E. Tee would play.

$$= \quad \frac{\text{Annual Season Ticket}}{\text{Saving on Each Round}}$$

$$= \quad \frac{\text{£140.00}}{\text{£ 7.00}}$$

$$= \quad 20 \text{ times}$$

E. Tee would have to play more than 20 times in the year before a season ticket and £2 payment for each round would be a worthwhile decision. Because E. Tee likes golf and intends to play twice a week for the whole year he purchases an annual season ticket for £140.

Simple so far, but true to life complications arise. One month later, he identifies another problem which he cannot solve. He has visited another golf club which is nearer to his home. There is a single payment of £360.00 for membership with no additional green fees. The course is not heavily used, and it takes approximately three hours to complete a round compared to the four hours at the present club. What should he do? What about the £140.00 he has recently paid for his annual season ticket? The £140.00 is not relevant to this decision. It has already been paid, is not refundable and it will be the same irrespective of the decision he takes. Only the additional costs (incremental costs) and the additional savings (incremental receipts) are relevant to this new decision, i.e. those costs which will change as a result of making the decision.

The incremental costs in this case would be the £360.00 membership fee, and the incremental savings would be the £2.00 per round he has to pay at the present club.

$$= \quad \frac{\text{Incremental Costs}}{\text{Incremental Savings}}$$

$$= \quad \frac{\text{£360.00}}{\text{£ 2.00}}$$

$$= \quad 180 \text{ times}$$

Therefore, E. Tee would have to play approximately three and half times a week in order for it to be financially worth his while joining the other golf club. If, on the other hand, E. Tee could save £1.00 on travel by joining the other golf club (which is nearer to his home), breakeven would be achieved after 120 rounds (£360 divided by [£2 + £1]). However, there are a number of other aspects not necessarily of a financial nature which should be considered in making a decision to change to another club. Examples are:

❐ The time taken to play and travel.

❐ The possibility of sharing travelling.

❐ Who else plays.

❐ The amenities and social aspects.

❐ The quality of the facilities.

2. Cost Relevance – An Example

A firm of boat builders has just had an order for a luxury yacht cancelled after it has been finished. The only potential buyer is Mr Apostolides; who said that he might buy the yacht on the following conditions:

1. that the price to him was no more than £37,500

2. that certain specified conversion work was undertaken

3. that he could take delivery within one month.

The firm's accountant submits the following price estimate to help management decide whether a sale to Mr Apostolides would be worthwhile and to decide the minimum price that could be charged.

Table 8.1   Cost of Building the Yacht: – Price Estimate

		£
Materials at Cost		21,000
Labour		18,000
		39,000
Variable Costs (100% on Direct Cost)		39,000
		78,000
less Deposit, retained when order cancelled		22,500
		55,500
Add, conversion work:		
Materials at Cost	4,500	
Labour	1,500	
	6,000	
Fixed Costs (100% on Direct Cost)	6,000	
Administration (25% on Production Cost)	1,500	
		13,500
Total Cost		69,000
Add, Profit Mark-up (5%)		3,450
Suggested Price to Mr. Apostolides		72,450

The following information is available:

1. Three types of materials were used in the original building of the yacht:

    a. Type one cost £10,500; but it could now only be sold to a scrap merchant for £3,000 but to put it in a suitable form for sale it would take 20 hours of labour at £5 per hour. This work would be undertaken by the firm's maintenance department which is very slack at this time.

    b. Type two cost £7,500 and it could now be sold as scrap for £3,000, again after 20 hours of labour had been spent on it by the maintenance department. Alternatively it could be kept for use next year as a substitute for a material which is expected to cost £4,500, but an additional 40 hours of highly skilled labour over and above that spent to make the material suitable for resale would then have to be hired at £7.50 per hour.

    c. Type three cost £3,000; it could now be sold for £2,250. Alternatively it could be kept until next year as a substitute for a material which is expected to cost £3,000, but because of its special nature would have to be stored at an additional cost of £300.

2. There are two further types of materials to be used for the conversion:

    a. Type four was ordered last year at a price of £3,000, delivery was delayed and its realisable value has fallen to £1,500. In recognition of this the suppliers have given the firm a discount of £900. The material could be used only for this one job.

    b. Type five has been in stock some time and originally cost £1,500. Because of its high content of precious metal it could now be sold for £3,750, but metal brokers would charge 10% commission for selling it.

3. Of the £1,500 conversion labour charge, £1,350 represents the skilled men that would have to be specially hired, the other £150 represents the time spent by the foreman who is a permanent employee.

4. The plans and specifications for the yacht could be sold for £3,750 if it is scrapped.

The accountants cost statement indicates that Apostolides's offer of £37,500 would be significantly below the cost of £72,450. Is that the right conclusion? If you think it necessary, redraft the original schedule in the way you think might be more helpful to management. Your answer should include any assumptions you have made.

Table 8.2   Value of Yacht, as is

			£
Material Type 1	Note 1		3,000
Material Type 2	Note 2		4,200
Material Type 3	Note 3		2,700
Value in Current State			9,900
Plans			3,750
		(A)	13,650
Conversion Cost:			
Material Type 4	Note 4		1,500
Material Type 5	Note 5		3,375
Labour			1,350
		(B)	6,225
Apostolides's Offer			37,500
less Minimum Price if Converted	(A − B)		19,875
Additional Contribution if Converted and Sold to Apostolides			17,625

Notes:

1. Realisable scrap value no labour charge as maintenance department over (under) capacity.

2. Replacement list value of £4,500 less skilled labour charge £300 (40 hours x 7.50 per hour). No maintenance labour as in Note 1.

3. Replacement cost less storage cost (£3,000 − £300).

4. Realisable value.

5. Realisable value.

6. Foreman, fixed cost.

8.1   The following data has been extracted from the budget of Hogan Ltd., for the six months ending 30th June 200X.

Sales (at £30 each)		£210,000
Variable Costs	£140,000	
Fixed Costs	£40,000	
		£180,000
		£30,000

REQUIRED

1. Calculate the break even point in units.

2. Assuming that each of the following are independent of one another, calculate the breakeven point assuming an increase in:

a   Fixed costs by 10%.

b   Variable costs by 5%.

c   Selling price by 4%.

d   Sales volume by 8%.

8.2   The following data relates to a new product due to be launched on the 1st March 200X.

Selling Price	£25.00	per unit
Forecast Volume	30,000	units
Variable Costs	£15.00	per unit
Fixed Costs	£200,000	

REQUIRED

Assuming that each of the following are independent of one another, calculate the

1. Break even point in units and £ sterling.

2. Break even point in units if variable costs per unit increase to £16.00.

3. Break even point in £ sterling if the fixed costs increase to £235,000.

4. Minimum selling price to meet a profit target of £70,000.

5. Volume of sales required at a selling price of £23.00 per unit.

6. Additional units required to cover an advertising campaign of £40,000.

8.3   A business makes and sells a single product from a plant with a capacity of 60,000 units per year. The results for the six months ended 31st December 1999 are shown below:

	£000	£000
Sales (20,000 units at £300 per unit)		6,000
Direct Materials	2,200	
Direct Labour	640	
Production Overheads (90% fixed)	1,600	
Selling and Administration Overheads (all fixed)	1,960	6,400
		– 400

The directors agree that this result is unsatisfactory. They propose cutting the price by £20, which they believe will stimulate sufficient sales to utilise all of the capacity during the six months to 30th June 2000.

REQUIRED

1. Calculate the break-even point in units for the six months to 31st December 1999.

2. Calculate the break-even point in units for the six months to 30th June 2000.

3. Calculate the profit for the six months to 30th June 2000 assuming that the increase in sales can be achieved.

4. Calculate the profit and break-even point for the next financial year if market conditions do not allow the price to be increased from the new level set by the directors, but fixed costs do increase by 10% and variable costs by 4%.

8.4   The following data have been collected: Selling price £84 per unit, Total variable costs £220,000, Forecast volume 5,500 units and Fixed costs £195,000.

1.   Profit for the period is:

2.   Break even point in units and sterling is:

3.   Break even point in units if variable costs increase by 10% is:

8.5   E. Tee Ltd., manufactures three models of electric powered golf trolleys, standard, super, and deluxe.

Budgeted fixed costs for the year ending 30th November 200X are £1,000,000.

The following data shows the selling prices and volumes together with the costs per unit for each of the models.

Models	Standard	Super	Deluxe
Sales Volumes	4,000	3,000	1,000
Selling Price	£300	£375	£550
Direct Materials	£90	£120	£160
Direct Labour	£45	£45	£90
Variable Overheads	£20	£30	£50

The Deluxe model has not been selling due to a cheaper import which has obtained an increased share in that market. E. Tee Ltd., has a choice, to drop their selling price of the Deluxe model by £75 which they feel will increase sales volume by 50%, or to drop the Deluxe model from their range.

The extra labour, which is currently employed on the Deluxe model could be transferred to increase the production of the Standard or the Super model, or of both models equally.

REQUIRED

1. State what the profit would be if E. Tee Ltd., continued with their budget plan.

2. Evaluate the choices available to E. Tee Ltd., and state which choice you would recommend.

8.6   The following data has been collected: Selling price £25.00 per unit, Variable cost £15.00 per unit, forecast volume 25,000 units and fixed costs are expected to be £200,000 for the period.

1.   The profit for the period is:

2.   The break-even in £ sterling is:

3.   The minimum selling price if fixed costs increase to £260,000 is:

(assume other relevant figures remain the same)

8.7   The following data relates to a new product due to be launched on the 1st July 200X:

    Selling Price   £35.00 per unit

    Forecast Volume   50,000 units

    Variable Costs   £26.00 per unit

    Fixed Costs   £350,000

REQUIRED

Assuming that each of the following are independent of one another, calculate the:

1.   Break even point in units and £ sterling.

2.   Break even point in units if variable costs decrease to £23.00 per unit.

3.   Break even point in units and £ sterling if fixed costs increase to £370,000.

4.   Minimum selling price to meet a target profit of £120,000.

5.   Volume of sales required at a selling price of £38.00 per unit.

6.   Additional units required to cover an advertising campaign of £60,000.

8.8   The following data has been collected: Selling price £24.00 per unit, Variable cost £16.00 per unit, forecast volume 35,000 units and fixed costs are expected to be £200,000 for the period.

1.   The profit for the period is:

2.   The break-even in £ sterling is:

3.   The minimum selling price if fixed costs increase to £260,000 is:

    (assume other relevant figures remain the same)

8.9   The decision to "make or buy" is often misunderstood. Discuss, with reference to examples.

8.10   The following data relate to a new product due to be launched on 1st August 200X:

Selling Price	£42.00 per unit
Forecast Volume	70,000 units
Variable Costs	£33.00 per unit
Fixed Costs	£490,000

REQUIRED

Assuming that each of the following is independent of one another, calculate the:

1.   Break even point in units and £ sterling

2.   Break even point in units if variable costs decrease to £30.00 per unit

3.   Break even point in units and £ sterling if fixed costs increase to £550,000

4.   Minimum selling price to meet a target profit of £180,000

5.   Volume of sales required at a selling price of £45.00 per unit.

6.   Additional units required to cover an advertising campaign of £72,000.

CHAPTER NINE

CONTRIBUTION ANALYSIS

When you have finished studying this chapter you should be able to:

❑ Prepare statements to show whether a company should continue with apparently unprofitable products, divisions, branches.

❑ Apply the concept of relevant costs to:

* identify the best use of scarce resources;
* the make our buy decision;
* competitive tendering.
* the decision to accept or reject a special order.

❑ Describe and understand the differences between Absorption costing and Marginal costing.

❑ Use a framework to aid the structuring of decisions.

9.1 Introduction

In the previous chapter we introduced the characteristics of financial information required for short-term decision making which must be differential as between alternative choices and relate to the future. We will reinforce these two requirements and, where appropriate, apply the principles of CVP analysis with reference to five common applications of short-term decision techniques.

❑ Whether to continue with apparently unprofitable products, divisions, branches.

❑ How to make the best use of available scarce resources.

❑ Whether to make/use internal resources or buy from outside.

❑ Whether or not to use competitive tendering.

❑ Whether or not to accept a special order.

To answer the above we need to use the technique of contribution analysis. What is contribution? In the previous chapter we saw that sales minus variable costs gave a contribution to fixed cost plus profit. Equally we saw that fixed cost plus profit equals contribution. Contribution analysis puts the emphasis on maximising contribution, which in turn will maximise profit. The focus on contribution also helps to highlight those variables that have an immediate impact on profit i.e. those items that will change OR can be changed.

9.2 Whether to Continue with Apparently Unprofitable Products, Divisions, Branches.

This application of short-term decision making techniques will consider using the following example:

> T.O. Wood Ltd manufactures and sells three products, X, Y and Z. The internally prepared product profitability statement for the company is shown in *Table 9.1*. Fixed overhead costs are absorbed as a percentage of labour costs and have been rounded to the nearest £100,000. Products X and Z are machine intensive while Product Y is labour intensive. Management is considering whether to drop Product Y because it is making a loss, the assumption being that they could increase the total profit of the company by £100,000 by dropping Product Y. Do you agree?

Table 9.1   T.O. Wood Ltd – Product Profitability Statement

		X £'000	Y £'000	Z £'000	Total £'000
(a)	Sales	1,500	1,600	800	3,900
(b)	Material Costs	500	400	100	1,000
(c)	Labour Costs	400	800	300	1,500
(d)	Fixed Costs	300	500	200	1,000
(e)	Total Costs	1,200	1,700	600	3,500
(f)	**Profit/(Loss)**	**300**	**–100**	**200**	**400**

With reference to line (d) Product Y is absorbing 50% of the total fixed costs many of which may not be avoided even if the company were to drop Product Y. In such a situation where there is a limited differential effect upon fixed costs in continuing or dropping Product Y, they are not relevant in making the decision.

On the assumption that fixed costs are not avoidable in the short-term we have rearranged the contents of *Table 9.1* to show a distinction between those costs likely to be avoidable and those that are not:

Table 9.2 T.O. Wood Ltd – Product Contribution and Profitability Statement

	X £'000	Y £'000	Z £'000	Total £'000
Sales	1,500	1,600	800	3,900
Material Costs	500	400	100	1,000
Labour Costs [1]	400	800	300	1,500
Total Variable Costs	900	1,200	400	2,500
Contribution	600	400	400	1,400
Fixed Costs				1,000
Profit				400
CONTRIBUTION/SALES %	40	25	50	

[1]   *Labour costs are usually considered to be variable costs because they do respond to changes in the level of activity, albeit that this response may not be immediate.*

In the rearranged *Table 9.2* the value of retaining Product Y is shown assuming that no fixed costs are avoidable. Product Y can be seen to contribute £400,000 towards the fixed costs. If dropped, T.O. Wood Ltd would lose this contribution, with the result being a reduction in the total contribution by £400,000. Furthermore, this £400,000 reduction in contribution would completely wipe out the £400,000 profit currently obtained from making all three products.

This example illustrates one issue which must be considered in short-term decision analysis that arises from the allocation of fixed costs. Where fixed costs have been identified with products, as in this example, it is tempting but usually wrong to assume that they will necessarily disappear when a product is dropped. In fact, in many organisations all that is known with any certainty is the total fixed costs likely to be incurred, their allocation across products or services is frequently heavily dependent upon judgement.

T.O. Wood Ltd is a useful illustration of CVP analysis. This technique can frequently be usefully extended by relating the contribution per product to the sales revenue to produce what is known as the contribution to sales (C/S) ratio. The contribution to sales ratio is potentially useful when costs have been separated into fixed and variable categories. This is because the effect on total profit of a given volume change for any product(s) can be assessed using knowledge of the contribution to sales ratio. Let us consider the calculation and application of the C/S ratio.

The contribution to sales ratios for X, Y and Z, are found by expressing the contributions of £600,000, £400,000 and £400,000 as a percentage of the sales revenues of £1,500,000, £1,600,000 and £800,000, respectively. The resulting contribution to sales ratios are 40%, 25% and 50%. The effect on profit of an extra £1,000,000 of sales revenue being generated by each of the products assuming that fixed costs would remain the same would be £400,000, £250,000 and £500,000, for X, Y and Z, respectively. Therefore, given the potential to increase sales revenue by £1,000,000 the first product to be selected would be Product Z which has the highest contribution to sales ratio. Thus the assumption that fixed costs are time related and remain unchanged for such an increase in activity, and, that there is no differential effect between products, then the highest profit will be generated from increasing sales of Product Z.

You will note that we have been able to consider the potential financial benefits of an increase in sales revenue by considering the C/S ratio alone. Given that the relationships in the model are understood it is not necessary to undertake lengthy calculations to gauge the benefit.

Of course we have assumed no resource constraints. Where these exist the contribution to sales ratio is not a useful distinguishing mechanism between alternative products, as we will see in the next section.

9.3   How to Best Use Available Scarce Resources

In some production and distribution decisions, management may be confronted with the question of how best to allocate the firm's limited resources. Where demand for the product is greater than the production or distribution capabilities available, a company should seek to maximise its total contribution margin from these limited resources.

Limited resources can arise from one, or a combination of the following:

❑   Shortages of raw materials or purchased goods.

❑   Shortage of certain labour skills.

❑   Restricted space for production, in the warehouse or in a retailing outlet.

❑   Maximum machine capacities.

It may not only be on the supply side that limitations prevail. It is also quite possible that a firm will face limitations upon the amount it can produce and/or sell because of:

❑   Customer demand for one or more products or services.

❑   Government restrictions.

In such circumstances the challenge is to obtain the maximum possible benefit from the market opportunities and the resources available.

Where there is one single constraint, it is possible to carry out an analysis to determine the best mix of products to maximise total contribution margin. At its simplest the analysis requires the contribution margin for a product to be divided by the unit of scarce resource i.e. limiting factor. That product or service with the highest contribution per unit of the scarce resource is the most desirable whilst the resource constraint operates. The application of the contribution per unit of scarce resource will be demonstrated with reference to T.O. Wood Ltd, where management is considering the most desirable mix of products to incorporate into their annual budget.

Market research information has produced the estimated sales of T.O. Wood's present products together with further estimates of two new products, P and Q. There is no sales constraint, but there is a constraint on machine capacity of 4,800 hours and, given this constraint, management needs to know the mix of products which should be produced so as to maximise total profit margin. The product data which has been summarised in *Table 9.3* is available:

Table 9.3   T.O. Wood Ltd – Possible Alternative Products

	Existing Products			New Products	
	X	Y	Z	P	Q
Machine Hours	2,000	800	2,000	800	1,000
	£'000	£'000	£'000	£'000	£'000
Sales	1,500	1,600	800	700	1,000
Material Costs	500	400	100	200	400
Labour Costs	400	800	300	200	200
Total Variable Costs	900	1,200	400	400	600
Contribution	600	400	400	300	400
Contribution to Sales Ratio	40%	25%	50%	43%	40%

Unfortunately, as we will illustrate, the current product analysis is inadequate for selecting the appropriate product mix to maximise profit. What is required is an analysis of the contribution yielded per machine hour for each product. This we have provided in *Table 9.4* which has been used to rank the products from those which show the highest contribution per machine hour through to the lowest.

Table 9.4   Best Use of Scarce Resources – Ranking

	Existing Products			New Products	
	X	Y	Z	P	Q
(a) Machine Hours	2,000	800	2,000	800	1,000
	£,000	£,000	£,000	£,000	£'000
(b) Contribution	600	400	400	300	400
Contribution Per	£	£	£	£	£
Machine Hour	300	500	200	375	400
[(b) ÷ (a)]					
Ranking	4	1	5	3	2

The analysis shows that Product Y ranked first, provides the highest contribution per machine hour. Each unit requires less of the scarce resource than the other products, and it contributes £500 per machine hour.

The ranking illustrated in the table provides the order which will result in the best use of scarce machine hours. Given the total constraint of 4,800 hours and the selection of Product Y which requires 800 hours, the remaining 4,000 hours would be allocated to products Q, P and X. This allocation to the four products does not exhaust the 4,800 hours available and 200 hours still remain unused. This 200 hours spare capacity could be used to ease production scheduling, or it might be used to produce a proportion of Product Z.

You will have doubtless noted by selecting the product mix using contribution per machine hour, Product Z with the highest contribution sales ratio is the least desirable. Whilst it may produce the largest effect on contribution for a given increase in sales, it suffers from being inefficient in terms of machine hour use. Hopefully, you will be thinking why not buy or lease a new machine or investigate subcontracting production. This line of thinking is entirely appropriate as is questioning whether T.O.Wood should focus more heavily on Product Y. However, your attention would not have been so readily directed at these questions in the absence of the analysis we have outlined.

Assuming that the 200 hours are retained to ease production scheduling, the following revised product income statement shows the results of maximising total contribution per machine hour available.

Table 9.5 Product Contribution and Total profit Statement

	Y	Q	P	X	Total
Machine Hours	800	1,000	800	2,000	4,600
	£'000	£'000	£'000	£'000	£'000
Sales	1,600	1,000	700	1,500	4,800
Material Costs	400	400	200	500	1,500
Labour Costs	800	200	200	400	1,600
Total Variable Costs	1,200	600	400	900	3,100
Contribution	400	400	300	600	1,700
Fixed Costs					1,000
Profit					700

Where more than one constraint exists the problem will be reliant upon operations research methods like linear programming for its solution. Such techniques are beyond the scope of this book.

9.4   The Decision to Make or Buy

If you are not involved in a manufacturing environment, you may be tempted to skip this section on the grounds that make or buy decisions will be irrelevant to you. Nothing could be further from the truth! This we will demonstrate in the next section which is concerned with the evaluation of providing internal services against the use of outside contractors, and represents a good illustration of an application of make or buy principles.

Stated very simply, in a make or buy decision, buying is preferable on economic grounds when the relevant costs for making are greater than the price quoted by the supplier. As with many decisions, what often confuses the analysis is the distinction between those costs that are relevant to making the decision and those that are not. The distinction between relevant and non–relevant costs for make or buy decisions is exactly the same as described earlier insofar as relevant costs are future orientated and differential. However, to aid your understanding of their applications to make or buy decisions we will relate it to the following example.

The purchasing manager of T.O. Wood Ltd has been investigating the possibility of buying a certain component from an outside supplier. L. Driver Ltd is prepared to sign a one year contract to deliver 10,000 top quality units as needed during the year at a price of £5.00 per unit. This price of £5.00 is lower than the estimated manufacturing cost per component of £6.00, which is made up as follows:

Table 9.6   Product Cost Statement

	Unit cost £.00
Direct Material Costs	1.20
Direct Labour Costs	1.80
Factory Variable Cost	0.60
Annual Machine Rental	0.40
Factory Fixed Cost – Allocated	0.50
– Apportioned	1.50
	£6.00

It appears at first sight that it will make better economic sense to buy rather than to make, however, let us consider whether all of the items within the product cost breakdown are relevant, i.e. 'If the decision is made to buy, which of the costs will be avoided?' An investigation of the components reveals that direct materials, direct labour, factory variable costs, annual machine rental and factory fixed costs – allocated would all be avoided. As the total of these relevant costs amounts to £4.50, which is less than the price of £5 quoted by the supplier, the decision should be to continue making the component. The remaining £1.50 of costs relating to apportioned fixed costs would presumably have to be borne elsewhere in the company and because they do not differ, irrespective of the course of action, are irrelevant.

Even if the analysis had indicated it to be more desirable to buy on economic grounds, there would still be factors to be considered other than purely the financial ones. For example loss of know-how in producing this component, the loss of certain skilled labour, not being able to control future cost increases and, therefore, final product prices, the ability to fill up capacity in slack times, and the possibility of finding it difficult to obtain supplies at a reasonable price during boom times, which must all be taken into consideration.

9.5   Competitive Tendering

As indicated, the principles used in the make or buy decision can also be applied to an evaluation of services to answer the question 'Do we provide service using our own resources or do we invite outside suppliers to compete to provide the service?'

There are many examples of organisations using competitive tendering in an attempt to obtain savings in the services they provide. These include, local authorities with refuse collection, health authorities with domestic, catering and building maintenance services, and even the Royal Navy with ship repair.

What is the basis used to determine whether an organisation should provide a service in-house or accept an offer from an outside supplier? The financial criteria are exactly the same as the make or buy decision, such that an organisation should provide an in-house service when the relevant costs associated with its provision are less than the price quoted by outside suppliers. These relevant costs are once again those costs which would be avoided if the provision of the service were to cease, and would tend to include materials consumed and wages. However, you must be constantly aware of irrelevant costs like historical as opposed to future values of stocks and other assets, and allocated costs which can often cloud a decision. A thorough review of all costs associated with such a service must be undertaken.

Once again please do note that our discussion has been concerned with financial criteria only. As we have emphasised on a number of occasions there will always be non-financial issues often of equal importance to take into consideration before a decision can realistically be taken.

9.6   The Decision to Accept/Reject a Special Order

One issue likely to be appropriate to all managers at some time in their careers is whether to accept what we will refer to as a special order. By this we mean 'Are there circumstances in which it might make sense in financial terms to sell products or services at a lower price than normal, or, alternatively to provide a service internally at less than its full cost?'

In considering such decisions it is most important to be quite clear about the meaning of the term *full cost*. In many organisations external and internal prices for products and services are generated with reference to the full or total cost of its provision plus a percentage margin, a practice known as *cost-plus pricing*. Within the full cost there will usually be allocated and apportioned fixed overheads required to be covered irrespective of whether a special order is accepted. Such non-relevant costs must be ignored since the criterion for accepting a special order must only consider whether the direct benefits which result exceed those costs that could be avoided by not taking it.

Such evidence as exists from surveys of pricing reveals that some organisations do accept special orders using some form of the contribution analysis, although the bias towards its use is not as significant as many textbooks would imply.

You should be aware that the acceptance of a special order with reference to direct costs and benefits can be problematic if it generates a special order 'culture'. If all orders are priced as special how will fixed overheads ever be recovered!

There are also other considerations to be taken into account that may have financial consequences. For example, if it became widely known that special orders were negotiable then the subsequent marketing and selling of products, or services, may be far more difficult, and require a good deal more effort to be expended than currently.

As a general guideline then, in these types of decisions a company must consider:

1   Whether the acceptance of a special order will tie up capacity which could be used for profitable orders at some time in the future. If it does so then it should avoid the special contract.

2   Whether the acceptance of a contract will affect the regular sales of the product and ultimately the future pricing structure of that product. Generally speaking a special contract should not be accepted if it will affect consumer behaviour adversely within the same market place. General knowledge of the availability of special orders may well lead to consumer games with the supplier. Special orders might relate to Government contracts or customers in a separate market segment; possibly in an overseas market.

In the example that follows we will produce:

1. Budgeted Income statement (without the special order)

2. Total Income Statement (including the special order)

3. Income Statement (showing incremental income and costs for special order)

Example

The Jolly Inc. company is considering whether it should accept a special order for 15,000 units from a customer in Malaysia who has offered an ex-factory cost of £48.00 per unit. The overseas customer will pay all delivery and insurance costs and sales will be restricted to its own country. In this example we will assume that the company does not sell any units in Malaysia. The following data relates to the volumes, prices and costs for the year.

Production Capacity;	80,000 units
Forecast Sales Volume;	60,000 units
Selling Price;	£72.00
Materials;	5kg at £3.00 per kg
Labour;	2 hours at £9.00 per hour
Variable Overheads;	£1.50 per labour hour
Fixed Production Overheads;	£420,000
Selling Costs;	£360,000
Administration Overheads;	£500,000

Table 9.7   Budgeted Income Statement

Forecast Sales Volume: 60,000 units

		£	£
Sales Revenue	(60,000 x £72.00)		4,320,000
Direct Materials	(60,000 x 5kg x £3.00)	900,000	
Direct Labour	(60,000 x 2hrs x £9.00)	1,080,000	
Variable Overhead	(60,000 x 2 hrs x £1.50)	180,000	
Fixed Overhead		420,000	
Total Production Cost			2,580,000
= Gross Margin			1,740,000
Selling Costs			360,000
			1,380,000
Administration Costs			500,000
= Net Profit			880,000

From the above statement it can be seen that the Jolly Inc. company is budgeted to make a profit of £880,000 for the year. It has used 60,000 units and has spare capacity of 20,000 units this year. Calculations are show where required. Fixed Overheads, Selling Costs and Administration Costs are all considered fixed costs.

Table 9.8   Total Income Statement including special order

Expected Sales Volume: 75,000 units

		£	£
Budgeted Sales	(60,000 x £72.00)		4,320,000
Sales from Special Order	(15,000 x £48.00)		720,000
TOTAL SALES REVENUE			5,040,000
Direct Materials	(75,000 x 5kg x £3.00)	1,125,000	
Direct Labour	(75,000 x 2hrs x £9.00)	1,350,000	
Variable Overhead	(75,000 x 2 hrs x £1.50)	225,000	
Fixed Overhead		420,000	
Total Production Cost			3,120,000
= Gross Margin			1,920,000
Selling Costs			360,000
			1,560,000
Administration Costs			500,000
= Net Profit			1,060,000

In *Table 9.8* the effect of the additional volume can be seen. We have added in the incremental sales of 15,000 units that increases total sales revenue to £5,040,000. We have also increase the total volume for materials, labour and variable overheads to 75,000 units and kept fixed production overheads, selling costs and administration costs at their budgeted level. Should there be additional costs associated with the special order, these would have to be included.

A comparison of *Table 9.7 and 9.8* shows that the net profit figure would increase from £880,000 to £1,060,000 if the special order was accepted. From a financial point of view the special order should be accepted. However, this might only be beneficial in the short-term; if volume was expected to expand within the existing customer base the company would not be able to obtain its expected market share. In general, special orders should be short-term, accepted to fill a capacity gap and contribute additional profit to the company i.e. incremental revenue exceeds incremental costs.

We now show an Income Statement that highlights incremental revenue and costs. This statement, shown in *Table 9.9* is prepared to show an alternative method of analysis. By taking the Budgeted Income Statement in *Table 9.7*, plus the Income Statement shown below, *Table 9.9* we obtain the same final result as *Table 9.8*.

Table 9.9   *Income Statement showing Incremental Income and Costs for special order*

Special Order for 15,000 units

		£	£
Sales Revenue	(15,000 x £48.00)		720,000
Direct Materials	(15,000 x 5kg x £3.00)	225,000	
Direct Labour	(15,000 x 2hrs x £9.00)	270,000	
Variable Overhead	(15,000 x 2hrs x £1.50)	45,000	
Total Production Costs			540,000
= Gross Margin			180,000

In the differential, or incremental statement shown above the total production costs of £540,000 is deducted from the sales revenue of £720,000 to give a gross margin of £180,000. Here we can see that fixed production overheads are not included since they have been 'recovered' from our existing budgeted activity. Similarly, selling costs are not included since it is unlikely that additional selling costs could be attributed to the special order. The same applies to the administration costs, the assumption being that there is sufficient capacity to deal with the special order i.e. no direct costs should be incurred.

9.7   Marginal Costing v Absorption Costing

We will complete this section of the book which has covered costing, cost-volume-profit analysis and contribution analysis with a look at the technique of marginal costing versus absorption costing.

Many of the examples in chapter assumed a marginal costing approach i.e. contribution analysis. You will have noticed the problem associated with using full cost to base decisions to

❑   drop a loss making product, division or business; or

❑   allocate the best use of scarce resources; or

❑   stop using facilities within the organisation and buy from outside; or

❑   accept or reject a special order.

In each case, the use of full costing i.e. Absorption costing gives an incorrect message to the decision maker.

Absorption costing

❑   Those in favour of absorption costing will be satisfied that all know costs are covered e.g. variable costs, fixed production costs, selling, distribution and administration costs.

❑   By valuing closing stock at full production cost it matches costs with revenues for the period i.e. a proportion of the costs are carried forward to the next period.

❑   Absorption costing removes the need to separate variable and fixed costs which is one of the main problems associated with marginal costing.

❑   With the final output being total costs i.e. all variable and fixed costs it can provide a basis for pricing for those businesses that operate on a cost plus method of pricing.

❑   Absorption costing would tend to be suited to low volume and/or large one-off items.

❑   Finally, absorption costing is the recommended method for external reporting; specifically, the valuation of stock.

Marginal costing

❏ Two of the main benefits of marginal costing are:

1. that it removes the need to decide on bases of apportionment for each element of fixed cost and, the calculation of overhead recovery rates such as machine hour rate and labour hour rates.

2. it removes the under/over absorption of fixed overheads due to changes in production volumes.

❏ The application of marginal costing simply requires that Fixed Costs are deducted as a 'lump' from contribution to give a profit figure.

❏ Marginal costing uses variable/direct costs that can be determined and located to a product.

❏ Marginal costing tends to suit high volume mass production products but is equally applicable to retail and similar environments.

❏ Provides data for short-term decision making e.g. most profitable products, make or buy, best use of scarce resources.

Example

In the example that follows we will show the difference in reported factory contribution/profit using marginal costing and absorption costing. We will then reconcile the difference between the two methods.

The following data has been collected prior to the preparation of absorption and marginal production cost statements for January and February.

Standard Costs per unit:

	£
Direct Materials	4.00
Direct Labour	7.00
Variable Manufacturing Overhead	3.00
Standard Variable Cost	14.00

Other data:

Fixed Manufacturing Overhead	£375,000 per month
Expected Production	75,000 units
Selling Price	£26.00

Actual production data:

	Jan	Feb
Opening Stock	0	11,000
Production	73,000	68,000
Sales	62,000	74,000
Closing Stock	11,000	5,000

Marginal Costing

Table 9.10 shows the calculation of Contribution after Factory Fixed Overheads. At the beginning of the table we repeat some of the basic data from the example. Tutorial notes are appended to support certain of the calculations. It is assumed that the reader is familiar with the contribution type layouts.

Table 9.10   *Marginal Cost of Production*

		Jan		Feb
Sales Volume		62,000		74,000
Production Volume		73,000		68,000
Closing Stock Volume		11,000		5,000
Selling Price per unit		£26.00		£26.00
Standard Variable Cost		£14.00		£14.00
	£	£	£	£
Sales (1)		1,612,000		1,924,000
Opening Stock (2)	0		154,000	
Factory Costs (3)	1,022,000		952,000	
	1,022,000		1,106,000	
less Closing Stock (4)	154,000		70,000	
		868,000		1,036,000
Contribution		744,000		888,000
less Factory Overheads		375,000		375,000
Contribution after Factory Ohds.		369,000		513,000

Tutorial notes:

1. The sales figure is calculated e.g. for February 74,000 units x £26.00 per unit = £1,924,000.

2. The opening stock figure is calculated; opening stock units time standard variable cost per unit e.g. for February (please note that the closing stock for January is the opening stock for February) 11,000 units x £14.00 per unit = £154,000.

3. Factory cost is calculated; production volume x standard variable cost per unit e.g. for February 68,000 units x £14.00 per unit = £952,000.

4. Closing stock is calculated; closing stock units times the standard variable cost per unit e.g. 5,000 units £14.00 per unit = £70,000.

Absorption Costing

Table 9.11 shows the calculation of Gross Profit. At the beginning of the table we repeat some of the basic data from the example. Tutorial notes are appended to support certain of the calculations. The main difference here is that an absorption rate must be calculated for Factory Fixed Overheads and added to the Standard Variable Cost. We will show this calculation after *Table 9.11*.

Table 9.11   Absorption Cost of Production

		Jan		Feb
Sales Volume		62,000		74,000
Production Volume		73,000		68,000
Closing Stock Volume		11,000		5,000
	£	£	£	£
Sales (1)		1,612,000		1,924,000
Opening Stock (2)	0		209,000	
Total Production Cost (3)	1,387,000		1,292,000	
	1,387,000		1,501,000	
less Closing Stock (4)	209,000		95,000	
		1,178,000		1,406,000
Gross Profit		434,000		518,000

The calculation of the absorption cost of production is as follows:

(Fixed Factory Costs / Budgeted Production Volume) + Standard Variable cost per unit

(£375,000 ÷ 75,000) + £14.00 = £19.00 per unit

Tutorial notes:

1. The sales figure is calculated e.g. for February 74,000 units x £26.00 per unit = £1,924,000. This is the same as the marginal cost method.

2. The opening stock figure is calculated; opening stock units times the absorption cost of production per unit e.g. for February (please note that the closing stock for January is the opening stock for February) 11,000 units x £19.00 per unit = £209,000.

3. Factory cost is calculated; production volume x the absorption cost of production per unit e.g. for February 68,000 units x £19.00 per unit = £1,292,000.

4. Closing stock is calculated; closing stock units times the absorption cost of production per unit e.g. 5,000 units £19.00 per unit = £95,000.

Reconciling the difference

The main differences between the marginal costing and absorption costing are that in absorption costing:

❑ Fixed Factory costs are absorbed based on budgeted production levels, with adjustments carried out for under or over absorption.

❑ Fixed Factory costs are absorbed into closing stocks and ultimately - opening stocks.

We will now reconcile the differences between the two methods.

Table 9.12   Reconciling the differences between Marginal and Absorption Costing

	Jan	Feb
Absorption Costing method (1)	434,000	518,000
Marginal Costing method (2)	369,000	513,000
	65,000	5,000
add Production Volume Variance (3)	– 10,000	– 35,000
Difference	**55,000**	**– 30,000**
Opening Stock (4)	0	55,000
Closing Stock (5)	55,000	25,000
Difference (6)	**55,000**	**– 30,000**

Tutorial Notes:

1. These figures are taken from *Table 9.10*.

2. These figures are taken from *Table 9.11*.

3. Production Volume Variance is calculated as follows:

    (Actual – Budget Production) x Fixed Cost Recovery Rate

    Therefore, for:

    January = (73,000 – 75,000) x £5.00 = – £10,000

    February = (68,000 – 75,000) x £5.00 = – £35,000

4. There was no opening stock in January. In February the opening stock is January closing stock of £55,000.

5. The closing stock for January is the difference between the closing stock in Table 9.10 and the closing stock in *Table 9.11*; i.e. £209,000 – £154,000 = £55,000.

    The closing stock for February is the difference between the closing stock in Table 9.10 and the closing stock in *Table 9.11*; i.e. £95,000 – £70,000 = £25,000.

6. Check on the January difference is as follows; (11,000 units – 0 units) = 11,000 x £5.00 = £55,000.

    Check on the February difference is as follows; (5,000 units – 11,000 units) = 6,000 x £5.00 = £30,000.

9.8   Structuring Decision Analysis

Clear thought and the application of certain key principles is critical for making sound decisions. We have offered these key principles by way of a number of applications which you may be able to apply to your own circumstances. All too often a major barrier to decision making is a lack of structure and we offer the following as a guideline:

❑ Clearly define exactly what the problem is for which a solution is sought.

❑ Consider all possible alternative courses of action which could lead to a solution.

❑ Discard those alternatives which on a common sense appraisal are 'nonstarters' for one reason or another.

❑ Evaluate the cost and benefit differences between each of the remaining courses of action.

❑ Weigh up the non-financial factors related to each course of action.

❑ Take into account both financial and non-financial factors important to the decision, make the necessary trade-offs and decide.

All common sense you might be thinking? We would agree, but in our experience it is all too easy to overlook, underestimate, or evaluate incorrectly one or more of the steps.

9.1   A company making a single product has a factory in Swindon and distribute its production through three depots situated in Swindon, Bristol and Reading.

It is estimated that during the coming year 99,000 units will be manufactured and sold at a price of £22 per unit, the sales being spread as follows:

Swindon	67,000 units
Bristol	22,000 units
Reading	10,000 units

Standard costs of production are:

Direct Materials	£6.50 per unit
Direct Labour	£3.40 per unit
Variable Production Overheads	150% on direct labour
Fixed Production Overheads	£250,000 per year

The cost of selling and distribution incurred by the depots are estimated as follows:

Fixed costs

Swindon	£70,000 per year
Bristol	£60,000 per year
Reading	£60,000 per year

Variable costs

Swindon	8% of Sales Revenue
Bristol	10% of Sales Revenue
Reading	12% of Sales Revenue

Management is considering closing the Bristol and/or Reading depots. If this is done it is expected that all sales in these areas will be lost, but the sales in Swindon will not be affected.

REQUIRED

1.   From the figures provided prepare a statement indicating why management is thinking of closing the depots in Bristol and Reading.

2.   Present additional information to help management make a decision in regard to this problem, and make recommendations from your figures.

9.2   A meeting has been arranged of the executives of W.E. Look Ltd., to consider the budget for the coming year. They are not convinced that the products they produce and the products they sell are giving the optimum profit. Until they move into the new factory in two years time there will be severe restrictions on capacity.

The current machine capacity is 160 hours per week with no other major restrictions (i.e. materials, labour etc.)

The following information has been collected for the products the company is able to sell per week with no seasonal trends.

Products	A	B	C	D	E	F	G
				£000			
Sales	7.0	2.0	2.0	4.0	6.0	2.0	4.0
Materials	4.0	0.8	0.7	2.5	3.0	0.6	0.6
Labour	2.0	0.6	1.0	1.0	1.0	0.6	2.0
Machine Hours	40	20	20	60	80	20	120

Fixed costs will remain constant at £115,440 per year, regardless of product mix.

REQUIRED

1. Prepare a statement showing which products should be produced to give the optimum profit from available capacity.

2. From the information obtained in above, prepare an income statement – for a single week.

9.3   Mouldit Ltd makes a range of products in expanded polystyrene (cups, trays, DIY materials etc.). The budget for the six months to 31st October 200X is as follows:

	£	£	£
Sales			780,000
Polystyrene (5,000 kg)	200,000		
Direct Labour (10,000 hours)	50,000		
Variable Overhead	150,000		
Total Variable Costs		400,000	
Fixed Overhead		250,000	
Total Cost			650,000
Budgeted Profit			130,000

You have been asked to quote for an order which is estimated to require 100 kg of polystyrene and 240 hours of direct labour.

REQUIRED

1. The order is from a regular customer. The company applies normal absorption costing principles. Variable overhead is assumed to be related to direct labour hours, and fixed overhead and profit are based on a loading of total variable cost and total cost respectively.

2. Labour is in short supply and the budget includes the maximum hours available. During the half year you expect to receive more order than you will be able to fulfil.

3. This is a potential new customer who is looking for a regular supplier. This is, in effect, a trial order and you would like to do business with them in the future. A competitor is believed to be quoting about £16,300.

9.4   Mars Packers Ltd has its own internal department which produces a standard size carton for packaging of the company's products. 360,000 of these cartons are used annually and the detailed budgeted costs of production are as follows:

Direct Materials	£84,000	Direct Labour	£18,000
Electricity (power costs)	£4,500	Depreciation of Plant	£13,500
Repairs to Plant	£3,000	Fixed Production Overheads	£15,000

An outside supplier has quoted to supply all the cartons on a regular basis throughout the year at a price of £325 per 1,000. In the event of accepting this offer the section will be closed and the specialist plant sold for £28,000. The company will also incur additional fixed costs of £9,000 per year for inspection and storage of the cartons.

REQUIRED

1. Prepare a financial statement to assist management to decide whether they should buy in the cartons.

2. Identify any other factors which should be taken into consideration.

9.5   The current availability of labour is 200 hours per week, with no other major restrictions. The following information has been collected for the products the company is able to sell, per week with no major restrictions:

Products	A	B	C	D
Sales	14,000	4,000	4,000	8,000
Materials	8,000	1,600	1,400	4,800
Labour	4,000	1,200	2,000	1,600
Labour Hours	80	40	40	80

REQUIRED

Prepare a table to show the ranking of products that would produce the greatest profit.

9.6   Whines Ltd., manufactures and assembles small electric motors. 32,000 units of part 1790 are manufactured each year to which the following production costs apply:

Direct Materials	£16,000
Direct Labour	£24,000
Variable Production Overheads	£16,000
Fixed Production Overheads	£32,000

Wedge Ltd., has offered to sell Whines Ltd., 32,000 units of part 1790 at £2.50 per unit. If the company accepts the offer, £12,000 of fixed overheads applied to part 1790 could be eliminated. Additionally, some premises used during the manufacture of part 1790 could be rented to a third party at an annual rental of £8,000.

REQUIRED

1.   Explain whether Whines Ltd. should accept the offer from Wedge Ltd. or not

2.   What other factors might the management of Whines Ltd. wish to consider before arriving at a decision.

9.7   Dymond Ltd. manufactures specialist jewellery for fashion shops. For the last year the company has been operating at 60 per cent of its capacity and its results were as follows:

Sales	(240,000 units at £12 each)	2,880,000
Variable Costs	(at £7.80 per unit)	1,872,000
Fixed Costs		700,000
Profit		308,000

A major retailer has offered to purchase the output from the excess capacity for the next three years at a price of £9.60 per unit. If the offer was accepted, fixed costs would increase by £150,000 per year.

Evaluate the offer from the major retailer.

9.8   The company accountant of L. Driver Ltd has drawn up the following statement to assist production management in their decision on product production during the coming year.

Product	A	B	C	D	E	F
Selling Price (£)	420	570	510	480	540	570
Materials	190	160	130	205	240	150
Labour	40	90	90	50	70	90
Variable Overheads	50	25	25	40	35	55
Fixed Overheads	60	135	135	75	105	135
	340	410	380	370	450	430
Profit Per Unit	80	160	130	110	90	140
Ranking for Production	6	1	3	4	5	2
Estimated Maximum Sales per annum (units)	400	1000	300	800	500	300

Specialist labour is required to produce the products and earns £8.00 per hour; the company can hire only 25,000 labour hours during the coming year. All other resources can be obtained in the desired quantities. Fixed overheads are charged at 150% of labour cost under the company's costing system.

REQUIRED

1. Produce an alternative method of ranking the company's products to make the best use of the shortage of specialist labour.

2. What other factors should be taken into consideration?

9.9 The current availability of labour is 160 hours per week, with no other major restrictions. The following information has been collected for the products the company is able to sell, per week with no major restrictions:

Products	A	B	C	D
Sales	16,000	6,000	6,000	10,000
Materials	9,000	2,600	2,400	5,800
Labour	4,000	1,200	2,000	1,600
Labour Hours	80	40	40	80

The Ranking is:

9.10 AMILL is a chemical used in the production of XZX Ltd's range of fertilisers. Because of a fire at the chemical works, supply is restricted to 12,000 kg per month, at a cost of £6.00 per kg.

Before supplies were restricted XZX's budget was:

	A	B	C	D
Sales (in kgs)	18,000	21,600	18,000	28,800
Selling Price (per kg)	£3.24	£4.92	£4.62	£6.00
Variable Costs per kg of output:				
Amill	£0.90	£1.44	£1.08	£2.40
Other Direct Materials	£0.30	£0.48	£0.48	£0.72
Direct Labour	£0.48	£0.66	£0.60	£0.84
Production Overhead	£0.12	£0.18	£0.12	£0.24
Fixed Costs	£30,000 per month.			

REQUIRED

Calculate the maximum profit possible, per month, while Amill is in short supply.

9.11   Sam and Ella Chick company are considering whether they should accept a special order for 35,000 units from a potential overseas customer who has offered an ex-factory cost of £18.00 per unit. The following data relates to the volumes, prices and costs for the year.

Production Capacity;	200,000 units
Forecast Sales Volume;	125,000 units
Selling Price;	£25.00
Materials;	2kg at £2.00 per kg
Labour;	1 hours at £7.00 per hour
Variable Overheads;	£2.00 per labour hour
Fixed Production Overheads;	£420,000
Selling Costs;	£200,000

REQUIRED

Prepare two income statements. The first to include budget forecast and special order; the second to show only the differential effect of the special order.

9.12   The following data has been collected prior to the preparation of absorption and marginal production cost statements for January and February.

Standard Costs per unit:

Direct Materials	£10.40
Direct Labour	£18.20
Variable Production Overhead	£7.80
Standard Variable Cost	£36.40

Other data:

Fixed Production Overhead	£975,000 per month
Expected Production	195,000 units
Selling Price	£67.60 per unit

Actual production data:	Jan	Feb
Opening Stock	0	30,000
Production	190,000	175,000
Sales	160,000	195,000
Closing Stock	30,000	10,000

REQUIRED

Prepare absorption and marginal cost statements for January and February.

CHAPTER TEN

BUDGETING
and
BUDGETARY
CONTROL

LEARNING OBJECTIVES

When you have finished studying this chapter you should be able to:

❏ Identify the diverse range of organisations to which budgeting is appropriate.

❏ Outline the activities which can be identified as being an integral part of the budgeting process.

❏ Describe the main budgeting techniques including flexible budgets, zero based budgeting and rolling budgets.

❏ Explain the key elements in administrating a budget.

❏ Prepare and interpret cash budgets.

10.1   Introduction

In *Chapter 1* we reviewed the main financial statements together with the accounting principles and policies important in drafting them. Here we place these financial statements into context by reviewing business planning, its links with budgeting, and how the main financial statements can be used effectively in business planning.

In common with earlier chapters it is important to stress that the purpose of this chapter is *not* to make you into a financial specialist. Although the output from the budgeting process may be expressed in financial terms, the purpose underlying budgeting is to ensure that scarce resources are allocated as efficiently and effectively as possible. In other words, budgeting is a *managerial process*.

The result of budgeting we will illustrate as being a set of financial statements in the form of a profit and loss account, balance sheet and cash flow forecast. These statements are prepared and approved prior to a defined future period, for the purpose of attaining specific objectives.

Budgeting is used in organisations of all types to help in the development and co-ordination of plans, to communicate those plans to the people who are responsible for carrying them out, to secure co-operation of managers at all levels and as a standard against which actual results can be compared. You will find budgeting used in a diverse range of organisations and activities including:

❑   Central and local government.

❑   The health service.

❑   Education.

❑   Large companies.

❑   Small businesses (such as the local garage).

❑   Churches.

❑   Charities.

❑   Television and radio networks.

❑   Local clubs.

❑   The family.

The analogy of our discussions with the family budget may be helpful. For example, a budget could be compared with the preparation of a shopping list. In its preparation we would be able to make changes to the list to ensure that personal objectives were met both for the goods obtained and money spent.

During the actual shopping activity, regular comparisons of actual spend against budget could be undertaken and, if necessary, changes could be made to attain our objectives.

Why budget? Consider the alternative of shopping without making a mental or written list. The outcome might be that many of the important items would not be bought and/or a situation of overspend reached, a feature of many bankrupt companies!

10.2 Planning the Business through Budgets

Organisations plan for the future in a number of ways. One useful way of looking at the process is to consider it in relation to the planning horizon – that is, the time span to be covered. One straightforward framework considers planning in the following three phases:

  – Long-term.

  – Medium-term.

  – Short-term.

There is no universally accepted definition of the period of time for which each plan should apply; it very much depends on the type of business – its markets, product life cycles, etc. However, the purpose of each phase in the planning process is quite clear.

Long-term planning is essentially a strategic exercise aimed at assessing trends and identifying and choosing between alternative courses of action over a period of many years.

Medium-term planning, is a more practical exercise aimed at optimising the use of resources over a manageable future period, bearing in mind the strategies identified in the long-term planning process.

Short-term planning, or budgeting, is a much more detailed process in which the medium-term objectives can be modified and adapted in response to immediate pressures and constraints. The short-term plan or budget normally covers periods of up to one year. It is this document (or set of documents) with which we will be most concerned in this chapter.

10.3   Budget Environment

Successful budgeting is difficult, particularly in large complex organisations. To achieve success attention has to be paid to a number of activities which can be identified as being an integral part of the budgeting process. These are:

❑   Defining Objectives.

❑   Planning.

❑   Organising.

❑   Controlling.

❑   Co-ordinating.

❑   Communicating.

❑   Motivating.

1. Defining Objectives

A budget must relate to and support the achievement of an organisation's financial objectives. Rational financial objectives should be set, bearing in mind the risk associated with them and the uncertainty of the future in relation to the return which shareholders expect from their investment.

Budget objectives or targets have two further characteristics. They should be capable of:

❑   Attainment by the managers concerned, and

❑   Objective measurement.

The budgeting process cannot be seriously undertaken until top management has defined in measurable terms the objectives of the business to be achieved during the period of the budget. Objectives might include:

❑   The achievement of a specified percentage return on capital employed.

❑   The reduction of borrowing by a specified amount.

❑   An increase in market share by a specified percentage.

❑   The introduction of a specified number of new products.

❑   The reduction of labour turnover by a specified figure.

A good framework is captured in the acronym S.M.A.R.T. which stands for the following; Specific, Measurable, Achieveable, Realistic and Time banded.

Whether the objectives set are acceptable will depend on:

❑ What has been achieved in the current and recent years

❑ Comparison with the performance of other business units working in similar business environments

❑ Management's opinion of what can be achieved in the business environment of the near future

The above are only a few examples of possible business objectives. They will usually relate to a range of activities within a company and not necessarily be restricted to purely financial or profit orientated objectives.

One key issue in defining objectives concerns those factors which limit the ability of an organisation to do exactly as it would wish. These are known as *limiting factors* and can be broken down into two types:

1. External factors over which an organisation has no direct control. The *external factors* might be the availability of:

    ❑ Sales demand in the marketplace.

    ❑ Raw materials.

    ❑ Scarce and specialised equipment.

    ❑ Skilled employees.

    In many cases external limiting factors can be related to the economic climate.

2. Internal factors over which it has a considerable amount of control. The factors which may limit the firm *internally* could include the following:

    ❑ Productive capacity of the company.

    ❑ Capacity and skill of the work force.

    ❑ Availability of cash.

All organisations will encounter constraints which limit their ability to do exactly as they wish. Some of these will be obvious, others not so obvious. The attainment of budgetary goals is limited by the capacity and commitments of the organisation as it currently exists. It is vital to identify and monitor closely the more important limiting factors in an organisation in order to set realistically attainable targets and budgets.

Limiting factors are identified in the external environment by the use of subjective judgement. Consideration of the social, technological, economic and political domains together with the competitive environment are a key part of strategic analysis and decision making which can be used to inform the budgeting process.

The limiting factors internal to the organisation are much less problematic. Objective measurements can be made of skills, capacities and other resources available which may limit the provision of goods or services to the market.

Careful and systematic consideration of both external and internal constraints may lead to the identification of previously unknown limiting factors, thus alerting management to problems likely to occur during implementation of a particular strategy.

Once top management has agreed overall company objectives then particular areas of responsibility can be assigned to lower levels of management and the budgetary process can commence.

2. Planning

Planning within the budgeting process takes place by the expression of departmental, functional or cost centre activities for the forthcoming year within individual budgets. These budgets will relate to the business objectives set by or agreed with top management for the year and will usually be a part of the overall budget, commonly called the 'master budget'.

Good planning provides the opportunity to evaluate alternative courses of action so that resources may be used effectively under conditions of minimum risk.

There are many different types of plans which will need to be developed into budgets, examples of which are:

❑ Sales plans.

❑ Purchasing plans.

❑ Manpower plans.

❑ Research and development plans.

❑ Capital expenditure plans.

❑ Marketing plans and business plans.

How are these plans linked and drawn together as budgets? As indicated in the last section, most organisations should have some idea of which aspects of the business limit their ability to generate profits; that is, where their major limiting factors are to be found. This should be the point at which they enter the budgeting process.

Very often, demand and the availability of the resources to meet it will be major constraints. For example, in times of buoyant sales prospects, actual sales may be limited by the maximum physical productive capacity of the organisation. On the other hand, where forecast sales demand is below the productive capacity of the business, the projected budget for the use of resources will be based on those sales forecasts.

Figure 10.1   *Master Budget and Financial Objectives*

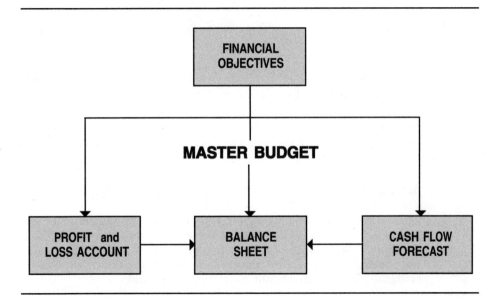

Theoretically, once the limiting factors have been identified the budgeting process should be simple to complete. In practice, however, the process is rather more complex, since the tendency is for the various budgets to be prepared in a predetermined sequence, each budget feeding information to the next. As problems of incompatibility between budgets occur, these are solved by going back through the process and re-budgeting as necessary. The entire exercise becomes one of negotiation and agreement between the various parties to the process.

Alternative scenarios can be analysed through a master budget which is illustrated in *Figure 10.1*. This consists of a profit and loss account, balance sheet and cash flow forecast. Once approved the master budget allows management to plan and co-ordinate the future direction of the business.

3. Organising

A budget will not happen on its own. The more physical and human resources that are involved the less likely is it to be conceived or achieved without good organisation.

Organising necessitates an understanding of the organisational structure, the tasks, the processes and systems, and the people involved if any agreed budget is to have any chance of success. In particular its success requires the following characteristics:

❏ The definition of the organisation structure so that possible areas of overlap can be identified and removed or at least reduced.

❏ The identification of tasks, responsibilities and the methods by which individuals will be measured.

❏ The means by which the budgeting activities will take place, including any training and/or documentation required.

❏ The recognition that budgeting can only be achieved through people and that they are an integral part of the process and any systems developed.

4. Controlling

Control is achieved by monitoring actual performance against the budget plan, noting deviations and taking corrective action where necessary. This is done by the analysis of variances similar to that of standard costing (discussed in *Chapter 11*). In addition, exception reporting is used to highlight only those deviations from the plan which warrant management attention.

The reporting of variances may be made before expenditure occurs where proposed spending is set against the budget or after the event when actual spending is compared to the plan. The former allows management to modify spending (for example, by seeking a cheaper source of supply) while the latter enables management to adjust future spending or ask for extra resources to conform to the plan.

5. Co-ordinating

Co-ordinating is an integral part of the budgeting process. Having organised, as discussed earlier, there is the need to look at the sequencing and interrelationships of the individual budget components.

As with limiting factors, it is difficult to view any process without considering its effect on other processes. Co-ordinating can be seen as a balancing activity which seeks to allocate priorities by predetermined agreement and also to unite a number of individual activities into a whole.

The different viewpoints of the co-ordinating process are usually apparent when agreeing company objectives. The activities will take into account the overall balance within the company, also such things as competitors and customers, economic political and social change, and if there is a need to change the future direction of the company.

6. Communicating

Within any budgeting system communication is important. Everyone concerned needs to know about:

❑ Objectives;

❑ Guidelines;

❑ Completed budgets and revisions;

❑ Actual results;

❑ Deviations from budget;

❑ Corrective action to be taken; and,

❑ Revisions to be included into forecasts which are provided to relevant management in an appropriate form.

7. Motivating

The budgeting process is often considered as a purely mechanical exercise. It is argued, however, that the process is just as much a political as a mechanical process. Any system which seeks to allocate scarce resources through a decision making hierarchy which is characterised by its unequal distribution of power, is bound to be influenced by internal politics. This may tend to upset the objective calculations of the designers.

Problems caused by political influences include the pursuit of personal or group objectives at the expense of the whole organisation (lack of goal congruence), built-in slack in budget estimates, where targets tend to be imposed from above and the adoption of short-term perspectives at the expense of long-term profit optimisation.

The problem is how can we know that if we take certain actions, then individuals will respond in a particular manner? For example, why do some managers like the budgeting process? Is it the challenge? Is it the power that information gives? Is it the 'games' they can play? Is it because they understand the system? Is it because they can see the purpose of the budgeting system? Is it because they are winning?

10.4 Budgetary Control

Of equal importance to planning in the budgeting process is the need to establish a monitoring system to ensure that budget targets are met. Such a system is concerned with the:

❑ Comparison of actual results against budget;

❑ Identification, recording and communication of controllable differences; and,

❑ Taking of corrective action either to maintain budget levels or to replan to meet recent developments.

The comparison of actual against budgeted performance requires that the budget is divided into monthly/four weekly periods against which actual results for each period may be compared.

To facilitate the control process, organisations may adopt approaches like flexible budgeting and/or rolling budgets. In the first case, differences in volume between the budget and actual performance are incorporated in a revised budget. In the second case, a re-forecasting process is used to update the original budget.

10.5 Budgeting Techniques

1. Fixed/Flexible Budgets

A fixed budget is one designed to remain unchanged irrespective of the level of activity. However, in most companies, levels of activity and operating conditions vary from month to month. Controlling against a fixed budget will lead to significant variances when activity levels are not as planned. To aid the control process, differences in volume between budget and actual performance are incorporated in a revised, or flexible, budget.

It is important to ensure that the comparison of budgeted and actual performances matches like with like. For example, if actual sales volumes are higher than budgeted, then certain items in the budget which are volume related should be increased. If this process was omitted a simple comparison would show an overspending on variable cost items, the result of which would be to record an unrealistic difference from budget. This is illustrated in *Table 10.1* below where the planned level of activity was the production and sale of 48,000 meals, whereas the reality was that 60,000 meals were produced and sold.

Table 10.1 Comparison of Budget and Actual

Budget Activity Level: 48,000 meals
Actual Activity Level: 60,000 meals

	Unit Cost per Meal £	Variable Cost 48,000 Meals £	Fixed Cost 48,000 Meals £	Total Budget 48,000 Meals £	Total Actual 60,000 Meals £	Variance £
Sales	1.75			**84,000**	**103,200**	**19,200**
Ingredients	0.35	16,800		16,800	20,280	–3,480
Wages	0.55	26,400		26,400	33,000	–6,600
Electricity	0.10	4,800	1,000	5,800	6,750	–950
Administration			12,000	12,000	11,500	500
Depreciation			9,000	9,000	9,000	0
Total Costs		48,000	22,000	**70,000**	**80,530**	**–10,530**
Profit				14,000	22,670	8,670

It can be seen that there are significant negative cost variances, which result in actual level of total cost being £10,530 higher than budget. However, this is offset by higher actual sales – £19,200 higher than budget – resulting in £8,670 profit greater than budget. On a line by line basis this is not very helpful for control purposes. For example, wage costs are significantly higher than planned, but they were for a different level of operation. What is needed is an understanding of how they match what should have been the level of cost at the level of actual activity. A flexible budget can be used to show this. Cost and revenues at the actual level of activity are recorded and matched against actual costs and revenues to identify the variances that are not related to differences in volume.

Obviously any variation in profit as a result of volume change is also important to know, but for control purposes, knowledge of variances due to efficiency and expenditure differences are vital. To produce the flexible budget a knowledge of those costs that change as activity levels change, as opposed to those that are fixed in the period is essential. *Table 10.2* illustrates the variances when actual performance (costs and revenues) is matched against the budget for the actual level of activity, i.e. actual costs and revenues for 60,000 meals and the budget for the 60,000 meals. It can be seen that the high unfavourable total cost variance of £10,500 when actual is compared to original budget, is more realistically reported as £1,470 favourable when the budget is flexed to represent the actual level of activity. However, because of the unfavourable sales variance, when the volume increase is taken into account the profit variance reported of £8,670 against the original budget becomes £330 unfavourable.

Table 10.2   Flexed Budget v Actual

Flexed Budget Activity Level: 60,000 meals
Actual Activity Level: 60,000 meals

	Unit Cost per Meal	Variable Cost 60,000 Meals	Fixed Cost 60,000 Meals	Total Flexed Budget 60,000 Meals	Total Actual 60,000 Meals	Variance
	£	£	£	£	£	£
Sales	**1.75**			**105,000**	**103,200**	**−1,800**
Ingredients	0.35	21,000		21,000	20,280	720
Wages	0.55	33,000		33,000	33,000	0
Electricity	0.10	6,000	1,000	7,000	6,750	250
Administration			12,000	12,000	11,500	500
Depreciation			9,000	9,000	9,000	0
Total Costs		60,000	22,000	**82,000**	**80,530**	**1,470**
Profit				23,000	22,670	−330

In summary, using flexible budgeting allows separation of the causes of variance between those that are volume related and those that are related to efficiency or expenditure.

4. Incremental/Zero Base Budgeting (ZBB)

In preparing a budget it is important to establish the base or starting point. One way, incremental budgeting, is to take the current levels as base data and to adjust for changes expected to occur during the budget period. For example, if salaries of a department are currently £100,000, with no increase in numbers expected, inflation is anticipated at 3%, the new budget figure would be £103,000. Although this may be an appropriate way of proceeding in such situations, the disadvantage of this approach is that it may allow past inefficiencies to become part of the new period's budget.

An alternative approach is the use of zero base budgeting, which is also sometimes known as priority based budgeting (PBB). The main aim of a zero base approach is to allow organisations to actively search for, learn from and adapt to changes in their environments. The Chartered Institute of Management Accountants' Official Terminology defines Zero Base Budgeting as:

> *A method of budgeting whereby all activities are reevaluated each time a budget is set. Discrete levels of each activity are valued and a combination chosen to match funds available.*

In practice this would mean that each manager has to budget ignoring the past, acting as though he were preparing a budget for the first time, and preparing a justification for the proposed spend. A decision package is prepared for each activity showing costs, purposes, alternatives, performance measurements and benefits. These packages are then screened and judged in a review process to determine benefits and the allocation of resources and funding. Advocates of this method claim that allocation of resources are more closely linked to need and benefit and it encourages an attitude which questions the status quo. However, it has to be said that it can take significant resourcing to undertake the activity, and as with all such areas of management there is a need to consider cost-benefit.

5. Rolling Budgets/Years Forecast or Out-Turn

Companies may choose to complement their annual budget with a regular (usually monthly) rolling or continuous forecast. This is intended to reflect changing circumstances and targets and aids in identifying corrective action. How is this achieved?

Assume that a company compares actual against budget every four week period. At the end of the first period a comparison is made against budget. Budget holders are required to forecast the effect any deviations from budget will have on the year end position and this is incorporated into a years forecast or out-turn. At the end of period six, budget holders will have sufficient actual results to be asked to forecast for the remaining six or seven periods. As the number of actual periods increase the importance of the original budget is reduced and the years forecast takes on a higher level of significance.

6. Activity Based Budgeting

In *Chapter 7*, the development of activity based costing was considered. Organisations that have adopted this approach may well extend their use of the activity based concepts, combining them with elements of priority based budgeting to budget on an 'activity base'. Such a budget will involve a form of matrix calculation of costs for major activities and the resource inputs (e.g. salaries, telecoms.) for each activity, with identification of the cost driver activity. We provide an illustration of an Activity budget schedule in *Table 10.3*.

Table 10.3   Illustration of an Activity Budget Schedule

	Receiving Purchase Requests	Vetting Supplies	Ordering Items	Expediting Delivery	Approving Payment	Supervising Dept. Work
Salaries						
Occupancy						
Telecoms						
Travel						
Training						
Stationery						
Total Cost						
Activity Cost Driver	No. of Requests	No. of Suppliers	No. of Items	No. of Deliveries	No. of Deliveries	No. of

10.6   Budget administration

What are the key elements in administering a budget? We recommend that you review those we provide and compare them with practice in your own organisation. See if you can identify possible areas for improvement.

1. Budget Guidelines

Budget guidelines are a means of conveying important budget assumptions to budget holders. They should be prepared at least annually and should include various percentages for budget holders to apply to expense items. They might also include information relating to overall movements in sales volumes, the increase/reduction in certain sectors of the business, or the requirement to implement a particular aspect of health and safety.

2. Budget Manual

A budget manual should contain sufficient information to enable managers to operate the budgeting system within a particular business, division or department. It should explain all the terms which are used in the budgeting system and provide worked examples of the main documents. A budget manual should not only deal effectively with the detail that a budget holder requires but also provide an overview of the total system.

3. Budget Period

The main budget period within business is usually one year. However, many companies consider their three year plan to operate within the budgeting system. The usual method of operating such a three year plan is that the annual budget forms the first year of a three year plan. The second year is usually shown in less detail, with the third year simply taking a broad overview.

4. Budget Factor

In any business there can be a number of factors which restrict its potential growth, a common one being sales volume. Whatever the factor that restricts potential growth it should be identified and made explicit. For example, if sales are considered to be such a factor then all other budgets should be prepared in an attempt to maximise sales. Other budget factors could include shortage of skilled labour, shortage of materials, storage of material, storage space or a specific item of plant within the manufacturing process.

5. Budget Timetable

In many large organisations budget preparation will often extend over the six months prior to the budget period. The complex nature of budget preparation demands that a detailed timetable be produced to ensure that each component within the overall activity will be completed in time for input into other components of the system.

Budget timetables should be produced to meet a number of key dates which relate to divisional and group board meetings.

6. Budget Training

If the budgeting system is to succeed it is important that the budget administration should include management training in the processes and techniques appropriate to a particular business. Such training should involve guided in-company instruction by staff familiar with the system and the specific responsibilities. It is not desirable to leave an individual with the manual and the responsibility – the training should precede the responsibility.

We have now set the scene for budgeting and budgetary control which is a vital area for all managers to understand. Budgeting is far more than simply working with numbers, as we have sought to illustrate with our review of key considerations within the budget environment, budgetary control and budget administration.

10.7 Preparation of Cash Budget

From the following information prepare a cash budget for the six months to 30th June 200X. The estimated cash balance at 1st January 200X is £4,000

	Sales	Purchases	Wages
200X-1	£	£	£
November	40,600	24,500	
December	48,000	23,200	
200X			
January	34,200	16,600	5,600
February	36,400	18,900	6,200
March	38,500	20,300	6,350
April	42,500	22,100	6,500
May	43,400	24,400	6,650
June	47,100	27,200	6,800

a. Credit allowed to customers   60% pay in one month
       40% pay in two months

b. Suppliers are paid one month in arrears

c. Other payments:

		£
January	Taxation	20,000
March	Equipment	40,000
June	Dividend	10,000

The steps to be taken in the preparation of a cash budget are shown below:

1   Enter the opening cash balance in January which is given i.e. £4,000

2. Calculate the receipts from Debtors, 60% pay in one month, 40% pay in two months following the month of sale, therefore:

Cash Received	60% of Sales in	40% of Sales in
January	December	November
February	January	December
March	February	January
April	March	February
May	April	March
June	May	April

3. Payment to creditors is delayed by one month. Therefore purchases in December will not be paid until January.

4. Complete the cash budget by entering the remaining figures and then calculate the monthly and cumulative balances to establish the cash flow picture.

Table 10.4   Monthly Cash Budget – for the Six Months Ending 30th June 200X

	Jan £'000	Feb £'000	Mar £'000	Apr £'000	May £'000	Jun £'000
Part A Receipts						
Sales	45,040	39,720	35,520	37,660	40,900	43,040
Subtotal A	45,040	39,720	35,520	37,660	40,900	43,040
Part B Payments						
Purchases	23,200	16,600	18,900	20,300	22,100	24,400
Wages	5,600	6,200	6,350	6,500	6,650	6,800
Taxation	20,000					
Equipment			40,000			
Dividend						10,000
Subtotal B	48,800	22,800	65,250	26,800	28,750	41,200
Part C						
Cash Flow (A–B)	–3,760	16,920	–29,730	10,860	12,150	1,840
Part D						
Balance b/f	4,000	240	17,160	–12,570	–1,710	10,440
Balance c/f (C+D)	240	17,160	–12,570	–1,710	10,440	12,280

In this case there will be a shortage of cash in March and April and we can use the statement to help identify the problem areas and possible courses of action. The main problem is the purchase of the capital equipment in March. As an alternative we could:

❑ delay the purchase of the capital equipment;

❑ negotiate terms for delayed payment;

❑ negotiate finance for the capital equipment;

❑ arrange hire or lease;

❑ obtain additional bank finance;

❑ reduce credit period allowed to customers, and/or;

❑ increase credit period taken (allowed) from suppliers.

Each course of action involves the consideration of an additional set of variables before arriving at a decision. For example, the last two items on the list above both affect the trading environment. If a company attempts either, it could lose customers and/or suppliers.

In February, May and June the statement show that there will be a surplus of cash. In this case a company should take steps to transfer funds into other activities which will generate interest. These include:

❑ bank deposit or building society;

❑ short-term money market. (Many large companies have departments whose function is to forecast closing cash positions on a daily basis and then negotiate terms on the overnight market).

10.1 E. Tee Ltd. prepares cash budgets on a monthly basis. The following forecasts are available for the four months ending 31st March 200X.

	Purchases	Sales	Overhead expense	Wages
	£000	£000	£000	£000
December 200X-1	90	270	33	57
January 200X	60	180	31	60
February	120	165	36	51
March	30	150	30	52

Other information is available as follows:

a   All purchases are on monthly credit terms – the suppliers being paid, less 2.5% cash discount, in the month following purchase.

b   20% of all sales are made on a cash basis, the remainder being sold to credit customers who pay in the month following the month of sale.

c   Overhead expenses include depreciation amounting to £4,500 each month. Payments are made in the month following the month in which expenses are incurred.

d   Wages are paid for in the month that they are incurred.

e   A new computer installation, costing £37,500, is to be paid for in February 200X. During March 200X, old fixtures and fittings, which originally cost £27,000 are to be sold for £1,500 cash.

f   The bank balance at 1st January 200X is expected to be £30,000.

REQUIRED

1. Produce a cash budget in tabular style for the quarter ending 31st March 200X showing the bank balance at each month end.

2. Comment on the results of your analysis, and suggest ways to deal with cash shortages and cash excesses.

10.2   Dream Ltd. is planning to open, on 1st January 200X, a new factory to manufacture tables.

Estimates for the first six months are as follows:

a   Sales will be £40,000 per month for the first three months and £60,000 per month thereafter. Payment for one half of these sales will be received in the month following the sale, the remainder will be received two months after the sale.

b   Production each month will equal that month's sales, i.e. no stocks.

c   Raw materials will cost 30% of sales value and will be paid for in the month following purchase.

d   Wages and salaries will cost 20% of sales value and will be paid in the month they occur.

e   Rent will be £40,000 per year, payable quarterly in advance.

f   Heat and light will cost £20,000 per year, payable at the end of each quarter.

g   Other expenses will cost £10,000 per month and will be paid at the end of each month.

h   Plant and machinery for the factory will be purchased on 1st January 200X at a cost of £50,000 and will be paid for in ten equal instalments.

i   The company's rate of depreciation for plant and machinery is 25% per year.

j   The new factory will be provided with a bank balance of £25,000 at 1st January 200X.

REQUIRED

1. Prepare a monthly cash budget for the factory for the six months ending 30th June 200X.

2. Prepare a budgeted profit and loss account for the six months ending 30th June 200X and a balance sheet as at that date.

3. Advise management on any action which might be required from the information disclosed by the cash budget.

10.3   Alastair Dryant is planning to commence business as a manufacturer on the 1st January 200X. The business is to be financed from capital of £25,000 provided by Dryant on the 1st January 200X and an overdraft limit of £15,000 agreed with the bank. Estimates of costs and revenues for the first six months are as follows:

a   Sales: January £9,000, February £12,000, March £18,000 and £20,000 per month thereafter. Half of the sales are expected to be for cash, the balance will be on one month's credit.

b   Production will take place during the month of sale, but raw materials are to be purchased in the month before production, except for the first month when two months stock will be obtained. Raw materials are 40% of sales value. Payment is made for raw materials in the second month following their purchase.

c   Direct wages and other direct expenses are expected to be a further 30% of sales value per month, they will be paid for in the month incurred.

d   Fixed expenses are budgeted at £2,200 per month, paid for in the month incurred.

e   During December 200X-1 machinery will be delivered, the cost of which has been quoted at £48,000. It has been decided to depreciate this machinery at 10% per annum on cost, and allowance for depreciation has been included in fixed expenses. Payment for the machinery will be in four equal instalments commencing February 200X.

f   Dryant will draw a managers salary of £2,000 per month.

REQUIRED

1. A cash budget for the first four months.

2. Comment on the situation revealed by the cash budget.

10.4 The executives of P.C Ltd are preparing budgets for the six months July to December 200X.

The budgeted Balance Sheet as at the 30th June 200X

Fixed Assets:		Capital and Reserves:	
Land and Buildings	100,000	Share Capital (£1 shares)	50,000
Plant and Machinery	160,000	Profit and Loss Account	115,000
		Loan Loans at 12%	250,000
Current Assets:		Current Liabilities:	
Stock	220,000	Creditors	65,000
Debtors	150,000	Bank Overdraft	150,000
	630,000		630,000

a The board has approved the purchase of a new machine in August 200X costing £40,000.

b Wages, assume 10% of monthly sales.

Fixed costs estimated at £5,000 per month (all cash payments).

c Depreciation is to be charged at £3,000 per month.

d Interim dividend of 20p per share, payable 15th July 200X.

e

	Jul	Aug	Sep	Oct	Nov	Dec
	£000	£000	£000	£000	£000	£000
Sales	50	70	80	100	60	40
Closing Stock	200	190	180	170	170	160

f Creditors at 30th June 200X are for purchases: May £40,000 and June £25,000. Debtors at 30th June 200X are for sales: April £70,000, May £40,000 and June £40,000.

Credit periods are expected to be the same during the second half of 200X i.e. two months for suppliers, and three months for customers.

g Gross profit to sales is budgeted at 30%. Assume purchases to be the balancing figure.

REQUIRED

1. Prepare a cash budget for the six months to 31st December 200X.

2. Describe the principle purposes of a cash budget.

10.5 The executives of Thrust Limited are concerned about possible cash shortages arising from a number of large payments due in the third quarter of 200X.

a The cash balance on 1st July 200X is forecast to be £30,000.

b A new machine is to be installed in August 200X costing £40,000 and will be paid for in September 200X.

c A sales commission of 2% on sales is to be paid in the month following the sale.

d Taxation of £110,000 is to be paid in August 200X.

e In July 200X and interim dividend of £50,000 is to be paid to ordinary shareholders (ignore taxation).

f Production costs are paid as incurred. The average delay in paying administration costs is one month.

g The average delay in paying wages is one week, with research and development costs averaging two weeks.

h To encourage payment of invoices, the company allows a cash discount of 5% if payment is made within the month of the sale, and 2% if payment is made in the month following the sale. It is estimated that 20% of the debtors pay within the month of the sale, and a further 50% of the debtors pay in the month following the sale. The remaining debtors are expected to pay their invoices in full, within two months.

i The period of credit allowed by suppliers averages three months.

j An issue of loan stock is expected to be made in August 200X which will result in £30,000 being received during that month.

A forecast of costs and revenues produced the following:

	Apr	May	Jun	Jul	Aug	Sep
				£000		
Sales	190	240	290	245	180	170
Purchases	60	55	80	50	40	45
Labour	50	45	65	40	30	35
Production Costs	20	18	20	25	20	18
Administration Costs	20	20	25	30	25	20
Research and Development	6	7	8	10	15	12

REQUIRED

Prepare a cash budget for the three months to 30th September 200X.

10.6 Findings Ltd are about to negotiate with the bank the short-term financing of a new venture until it has concluded arrangements for permanent finance. Budgeted Profit and Loss account to 30th April 200X.

	Jan £000	Feb £000	Mar £000	Apr £000
Credit Sales	120	130	84	132
Materials	40	42	28	46
Labour	34	34	26	36
Production Costs	7	8	7	8
Administrative Costs	8	8	8	8
Selling and Distribution Costs	8	9	6	10
Net Profit	23	29	9	24

The following additional information is available:

a   There are no stocks of finished goods.

b   Cost of materials has been arrived at as follows:

	Jan £000	Feb £000	Mar £000	Apr £000
Opening Stock	0	22	30	42
Purchases	62	50	40	50
less Closing Stock	22	30	42	46
Cost of Raw Materials	40	42	28	46

c   The period of credit allowed by suppliers of materials is one month.

d   To encourage early payment of invoices, Findings Ltd. allows a cash discount of 10% if payment is made within the month of sale. It is estimated that 10% of the debtors each month will take this discount, and a further 50% of the debtors of each month will pay in the following month. The remaining 40% are expected to pay their invoices in full, two months after the month of sale.

e   The overhead costs include the following items which have been allocated on an equal monthly charge but which are payable as follows:

Costs	Monthly charge	Amount and date of payment
Production	£1,000	£4,000 in January
Administration	£800	£2,000 in January
Selling and distribution	£500	£1,500 in March

f   Depreciation has been charged and included in production overhead at £1,500 per month.

g   The capital budget indicates that capital payments will be made as follows:

January £180,000   March £20,000.

h   Unless stated otherwise, items can be treated on a cash basis.

REQUIRED

1.   Prepare a monthly cash budget to determine the finance required.

2.   Discuss the importance of cash budgets in a system of budgetary control.

CHAPTER ELEVEN

STANDARD COSTING

LEARNING OBJECTIVES

When you have finished studying this chapter you should be able to:

❏ Understand who would set the standards for materials and labour in a standard costing system.

❏ Describe, calculate and interpret:

- Labour variances including, cost, efficiency and rate.
- Material variances including, cost, usage and price.
- Sales variances including, total, volume and price.
- Variable overhead variances including, cost, efficiency and expenditure.

11.1 Introduction

An early CIMA definition for standard costing states:

> *"A standard cost is a predetermined cost calculated in relation to a prescribed set of working conditions, correlating technical specification and scientific measurement of materials and labour to the prices and wage rates expected to apply during the period to which the standard cost is expected to relate with an addition of an appropriate share of budgeted overhead."*

That being said, we all practice the basic techniques of standard costing in our daily lives. For example, driving to work – we normally have a standard time in mind that can be used to compare our actual time taken, the difference being the variance from the standard time (allowed). When setting our standard time we would have to take into account, the likely road conditions, the performance of the car and the abilities of the driver. If we completed the journey in less time (or more time) we could explain the reason(s) why.

Driving to work is a repetitive activity, therefore, it lends itself to the development of a standard. In business, standard costing is applied to the planning and control of direct materials and direct labour, although it can be used to develop a full standard cost and price for a product or service.

11.2 Setting the Standards

Who Would Set the Standards for Materials?

An engineer, designer, chemist or similar person would prepare a specification of material required, both quality and quantity. The recipe in a cookery book is a good example. It not only gives a listing of the ingredients and quantities but also specifies the method to be used.

The method to be used would dictate the prescribed set of working conditions (the driving to work example), in terms of location, equipment and people.

Standard prices are determined for each material. These will be prepared by the appropriate purchasing specialist and will apply throughout the period to which the standards have been developed, normally in line with the budget period.

Who Would Set the Standards for Labour?

An industrial engineer will determine the best working method (using method study) and will then carry out timings to find out the time taken to complete each part of the process including the number of people and their grades.

It is important to recognise that should the working method change then the standard times will change. Often the labour standards have been reduced in the standard costs, in anticipation of the revision to the working method – normally a saving in labour through increased mechanisation.

Standard labour rates are determined for each grade of labour. The Personnel Director would be responsible for setting a base labour rate from which all other rates would be adjusted. When setting standard labour rates it is important to take into account holiday pay, normal bonus payments, normal overtime working and the mix of labour grades for each process.

What is a Normal Standard?

A normal standard is one that considers normal working conditions and a normal (achievable) level of activity. It is a standard that a worker can achieve without resorting to changes in working methods. If a standard is set too tight and is not achievable, it is unlikely that the workforce will recognise the standard and will not produce the desired result.

3. Variance Analysis

In budgeting systems, budget holders develop their budgets for the coming year. Once approved, these are used to compare actual expenditure and identify variances from budget. The same principle applies in standard costing systems where standard costs are developed for each product or service. Once approved, these are used to compare actual costs and identify variances from standard costs.

In standard costing these variances are used to determine who is responsible for each variance. For example, the material cost variance is split into a material usage variance and a material price variance. The former would be the responsibility of the production manager/supervisor, while the latter would be the responsibility of the purchasing specialist.

11.3   Labour, material and sales variances

1. Calculation of Labour Variances

A company manufactures a component with the following specification for direct labour:

Standard Direct Labour Hours   20 hours

Standard Direct Labour Rate   £5.00 per hour

During the month 250 components were produced, and the actual wages paid amounted to £30,800 for 5,600 hours worked.

Table 11.1   Calculation of Standard Costing Variances – Labour

Column A Standard Hours times Standard Rate			Column B Actual Hours times Standard Rate			Column C Actual Hours times Actual Rate		
Hours	Rate	£	Hours	Rate	£	Hours	Rate	£
5,000	5.00	25,000	5,600	5.00	28,000	5,600	5.50	30,800

£3,000 adverse
Labour Efficiency Variance

£2,800 adverse
Labour Rate Variance

£5,800 adverse
Labour Cost Variance

The steps to be taken in the calculation of the labour variances are shown below:

1. Enter actual hours and actual wages paid in Column C, i.e. 5,600 hours and £30,800. Optional, divide the actual wages paid by the actual hours to arrive at the actual rate, i.e. £30,800 ÷ 5,600 hours = £5.50. *We will use this actual rate when interpreting the labour rate variance, see below.*

2.   Enter actual hours in Column B.

3.   Enter standard labour rate in Column B, then multiply the actual hours by the standard rate, i.e. 5,600 hours x £5.00 = £28,000.

4.   Calculate the standard labour hours (number of components multiplied by the standard hour per component), i.e. 250 components x 5 hours = 5,000 hours. Enter the result in Column A.

5.   Multiply the standard hours by the standard rate, i.e. 5,000 hours x £5.00 = £25,000. Enter the result in Column A.

6.   Calculate and interpret the variances:

Labour Cost Variance. This is the total variance and is calculated by taking Column A minus Column C, i.e. £25,000 – £30,800 = £5,800 adverse. Interpretation; we were 'allowed' £25,000 to produce the 250 components. We actually paid £30,800 in wages, therefore, the adverse variance of £5,800. Interpretation; it is not possible to say much about this variance other than it is favourable or in this case adverse. We must look at the two subsidiary variance, labour efficiency and labour rate, to find out the causes.

Labour Efficiency Variance.   This is a sub-variance of the labour cost variance and is found by taking Column A minus Column B i.e. £25,000 – £28,000 = £3,000 adverse. Interpretation; we were 'allowed' 5,000 hours to produce the 250 components. We actually took 5,600 hours, i.e. 600 hours more at the standard labour rate of £5.00 per hour = 600 hours x £5.00 = £3,000 adverse. Consider reasons for the labour efficiency variance between the standard hours 'allowed' and the actual hours taken; could be caused by using incorrect skill of labour.

Labour Rate Variance. This is a sub-variance of the labour cost variance and is found by taking Column B minus Column C i.e. £28,000 – £30,800 = £2,800 adverse. Interpretation; for 5,600 hours worked, we were 'allowed' £28,000 at the standard labour rate. The actual wages paid were £30,800. This can be checked by taking the actual hours worked and multiplying by the difference between the standard labour hour rate and the actual labour hour rate, i.e. 5,600 hours x (£5.00 – £5.50) = £2,800 adverse. Consider reasons for the labour rate variance;   increase in actual labour rates above those incorporated into the standard labour rate, similar with overtime rates; could have used a different (more expensive) grade of labour.

2. Calculation of material variances

A company manufactures a unit with the following specification for direct material:

Standard Quantity of Material   8 kgs.

Standard Material Price   £4.00 per kg

During the month 2,000 units were produced, and the value of the actual materials issued from stores was £65,520 for a quantity of 15,600 kgs.

Table 11.2   Calculation of Standard Costing Variances – Material

Column A			Column B			Column C		
Standard Quantity times Standard Price			Actual Quantity times Standard Price			Actual Quantity times Actual Price		
Qty.	Price	£	Qty.	Price	£	Qty.	Price	£
16,000	4.00	64,000	15,600	4.00	62,400	15,600	4.20	65,520

£1,600 favourable   £3,120 adverse
Material Usage Variance   Material Price Variance

£1,520 adverse
Material Cost Variance

The steps to be taken in the calculation of the material variances are shown below:

1. Enter actual quantity and actual value of materials issued from stores in Column C, i.e. 15,600 kgs and £65,520. Optional, divide the actual value of materials by the actual quantity to arrive at the actual price, i.e. £65,520 ÷ 15,600 kgs = £4.20 per kg. *We will use this actual price when interpreting the material price variance, see below.*

2. Enter actual quantity of materials issued from stores in Column B.

3. Enter standard material price in Column B, then multiply the actual quantity by the standard price, i.e. 15,600 hours x £4.00 = £62,400.

4. Calculate the standard quantity of materials allowed (actual units produced multiplied by the standard quantity), i.e. 2,000 x 8 kgs = 16,000 kgs. Enter the result in Column A.

5. Multiply the standard quantity by the standard price, i.e. 16,000 kgs x £4.00 = £64,000. Enter the result in Column A.

6. Calculate and interpret the variances:

Material Cost Variance. This is the total variance and is calculated by taking Column A minus Column C, i.e. £64,000 – £65,520 = £1,520 adverse. Interpretation; we were 'allowed' £64,000 to produce the 2,000 units. We actually issued £65,520 worth of materials from stores, therefore, the adverse variance of £1,520. Interpretation; it is not possible to say much about this variance other than it is favourable or in this case adverse. We must look at the two subsidiary variances; material usage and material price, to find out the causes.

Material Usage Variance. This is a sub-variance of the material cost variance and is found by taking Column A minus Column B i.e. £64,000 – £62,400 = £1,600 favourable. Interpretation; we were 'allowed' 16,000 kgs to produce the 2,000 units. We actually used 15,600 kgs, i.e. 400 kgs less at the standard material price of £4.00 per kg = 400 hours x £4.00 = £1,600 favourable. Consider reasons for the material usage variance between the standard quantity 'allowed' and the actual quantity used; possible reasons for the favourable variance could be difference in batch sizes and/or less waste.

Material Price Variance. This is a sub-variance of the material cost variance and is found by taking Column B minus Column C i.e. £62,400 – £65,520 = £3,120 adverse. Interpretation; for 15,600 kgs issued from stores, we were 'allowed' £62,400 at the standard material price while the actual value of the materials issued from stores was £65,520. This can be checked by taking the actual quantity and multiplying by the difference between the standard material price per kg and the actual material price per kg, i.e. 15,600 kgs x (£4.00 – £4.20) = £3,120 adverse. Consider reasons for the material price variance; could be due to change in supplier, lower trade discounts, higher delivery costs or higher grade of material.

3. Calculation of sales variances

A company sells a component and has achieved the following results for the month of March:

Budgeted Volume   6,000 components

Budgeted Selling Price   £6.00 per component

During the month 8,000 components were sold at an actual price of £5.00 per component.

Table 11.3   Calculation of Standard Costing Variances – Sales

Column A Standard Volume times Standard Price			Column B Actual Volume times Standard Price			Column C Actual Volume times Actual Price		
Vol.	Rate	£	Vol.	Rate	£	Vol.	Rate	£
6,000	6.00	36,000	8,000	6.00	48,000	8,000	5.00	40,000

£12,000 favourable   £8,000 adverse

Sales Volume Variance   Selling Price Variance

£4,000 favourable

Total Sales Variance

The steps to be taken in the calculation of the labour variances are shown below:

1. Enter actual sales volume and actual selling price in Column C, i.e. 8,000 hours and actual selling price i.e. £5.00 per component. Multiply to give actual sales revenue.

2. Enter actual sales volume in Column B.

3. Enter budgeted selling price in Column B. Multiply the actual sales volume by the budgeted selling price, i.e. 8,000 components x £6.00 = £48,000.

4. Enter the budgeted sales volume in Column A together with the budgeted selling price.

5. Multiply the budgeted sales volume by the budgeted selling price, i.e. 6,000 components x £6.00 = £36,000. Enter the result in Column A.

6. Calculate and interpret the variances:

   Total Sales Variance. This is the total variance and is calculated by taking Column C minus Column A, i.e. £40,000 – £36,000 = £4,000 favourable. Interpretation; the budgeted sales were set at £36,000 while the actual sales were £40,000. The company has achieved a higher level of sales revenue. Interpretation; it is not possible to say much about this variance other than it is favourable. We must look at the two subsidiary variance, sales volume and selling price, to find out the causes.

   Sales Volume Variance. This is a sub-variance of the total sales variance and is found by taking Column B minus Column A i.e. £48,000 – £36,000 = £12,000 favourable . Interpretation; the budgeted sales were set at 6,000 components at £6.00 per component. The actual sales was 8,000 components. The sales volume variance is the difference in the sales volume times the standard selling price i.e. (8,000 – 6,000) x £6.00 = £12,000 favourable. Possible reason for this variance could be that the company has decided to reduce its selling price in order to obtain an increase in volume (and market share).

   Selling Price Variance. This is a sub-variance of the total sales variance and is found by taking Column C minus Column B i.e. £40,000 – £48,000 = £8,000 adverse. Interpretation; the actual sales were 8,000 components at £5.00 per component while the budgeted selling price was set at £6.00 per component. The selling price variance is the actual components times the difference between the actual selling price less the budgeted selling price i.e. 8,000 components x (£5.00 – £6.00) = £8,000 adverse. One possible reason for this variance is given in the sales volume variance above. Also, it might be that the company can't achieve £6.00 per component or that the trade discounts have had to be increased.

11.4 Comprehensive Example

In this example we will produce the following:

1. A flexible budget

2. Variance analysis covering:

   Sales variances

   Material Variances

   Labour Variances

   Variable Overhead Variances

3. A statement showing revenue and costs for the period together with a summary of variances.

Budget and actual data is given below

Budget	Units	Price/Rate	
Sales	8,000	22.00	176,000
Direct Materials	11,000	5.50	60,500
Direct Labour	5,000	8.00	40,000
Variable Overhead	5,000	3.00	15,000
Contribution Margin			60,500

Actual			
Sales	7,400	24.00	177,600
Direct Materials	9,500	6.00	57,000
Direct Labour	5,500	7.60	41,800
Variable Overhead	5,250	2.80	14,700
Contribution Margin			64,100

It would not be appropriate to calculate variances based on the difference between budget and actual. For example, the actual sales are 600 units less than budgeted, therefore, the costs in the budget are for 8,000 units while the costs in the actual relate to 7,400 units. In order to compare like with like we adjust the costs to take account of the differences in volume as shown in Table 11.4 below. The selling prices per unit and costs are at budgeted levels. The result in *Table 11.4* shows the budget contribution margin to be £55,962.

Table 11.4 Flexible Budget on actual volume (i.e. 8,000 to 7,400 units)

	Volume	Price/Rate	£
Sales	7,400	22.00	162,800
Direct Materials [1]	10,175	5.50	55,963
Direct Labour [2]	4,625	8.00	37,000
Variable Overhead [3]	4,625	3.00	13,875
Contribution Margin			55,962

Notes:

[1] Budgeted Direct Materials x Actual Volume divided by Budgeted Volume. i.e. 11,000 x 7,400 ÷ 8,000 = 10,175.

[2] Budgeted Direct Labour x Actual Volume divided by Budgeted Volume. i.e. 5,000 x 7,400 ÷ 8,000 = 4,625.

[3] Budgeted Variable Overhead x Actual Volume divided by Budgeted Volume. i.e. 5,000 x 7,400 ÷ 8,000 = 4,625.

It is now possible to see the result of preparing the flexible budget. In *Table 11.5* we show the total variances, sales £14,800 favourable while the costs are £6,662 adverse i.e. (1,037 + 4,800 + 825). We will now calculate variance for Sales, Materials, Labour and Variable Overheads.

Table 11.5 Flexible Budget, Actual and Variance

	Flexible Budget	Actual	Variance
Sales (after volume)	162,800	177,600	14,800
Direct Materials	55,963	57,000	– 1,037
Direct Labour	37,000	41,800	– 4,800
Variable Overhead	13,875	14,700	– 825
Contribution Margin	55,962	64,100	8,138

Calculation of variances

In this example we will use an alternative method to calculate the variances. In the earlier examples we used a tabular form which is widely used. Here we are using a simple list method which again, is widely used. Check this alternative approach with the previous examples.

Sales Variances

We will calculate the total sales variance then two subsidiary variances as shown in *Figure 11.1*.

Figure 11.1   Standard Costing Sales Variances

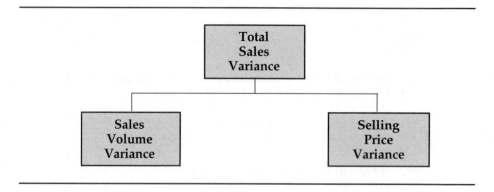

Table 11.6   Calculation of Standard Costing Variances – Sales

Total Sales Variance		
Actual Sales x Actual Price		177,600
Budgeted Sales x Budgeted Price		176,000
		1,600
Sales Volume Variance		
Actual Sales x Budgeted Price	(7,400 x £22.00)	162,800
Budgeted Sales x Budgeted Price	(8,000 x £22.00)	176,000
		– 13,200
Sales Price Variance		
Actual Sales x Actual Price	(7,400 x £24.00)	177,600
Actual Sales x Budgeted Price	(7,400 x £22.00)	162,800
		14,800

Interpretation of Sales Variances

The total sales variance is the difference between the actual sales less the budgeted sales. In this example we have a favourable variance of £1,600. The reasons for the difference can be found by an examination of the two subsidiary variances.

The first is the sales volume variance which is the difference between the actual sales less the budgeted sales times the budgeted selling price. In this example the difference between the actual and budget sales is 600 units (adverse) times £22.00 per unit that gives – £13,200.

The second is the sales price variance which the actual sales volume times the difference between the actual price less the budgeted sales price. In this example the actual sales volume is 7,400 units times (the actual price of £24.00 less the budgeted price of £22.00) that gives £14,800 favourable.

Reasons for sales variances could be:

Sales volume	Better/worse economic conditions
	Higher/lower selling price
	Changes in competitive advantage
Selling price	Competition
	Economic conditions
	Increase/decrease in costs; hence selling price

Material Variances

We will calculate the material cost variance then two subsidiary variances as shown in *Figure 11.2*.

Figure 11.2 Standard Costing Material Variances

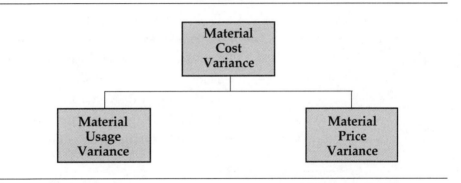

Table 11.7   Calculation of Standard Costing Variances – Material

Material Cost Variance

Actual Quantity x Actual Price		57,000
Standard Quantity x Standard Price		55,963
		– 1,037

Material Usage Variance

Actual Quantity x Standard Price	(9,500 x £5.50)	52,250
Standard Quantity x Standard Price	(10,175 x £5.50)	55,962
		3,713

Material Price Variance

Actual Quantity x Actual Price	(9,500 x £6.00)	57,000
Actual Quantity x Standard Price	(9,500 x £5.50)	52,250
		– 4,750

Interpretation of Material Variances

The material cost variance is the difference between the actual materials (issued from stores) at actual prices less the standard quantity (allowed) at the standard price. In this example we have an adverse variance of £1,037. The reasons for the difference can be found by an examination of the two subsidiary variances.

The first is the material usage variance which is the difference between the actual materials (issued from stores) less the standard quantity (allowed) times the standard material price. In this example the difference between the actual and budget quantities is 675 units (favourable) times £5.50 per unit that gives £3,713.

The second is the material price variance which the actual materials (issued from stores) times the difference between the actual price less the standard material price. In this example the actual materials is 9,500 units times (the standard price of £5.50 less the actual price of £6.00) that gives £4,750 adverse.

Reasons for material variances could be:

Material usage	Difference in quality or batch sizes
	Deterioration, obsolescence, loss, theft
	Increase/decrease in waste allowance
Material price	Higher/lower trade discounts
	Higher/lower delivery costs
	Higher/lower grade of materials
	Change in supplier/procedures

Labour Variances

We will calculate the labour cost variance then two subsidiary variances as shown in Figure 11.3.

Figure 11.3 Standard Costing Labour Variances

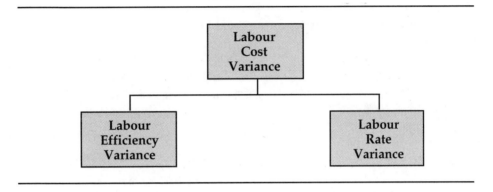

Table 11.8 Calculation of Standard Costing Variances – Sales

Labour Cost Variance		
Actual Hours x Actual Rate		41,800
Standard Hours x Standard Rate		37,000
		− 4,800
Labour Efficiency Variance		
Actual Hours x Standard Rate	(5,500 x £8.00)	44,000
Standard Hours x Standard Rate	(4,625 x £8.00)	37,000
		− 7,000
Labour Rate Variance		
Actual Hours x Actual Rate	(5,500 x £7.60)	41,800
Actual Hours x Standard Rate	(5,500 x £8.00)	44,000
		2,200

Interpretation of Labour Variances

The labour cost variance is the difference between the actual wages paid less the budgeted wages. In this example we have an adverse variance of £4,800. The reasons for the difference can be found by an examination of the two subsidiary variances.

The first is the labour efficiency variance which is the difference between the standard hours (allowed) less the actual hours times the standard rate. In this example the difference between the budget and actual hours is 875 (adverse) times £8.00 per hour that gives £7,000 adverse.

The second is the labour rate variance which the actual hours times the difference between the standard rate less the actual rate per hour. In this example the actual hours (worked) is 5,500 hours times (the standard rate of £8.00 less the actual rate of £7.60) that gives £2,200 favourable.

Reasons for labour variances could be:

Labour efficiency	Changes in working conditions
	Changes in grade of labour
	Changes in supervision
Labour rate	Changes in grade of labour
	Higher/lower overtime, productivity bonuses
	Higher/lower wage negotiations

Variable Overhead Variances

We will calculate the variable overhead cost variance then two subsidiary variances as shown in *Figure 11.4*.

Figure 11.4 Standard Costing Variable Overhead Variances

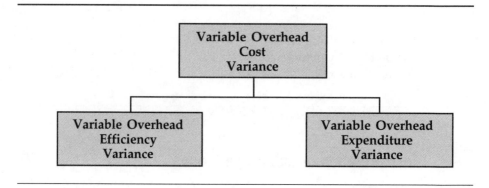

Table 11.9   Calculation of Standard Costing Variances – Variable Overheads

Variable Overhead Cost Variance		
Standard Hours Allowed x Standard Cost per hour		13,875
Actual Hours Worked x Actual Cost per hour		14,700
		– 825
Efficiency Variance		
Standard Hours Allowed x Standard Cost per hour	(4,625 x £3.00)	13,875
Actual Hours Worked x Standard Cost per hour	(5,250 x £3.00)	15,750
		– 1,875
Expenditure Variance		
Actual Hours Worked x Standard Cost per hour	(5,250 x £3.00)	15,750
Actual Hours Worked x Actual Cost per hour	(5,250 x £2.80)	14,700
		1,050

Interpretation of Variable Overhead Variances

The variable overhead cost variance is the difference between the standard hours allowed less the actual hours worked. In this example we have an adverse variance of £825. The reasons for the difference can be found by an examination of the two subsidiary variances.

The first is the variable overhead efficiency variance which is the difference between the standard hours allowed less the actual hours worked times the standard rate. In this example the difference between the standard hours allowed and actual hours worked is 625 hours (adverse) times £3.00 per hour that gives – £1,875.

The second is the variable overhead expenditure variance which the actual hours worked times the difference between the standard rate less the actual rate. In this example the actual hours worked is 5,250 hours times (the standard rate of £3.00 less the actual rate of £2.80) that gives £1,050 favourable.

Reasons for variable overhead variances could be:

Efficiency	Changes in working conditions
	Changes in equipment
Expenditure	Higher/lower variable costs
	Changes in suppliers/rates

Summary of Standard Costing Variances

In *Table 11.10* we now show a summary of the standard costing variances. There are many different possibilities for the layout of such a summary. Here we have chosen to start with the budgeted sales revenue, adjust for the sales variances to arrive at the Actual Sales Revenue then deduct the Standard Cost of Production to give the Actual Sales at Budgeted Costs. Finally, a listing of the Production Cost Variances is deducted from the Actual Sales at Budgeted Costs to give the Actual Sales at Actual Costs.

Table 11.10   Summary of Standard Costing Variances

Budgeted Sales Revenue			176,000
Sales Volume Variance	(7,400 – 8,000) x £22		– 13,200
Actual Sales at Budget Prices			162,800
Sales Price Variance	7,400 x (£24 – £22)		14,800
Actual Sales Revenue			177,600
less Standard Cost of Production	(55,963 + 37,000 + 13,875)		106,838
Actual Sales at Budgeted Costs		(A)	70,762
Production Cost Variances:			
Material Usage Variance			
(Standard Quantity – Actual Quantity) x Standard Price			
	(10,175 – 9,500) x £5.50		3,713
Material Price Variance			
Actual Quantity x (Standard Price – Actual Price)			
	9,500 x (£5.50 – £6.00)		– 4,750
Labour Efficiency Variance			
(Standard Hours – Actual Hours) x Standard Rate			
	(4,625 – 5,500) x £8		– 7,000
Labour Rate Variance			
Actual Hours x (Standard Rate – Actual Rate)			
	5,500 x (£8.00 – £7.60)		2,200
Variable Overhead Expenditure			
Actual Hours Worked x (Standard Rate – Actual Rate)			
	5,250 x (£3.00 – £2.80)		1,050
Variable Overhead Efficiency			
(Standard Hours Allowed – Actual Hours Worked) x Standard Rate			
	(4,625 – 5,250) x £3.00		– 1,875
Total Production Variances		(B)	– 6,662
Actual Sales at Actual Costs		(A – B)	64,100

To finish this example we now show a brief summary of the variances. This time we start at the Actual Sales at Budget Prices and Costs, £55,962 – *Table 11.4*, (which is already adjusted for the adverse sales volume variance. We add the Sales Price Variance then add the total of the Production Cost Variances to give the Actual Sales at Actual Costs of £64,100.

Table 11.11   Flexible Budget to Actual Contribution Margin

	£
Actual Sales at Budget Prices and Costs	55,962
add Sales Price Variance	14,800
Actual Sales at Budget Costs	70,762
add Production Cost Variances	– 6,662
Actual Sales at Actual Costs	64,100

11.5 Final Example

To complete this chapter we will consider a problem where we are given certain variances and some of the data and required to determine other pieces of data.

Given that the standard labour rate is £8.00 per hour, the actual hours (worked) is 350 hours, the total labour cost variance is £400 adverse and that the labour rate variance is £800 adverse, calculate the actual wage rate and the standard hours (allowed).

To answer this question we will use the columnar layout described earlier in this chapter and shown in *Table 11.12*.

Table 11.12 Standard Costing Variances – Labour

Column A Standard Hours times Standard Rate			Column B Actual Hours times Standard Rate			Column C Actual Hours times Actual Rate		
Hours	Rate	£	Hours	Rate	£	Hours	Rate	£
400	8.00	3,200	350	8.00	2,800	350	10.29	3,600

£400 favourable   £800 adverse
Labour Efficiency Variance   Labour Rate Variance

£400 adverse
Labour Cost Variance

Notes:

1. Determine the Labour Efficiency Variance i.e. £400 favourable.

2. Calculate Column B, i.e. 350 x £8.00 = £2,800.

3. If Column B is £2,800 and the Labour Rate Variance is £800 adverse then the total of Column C is £2,800 + £800 = £3,600.

4. The Actual Wage Rate is £3,600 ÷ 350 hours = £10.29 per hour

5. If Column B is £2,800 and the Labour Efficiency Variance is £400 favourable then the total of Column A is £2,800 + £400 = £3,200.

6. The Standard Hours Allowed = £3,200 ÷ £8.00 = 400 hours.

11.1   A company manufactures a component with the following standard specification for direct labour:

Grade 1   3 hours at £4.00 per hour

Grade 2   2 hours at £4.50 per hour

Grade 3   2 hours at £6.00 per hour

During the period 3,000 components were produced, and the direct labour recorded and paid was as follows:

Grade 1   6,000 hours   £26,400

Grade 2   7,000 hours   £34,650

Grade 3   7,000 hours   £46,200

REQUIRED

Calculate the labour variances

11.2   The standard raw material mix for one batch of finished product is:

Material	A	770 lbs	at	£0.70 per lb
	B	200 lbs	at	£0.28 per lb
	C	500 lbs	at	£0.49 per lb
	D	60 lbs	at	£2.80 per lb

Material issued from stores for the week ending 30th November 200X was as follows:

Material	A	5,200 lbs	at	£0.84 per lb
	B	1,300 lbs	at	£0.35 per lb
	C	3,700 lbs	at	£0.42 per lb
	D	450 lbs	at	£2.50 per lb

Seven batches were produced during the period.

REQUIRED

Calculate the material variances

11.3   Fairway Limited uses a standard costing system to control material and labour costs.

Details of the standard specification for materials and labour for one of its products, Fairway 300, is as follows:

Materials:	Stock Code	Standard Quantity	Standard Price
	A708	4 units	£3.00
	A022	6 units	£7.50

Labour:	Cost Centre	Standard Hours	Standard Rate
	Turning	2 hours	£8.00
	Finishing	1 hour	£10.00

Material A708 is used only in the turning cost centre and Material A022 only in the finishing cost centre. Details of the materials and labour used to produce 60 units of product Fairway 300 during the period ended 30th June was as follows:

Materials:	Stock Code	Actual Quantity	Actual Price
	A708	230 units	£2.50
	A022	370 units	£7.00

Labour:	Cost Centre	Actual Hours	Actual Rate
	Turning	130 hours	£975.00
	Finishing	58 hours	£580.00

REQUIRED

1. Prepare an analysis of the standard cost variances arising from the production for the month of June.

2. Indicate which variances the purchasing manager and the manager of each cost centre might be held responsible for and explain how the variances might have arisen.

11.4 The plant manager of JR Components arranged a meeting with the supervisor from the Mixing Department to discuss the standard cost variances for the four weeks ending 30th November 200X.

The plant manager gave the supervisor the following details:

Standard Material Cost	£52,500
Actual Materials Issued from store	£54,400
Standard Material Cost Variance	£1,900 adverse

The supervisor then went to the costing department and asked for further details of the variance. It was shown that 2,000 units had been produced for the period and that the materials issued from store were as follows:

Material A   32,000 lbs   at   £0.80 per lb
Material B   16,000 lbs   at   £1.80 per lb

The standard materials required to produce one unit of finished product were as follows:

Material A   15 lbs   at   £0.75 per lb
Material B   10 lbs   at   £1.50 per lb

REQUIRED

From the information available, evaluate further variances and draft a memorandum to the plant manager explaining the results for the period.

11.5   You are required to calculate the Labour Efficiency Variance and the Labour Rate Variance given the following:

Standard labour hours (allowed) to produce one unit   3 hours

Standard labour rate   £6 per hour

During the period, 100 units were produced.

Actual wages paid   £1,800

Actual hours worked   360 hours

11.6   Standard quantity of materials required to make one batch is 300 kg, with a standard price of £3 per kg. The actual materials issued from store for one batch was 250 kg with an actual cost of £1,000.

a.   Material Usage Variance is

b.   Material Price Variance is

11.7   The standard quantity of materials required to make one batch is 250 kg, with a standard price of £5 per kg. During the period, the actual materials issued from stores for five batches was 1,100 kg with an actual cost of £5,720.

a.   The Material Usage Variance is:

a.   The Material Price Variance is:

11.8   Concern has been expressed about the standard costing variances for the month of April.

The plant manager has given the supervisor the following details:

Standard material cost	£262,500
Actual materials issued	£272,000
Standard material cost variance	£9,500 adverse

The supervisor then went to the costing department and asked for further details of the variance. It was shown that 2,000 units had been produced for the month and that the materials issued from store were as follows:

Material A   32,000 lbs at £4.00 per lb

Material B   16,000 lbs at £9.00 per lb

The supervisor also obtained details of the standard materials required to produce one unit of finished product:

Material A   15 lbs at £3.75 per lb

Material B   10 lbs at £7.50 per lb

REQUIRED

From the above information evaluate further variances and draft a memorandum to the plant manager explaining the results.

CHAPTER TWELVE

CAPITAL INVESTMENT APPRAISAL

LEARNING OBJECTIVES

When you have finished studying this chapter you should be able to:

❑ Understand the need of organisations to identify and invest in high quality capital projects.

❑ Prepare a list of the main financial variables required for project appraisal.

❑ Identify the main points to consider when assessing the quality of input data.

❑ Evaluate capital projects using traditional methods of investment appraisal such as:

Simple Payback and Accounting Rate of Return (ARR);

Net Present Value (NPV) and Profitability Index (PI);

Internal Rate of Return (IRR).

12.1   Introduction

Growing a business by internal development, as opposed to external investment in other organisations, requires sound commercial judgement. Such growth only occurs when the future returns from internal investment exceed the present costs; this means that managers must test their judgement against the difficulties presented by a highly unpredictable and uncertain future.

In considering this problem we ask:

❏   Are there any tools or techniques available from the realms of accounting and finance to help assess the desirability of particular investments?

❏   What are the differences between these tools and techniques?

We will consider these questions and other important issues in this chapter in relation to the evaluation of investments within the business. Such evaluations are similar to those made by private individuals when say, buying a car. The decision needs first to be weighed against other spending priorities. Various models would then be considered evaluating the costs and benefits of each before the actual choice is made. After the purchase a conscious or perhaps subconscious evaluation would be undertaken on the quality of the decision.

The process is roughly the same for commercial decisions except that the financing of capital expenditure projects is treated separately.

12.2   Organising Investment Decisions

A major stimulus for much investment is often the concern about the future performance of the business if investment does not take place. However, in practice many businesses actually consider investment requirements according to the particular needs to be addressed. Let us consider such needs with reference to the following four categories of investment:

1.   Asset replacement.

2.   Cost saving.

3.   Expansion.

4.   Reactive.

1.   Asset Replacement

If a company fails to replace those assets which currently generate its cash flow and profit, then in the absence of any other investment, its performance will decline, whether quickly or slowly. If the current profile of activities are appropriate to future long term plans then, in order to continue to generate adequate cash flows and profit, the business must replace assets as they become worn out or obsolete.

2.   Cost Saving

Cost saving projects are critical to companies which have products or services where sales revenues have reached the maximum level that can be sustained by the market. Irrespective of whether this maximum is temporary because of depressed economic conditions, or more permanent because the maximum achievable share of a mature market has been reached, a reduction in the firm's costs is possible by improving the efficiency of existing asset use. Sales generation ratios (described in *Chapter 6*) can be used to identify possible areas for improvement, such as the automation of a previously labour intensive production system. This usually involves the substitution of an avoidable variable cost with an unavoidable fixed cost in order to secure forecast savings.

Finally, cost saving projects may be important to the not-for-profit organisation in which there may be no revenues associated with a project. The analysis of cost savings enables comparisons to be made with existing practice and between alternatives.

3.   Expansion

Business growth can result from internal or organic expansion or by focusing upon external targets via an acquisitive strategy. Much investment activity can be related to the desire to achieve growth which many organisations (particularly smaller ones) will attempt to achieve internally. Successful internal growth will eventually permit an organisation to contemplate external expansion, particularly where its shares may be traded publicly. However, even companies with a successful track record of acquisitions will undertake internal investment resulting in business expansion to achieve growth.

4.   Reactive Investment

Reactive investment covers two particular types of capital expenditure. The first is that which is required as a defensive response to threatening changes in the commercial environment. For example, some of the changes which can be observed in the major U.K. clearing banks services are the result of substantial investment caused by threats from previously dormant players in the financial services sector, such as Building Societies, in recent years. The second embraces that imposed upon the business because of legislative or other reasons where the benefits of the expenditure are not always readily measurable. It is perhaps, best illustrated by the following examples;

❏ As a result of new legislation, the U.K. furniture industry was required to undertake substantial investment in fire resistant foam filling.

❏ Following the Piper Alpha disaster, North Sea Oil companies have been required to undertake safety modifications to offshore installations estimated to cost hundreds of millions of pounds.

5.   Managerial Responsibility for Investment

In larger organisations managerial responsibility for investment is usually delegated from top management to lower levels of management. This delegation will usually exclude the raising of finance other than from short-term sources. Decisions about sources of finance with long-term implications are usually taken by top management who will try to balance proportions of debt and equity so as to minimise the cost of capital to the business.

The delegation of managerial responsibility for the evaluation of capital expenditure can be achieved by specifying cut-off levels, the amount of which corresponds with given levels of seniority. For example, senior divisional management may be responsible for capital expenditure up to an agreed cut-off sum, and approval would have to be obtained from top management for capital expenditure above the agreed cut-off. In addition, such senior divisional management may also be required to approve submissions for capital expenditure from its divisional management, where the capital expenditure required exceeds the level of delegated responsibility.

12.3   Appraising Investment Opportunities

In this section we provide a background to the financial appraisal of potential investment opportunities. In common with many areas of accounting and finance, numerous terms are used to describe the financial appraisal process of which investment appraisal, project appraisal and capital budgeting are common. To avoid confusion and to reinforce the point that our concern is not with investing in securities of other organisations, we will adopt the term *project appraisal* to refer to the evaluation of capital expenditure.

You may find it easy to become lost in the detail of the financial issues associated with project appraisal, so let us take stock of the key financial requirements to be met:

❏ only those projects which meet the objectives of the business should be selected, i.e. those which provide what the business regards as a satisfactory return for the risks involved;

❏ the return to be expected from a project must exceed the financing cost that the capital expenditure will necessitate, and;

❏ the most financially desirable project must be selected from the range of opportunities available (assuming, as is normally the case, that resources are limited and that not all projects can be undertaken).

In addition to these financial requirements it is important to stress that for many investments non-financial factors may be very important. Therefore account must also be taken of these so that both financial and non-financial considerations are given appropriate weight.

With these points in mind and before we consider individual techniques for gauging the financial benefit, let us consider the main financial variables of a project appraisal. A definitive list is impossible, but the following items will usually occur in one form or another:

❑ The initial capital outlay including the cost of fixed assets, working capital and, if appropriate, deliberate start-up losses.

❑ The expected useful economic life of the project.

❑ An estimate of the residual value of assets remaining at the end of the project's useful economic life.

❑ The amounts and timing of all cost and revenue components associated with the project.

❑ Expected price level changes for each cost and revenue component.

❑ Taxation assumptions and any regional grants likely to affect the corporate position.

❑ The relevant cost of financing the project (cost of capital).

❑ Likely estimates of variation for each of the above variables.

Many of these financial variables will be discussed in the next section outlining the major project appraisal techniques. It is all to easy to focus upon the mechanics of the techniques themselves whilst losing sight of their limitations in the absence of good quality input data. It cannot be over-stressed that the benefit to be derived from any technique used for appraising a project can be no better than the quality of the input data employed.

12.4 Assessing the Quality of Input Data

The main points to consider in assessing the quality of input data are:

1. Future Orientation

The only capital outlay, operating costs and revenues relevant to a proposed capital project are those that concern the future. Sunk, past costs are irrelevant even though there may be a temptation to treat them otherwise, as are costs to be found in a company's cost or management accounting system. This is the case whether they are past or present and they are useful only as a guide in forecasting future cost levels.

It is not only the costs themselves that are irrelevant but also the patterns of cost behaviour. Such patterns may be appropriate to the routine accounting functions of budgeting and variance analysis, but may not be suitable for decisions where the relevant time span is longer than that required for effective control. Assumptions which ordinarily permit different costs to be described as fixed, variable or semi-variable in their behaviour may need to be adapted when five or ten year time scales are involved, since at the time a capital project decision is being made all costs relevant to the decision are variable. It is only when the project is accepted and implemented that project associated costs become fixed.

2. Attributable Costs and Revenues

The costs and revenues relevant to a capital project are only those which can be legitimately attributed to it rather than any other source. Whilst this notion is simple and manageable in principle at the level of the individual project, difficulties can be encountered in practice when the cumulative effects of several proposed capital projects need to be anticipated.

3. Differential Costs and Revenues

Where decisions require more than one course of action to be examined, the only costs and revenues to be considered are those that will differ under the alternative courses of action. Common costs and revenues may be ignored, provided they are expected to behave identically in each of the alternatives under consideration.

4. Opportunity Costs and Benefits

These costs and benefits are usually the most difficult of all to deal with. Nevertheless, opportunity costs and benefits must be included in any project decision. For example, if a consequence of introducing a new model of a product currently sold at a profit is that sales of the existing product will be lost, then the lost contribution on the existing product is an opportunity cost of the new model which must be included in the appraisal.

5.   Financing Costs

It is often tempting, but incorrect, during a project appraisal to include the financing costs associated with a proposal within the estimated operating costs. As we will show in the next section, how the financing costs are compared with the financial benefits does vary according to the appraisal techniques used, but they should not be included with the estimated operating costs.

6.   Uncertainty and Inflation

It is important that the risk and uncertainty associated with projects is incorporated within any appraisal, together with expectations about changes in costs and prices. Any failure to make appropriate allowances for risk, uncertainty and inflation can result in an appraisal of questionable value.

7.   Qualitative Issues

A serious limitation of conventional project appraisal is the omission of non-financial issues, such as improvements in product quality for corporate image, or a lower susceptibility to adverse social pressures. Whilst such benefits are often extremely difficult to assess, they should not be ignored.

12.5 Project Appraisal Techniques

We have now set the scene for project appraisal in our discussions of the financial variables required and important issues associated with the quality of cost and revenue inputs. The important issue for consideration now is how such data is organised for purposes of appraising a project. This we will illustrate with reference to the four major project appraisal techniques. Where we have deliberately omitted issues such as inflation and taxation which sit more comfortably with the discussions which follow in the next chapter.

1. Payback period.

2. Accounting rate of return.

3. Net Present Value (NPV) and Profitability Index.

4. Internal Rate of Return (IRR).

The distinguishing characteristics of these four project appraisal techniques and their respective advantages and disadvantages are best illustrated with financial data. Accordingly we will use data for an imaginary organisation contemplating the following four alternative projects which are summarised in *Table 12.1* below.

Table 12.1 Basic Data for Four Projects

	Project A £'000	Project B £'000	Project C £'000	Project D £'000
Capital Outlay	−15,000	−18,000	−10,000	−18,000
Net Cash Inflows:				
Year 1	7,000	6,000	5,000	4,000
Year 2	4,000	6,000	5,000	5,000
Year 3	3,000	6,000		6,000
Year 4	2,000	6,000		7,000
Year 5	1,000	6,000		8,000

1. Payback Period

The payback period is calculated with reference to cash flow data. It is expressed in terms of a number of years (or years and months) and summarises the time required for a project to recover its capital outlay from cash inflows. For example, for Project B which has a capital outlay of £18 million and cash inflows of £6 million for each year of its five year expected economic life, the payback is exactly three years:

Capital Outlay		£18 million		
———————————	=	———————————	=	3 years
Net Cash Inflow		£ 6 million		

Project B is straightforward because the payback period occurs exactly at the end of year three, but this is not usually the case. For example, if you try to calculate the payback period for projects A and D you will find that it does not occur at the end of a single year. Let us see how this can be dealt with using the data for Project A. The first step is to accumulate the cash flows as follows:

Table 12.2   Calculation of Payback Period – Project A

	£'000			
Capital Outlay	−15,000			
Net Cash Inflows:	(i)		(ii)	(iii)
	Annual		Annual to Payback	Cumulative to Payback
	£'000		£'000	£'000
Year 1	7,000		7,000	7,000
Year 2	4,000		4,000	11,000
Year 3	3,000		3,000	14,000
Year 4	2,000		1,000	15,000

The figures in column (iii) show that in each of the first three years the whole of the net cash inflows are used to accumulate to £14 million. In the fourth year, only £1 million of the net cash flows are required to make the accumulated net cash flows equal to the capital outlay. Therefore, the payback period takes place in three and one half years i.e. three years, plus £1 million out of £2 million.

The results for all four projects may be summarised as:

	Project A	Project B	Project C	Project D
Payback Period (years)	3.5	3.0	2.0	3.4

The main aim in using any project appraisal technique is to find out which project should be selected from a number of competing projects. A simple ranking, this case based on the project offering the shortest payback period, would reveal that Project C is the best project. However, some companies will evaluate the payback period in relation to the project's useful economic life. This means that Project B which pays back after three years of its estimated five year life may be viewed far more favourably than Project C, which pays back at the end of its useful economic life. The relationship between the payback period and the useful economic life for each of the projects may be summarised as:

	Project A	Project B	Project C	Project D
Payback Period (years)	3.5	3.0	2.0	3.4
Useful Economic Life (years)	5	5	2	5
Payback ÷ Economic Life	0.70	0.60	1.00	0.68

Payback period has a major advantage over other methods because it is simple to calculate, understand and implement. Against this, the payback period focuses upon time taken to recover the capital outlay but cash flows generated after the payback period may not be taken into consideration. One other major shortcoming, the substance and importance of which will become evident shortly in our discussion of the discounting principle, is that unless the cash flows are specifically adjusted, the time value of money is ignored.

2. Accounting Rate of Return

The accounting rate of return differs from the payback period since its calculation draws on data relating to the whole life of a project. You must be aware, however, that it is calculated using a project's profit, rather than cash flows and thus suffers, as we saw earlier, from the ambiguity of the definition of profit. Once profit is defined the accounting rate of return is relatively straightforward to calculate. Take note that different users may arrive at different accounting rates of return using the same input data, and what is even more confusing is that none of the resulting calculations are necessarily incorrect!

The first step in calculating the rate of return is to add the estimated annual profit flows to establish the total profit of the proposed project. If only cash flow information is available then the annual cash flows must be added together to find the total cash flows, which in our example are £17 million, £30 million, £10 million and £30 million for Projects A, B, C and D, respectively. From this total the capital outlay (the total depreciation) is deducted to give the total profit. The average annual profit required for the calculation is found by dividing the total profit by the life of the project. This is illustrated for our four example projects in *Table 12.3*.

Table 12.3 Calculation of Accounting Rate of Return

		Project A £'000	Project B £'000	Project C £'000	Project D £'000
Total Net Cash Inflow	(A)	17,000	30,000	10,000	30,000
Capital Outlay	(B)	−15,000	−18,000	−10,000	−18,000
Total Profit	(C)=(A)–(B)	£2,000	£12,000	0	£12,000
Life (years)	(D)	5	5	2	5
Average Annual Profit	(C)÷(D)	£400	£2,400	0	£2,400

The accounting rate of return is then calculated by dividing the average annual profit by the capital outlay. For Project A, the calculation is:

$$\text{Accounting Rate of Return (\%)} = \frac{\text{Average Annual Profit}}{\text{Capital Outlay}} \times 100$$

$$= \frac{\text{£0.4 million}}{\text{£15 million}} \times 100$$

$$= 2.7\%$$

Similar calculations for Projects B, C and D produce accounting rates of return of 13.3%, 0% and 13.3% respectively. A simple ranking from highest to lowest rate of return shows that Projects B and D are ranked equal.

	Project A	Project B	Project C	Project D
Accounting Rate of Return %	2.7	13.3	0	13.3
Ranking	3	1 =	4	1 =

It was indicated earlier that using the same input data, different accounting rates of return can be produced. How can this happen? It is conceivable that one might use some notion of average capital outlay rather than the total capital outlay adopted in our example and, indeed, some organisations do just this. As you will appreciate, anything which has the effect of reducing the capital outlay in the calculation will increase the accounting rate of return. Consider for example the effect on Project B if the average capital outlay was calculated as being £9 million. The rate of return percentage would double!

The potential ambiguity in accounting rate of return results is sometimes presented as being a shortcoming. Nevertheless, the technique is used and with some success particularly where manuals of capital expenditure procedure provide a specific definition of the items to be used in accounting rate of return calculations.

3. The principle of discounting

The two remaining techniques for discussion, the net present value (NPV), and the internal rate of return (IRR) are both reliant upon a principle which involves discounting, or scaling-down, future cash flows. In order to appreciate the principle involved we will compare discounting with the more familiar but related technique of compounding.

Compounding is applied to a sum of money so that its value in future may be calculated given a required rate of interest. Discounting is the reverse. Future cash inflows are discounted at a given rate of interest so that they may be directly compared to the present outlay of cash.

Figure 12.1 Compounding and Discounting Cash Flows

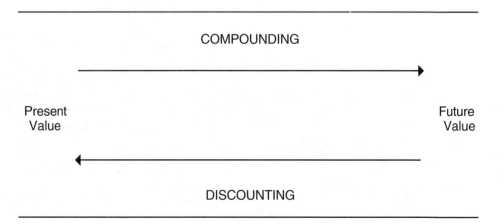

How is this discounting achieved? Cash flows can be discounted using factors which are readily available in statistical tables. The basis for their calculation is similar to the principles used in calculating compound interest. We will use the information in *Table 12.4* to show the relationship between compounding and discounting. There we make specific reference to the factors used to compound and discount cash at a 10% rate.

Table 12.4   *Compound Interest and Discounted Cash Flow Factors*

	Compound interest factors 10%	Discounted cash flow factors (DCF) 10%
Year 0	1.000	1.000
Year 1	1.100	0.909
Year 2	1.210	0.826
Year 3	1.331	0.751
Year 4	1.464	0.683
Year 5	1.611	0.621

Using the factors in *Table 12.4*, £1,000 invested today at 10% compound interest would yield £1,210 at the end of year two i.e. £1,000 x 1.21. The reverse can be seen if we assume a forecast cash flow of £1,210 at the end of year two, discounted at 10% back to a present value would produce £1,000 i.e. £1,210 x 0.826. The principle of discounting thus operates by scaling down future cash flows to produce a present value. In this way future cash flows can be readily compared with the present value of capital outlays. The reduction in the value of future cash flows using the discounting process is dependent upon the rate of interest. The higher the rate of interest, the more severely the cash flows will be scaled down. The technique of adjusting cash flows might seem tedious but the discount factor tables are readily available at the end of the book. In this table the present value of £1 has been calculated for a wide range of interest rates.

4.   Determining the Relevant Discount Rate

In order to calculate the net present value technique (and other discounting techniques such as, the profitability index, or the discounted payback period that we will discuss), the relevant discount factor must be known. This discount factor should be the company's required rate of return (sometimes known as the hurdle rate from the sporting analogy where hurdles have to be jumped to even stand a chance of being successful). This rate as represented by the company's cost of capital, is the projects' break even point. Projects undertaken yielding a return above this *hurdle* rate will increase the value of the business whilst those below will decrease value.

The components involved in the determination of a company's cost of capital have been the subject of much academic research and debate. However, there does seem to be some agreement that the appropriate rate should comprise the weighted average of the after tax cost of debt capital and the equity cost of capital. In the case of debt capital the after tax cost is used because, interest is deductible before tax thus providing a reduced real cost. This is unlike dividend payments which have to be met from after tax profits. How this cost of capital is arrived at is best understood from the following example: *A* company has an after tax cost of debt of 6 per cent, an estimated cost of equity of 16 per cent and future gearing comprising 20 per cent debt and 80 per cent equity. In this simple case, the company's weighted average cost of capital is 14%, and the basis for the calculation is illustrated in *Table 12.5*.

Table 12.5   Weighted average cost of capital   (WACC)

	Weight A (%)	Cost B (%)	Weighted cost A x B % (%)
Debt	20	6	1.2
Equity	80	16	12.8
			14.0

This cost of capital includes the returns demanded by both debt-holders and shareholders because pre-interest cash flows are those to be discounted. Given that both debt-holders and shareholders have claims against these, the appropriate cost of capital will be one that incorporates the relative capital contribution of each group. Thus, total pre-interest cash flows which are attributable to both lenders and shareholders are discounted by a weighted cost of capital to yield a value to the business.

It is important to realise that the relative weights attached to debt and equity within the calculation should be based on the relative proportions of each estimated for the future. This is because the concern of a capital project appraisal is with the future and not with the past. Thus, the present or previous debt to equity proportions are irrelevant, unless they apply to the future. There is also a useful analogy with the matching principle introduced in relation to accounting in *Chapter 1*. The objective is to compare like with like, hence the use of a future orientated gearing ratio for establishing the cost of capital at which to discount future cash flows.

The determination of the relevant discount factor is important not only to project appraisal. In recognition of its importance it is discussed more fully in a later chapter.

5.   Net Present Value   (NPV)

We will now illustrate the application of the net present value (NPV) technique, where for a given rate of interest, future cash flows are discounted using the principle discussed in the previous section. The sum total of these discounted future cash flows is compared with the capital outlay and where it is greater than that outlay, the NPV is said to be positive and the project is acceptable on economic grounds. Conversely, if a negative NPV results (capital outlay is greater than the sum of discounted future cash flows) the project is not acceptable on economic grounds.

Using basic data for the four proposed projects illustrated earlier, and assuming a 10% cost of capital, the following NPV analysis can be carried out for Project B.

Table 12.6   Calculation of Net Present Value − Project B

Year	Column 1 Discount Factor 10%	Column 2 Cash Flows £000	Column 3 (Col. 1 x Col. 2) Present Value £000
1	0.909	6,000	5,454
2	0.826	6,000	4,956
3	0.751	6,000	4,506
4	0.683	6,000	4,098
5	0.621	6,000	3,726
Present Value of Cash Inflows			22,740
less Capital Outlay			18,000
Net Present Value			£4,740

The annual net cash flows shown in column 2 are multiplied by the 10% discount factors in column 1 to produce the annual present value of the cash flows in column 3. These annual present values are then added together to give the total present value of the cash inflows of £22.740 million. The net present value is calculated by deducting the capital outlay from the total present values of the cash inflows (i.e. £22.740 million − £18.000 million) giving £4.740 million. The effect of discounting the cash flows is also illustrated in *Figure 12.2*.

Figure 12.2   Comparison of Cash Flows − Project B

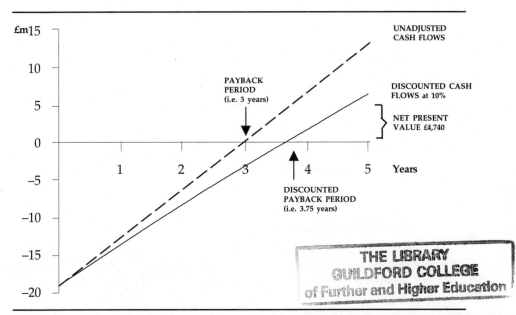

The capital outlay of £18 million is the starting point of the upper diagonal which is constructed from accumulating the annual net cash inflows of £6 million. The result is a cumulative cash inflow of £30 million at the end of year five. When these annual cash inflows of £6 million are discounted at 10% and plotted in the diagram, the lower diagonal results. The application of the 10% discount factor can be seen to cause a scaling-down which results in a net present value of £4.740 million. Raising the discount factor would scale-down the cash flows even further, thereby resulting in a lower net present value. One other observation from the diagram is the effect upon the payback period when discounted rather than undiscounted annual net cash inflows are used. You will see from the diagram that the *discounted payback period* is 3.75 years rather than the original three years when the net cash inflows are discounted at 10%. Furthermore, should the discount factor be increased resulting in a greater scaling down of cash flows, the discounted payback period becomes even longer.

We will consider the discounted payback and profitability index once we have reviewed the net present value calculations for all four projects.

Table 12.7 Comparison of Net Present Values

	Project A £000	Project B £000	Project C £000	Project D £000
Present Value of Cash Inflows	13,907	22,740	8,675	22,021
Capital Outlay	15,000	18,000	10,000	18,000
Net Present Value	£–1,093	£4,740	£–1,325	£4,021

The results show that only Projects B and D produce a positive net present value and on economic grounds would be acceptable because they:

❏ exceed the required rate of return (cost of capital) of 10%;

❏ cover the capital outlay; and,

❏ produce a sum in excess of the capital outlay which is referred to as the net present value.

Discounted Payback

The discounted payback period is similar in principle to the simple payback period, the only difference being that we use the discounted annual flows, and accumulate them until their sum equals the capital outlay.

In *Figure 12.2* we illustrated the discounted payback period for Project B of 3.75 years, but how is this calculated? Using the discounted annual cash flows for Project B, the discounted payback period can be calculated in a similar manner to simple payback:

Table 12.8   Calculation of Discounted Payback – Project B

	£'000		
Capital Outlay	−18,000		
Discounted Cash Flows:	(i) **Annual**	(ii) **Annual to** **Payback**	(iii) **Cumulative** **to Payback**
	£'000	**£'000**	**£'000**
Year 1	5,454	5,454	5,454
Year 2	4,956	4,956	10,410
Year 3	4,506	4,506	14,916
Year 4	4,098	3,084	18,000

Note.   The adjusted cash flows shown in column (i) have been extracted from Table 12.6

The discounted cash flows to achieve the £18 million capital outlay can be monitored from column (iii). At the end of Year three £14.916 million will be recovered, leaving £3.084 million to be recovered in Year four. Given that £4.098 million will be recovered from Year four, the proportion of a year represented by £3.084 million can be readily calculated. Thus discounted payback is achieved in three years plus £3.084 million divided by £4.098 million, which equals approximately 3.75 years.

Similar calculations for the discounted payback can be performed for Projects A, C and D to produce the following results:

Table 12.9   Comparison of Discounted Payback

	Project A	Project B	Project C	Project D
Discounted Payback (years)	n/a	3.75	n/a	4.19

Profitability Index

Where the capital outlay differs from project to project the *profitability index* is calculated and provides useful information to assist in the decision making process. The profitability index is a ratio which relates the present value of the cash inflows from a project to its capital outlay. For Project A this would be £13.907 million divided by £15 million which gives 0.93 and for Projects B, C and D it is 1.26, 0.87 and 1.22, respectively. It is now possible to rank all projects competing for limited funds using the profitability index – all other things being equal, the higher the profitability index the better.

Table 12.10 Calculation of Profitability Index

		Project A £000	Project B £000	Project C £000	Project D £000
Present value of Cash net Inflows	(A)	13,907	22,740	8,675	22,021
Capital Outlay	(B)	15,000	18,000	10,000	18,000
Profitability Index (A) ÷ (B)		0.93	1.26	0.87	1.22

The index of 1.26 for Project B means that the capital outlay is covered once plus an additional 26% and that where capital is restricted, should be preferred to the other alternatives on economic grounds. Where the profitability index is less than 1, e.g. Project A, this means that the project does not cover its capital outlay, therefore, does not provide the minimum return i.e. company's cost of capital. However, before drawing any further conclusions let us consider the internal rate of return.

6. Internal Rate of Return (IRR)

The net present value, the profitability index and the discounted payback calculations require knowledge of the company's cost of capital as necessary data input for their calculation, but internal rate of return (IRR) does not.

The IRR is a discounted cash flow method which seeks to find the discount rate at which the present value of net cash inflows from a capital project exactly equal the capital outlay, in other words at the IRR the net present value is zero.

The IRR can best be understood with reference to *Figure 12.3* in which you can see that the lowest line corresponds with a NPV of £0. This is achieved by scaling–down the net cash inflows by applying a discount factor corresponding with the IRR percentage. Thus the percentage which when converted to a discount factor and multiplied by the net cash inflows gives a present value equal to the capital outlay is the internal rate of return.

Figure 12.3   Graph Showing Internal Rate of Return (IRR)

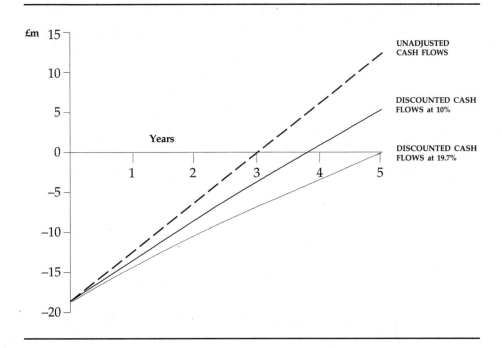

Once determined the IRR percentage should then be compared with the company's cost of capital in order to establish the economic acceptability of a project. The principle is that if the IRR exceeds the cost of capital then a project is acceptable on economic grounds. On the other hand, if the IRR from a project is lower than the cost of capital the project is not acceptable on economic grounds.

The calculation of the IRR is based on trial and error to find the discount rate corresponding to a zero net present value. As such several calculations may need to be made and are best facilitated with the aid of a computer. The calculations necessary to find the IRR for Project B are based upon data summarised in *Table 12.11.*

Table 12.11   Trial and Error Calculation of Internal Rate of Return (IRR) – Project B

Year	Cash Inflows £'000	DCF factor 18%	Present value £'000	DCF factor 21%	Present value £'000
1	6,000	0.847	5,082	0.826	4,956
2	6,000	0.718	4,308	0.683	4,098
3	6,000	0.609	3,654	0.564	3,384
4	6,000	0.516	3,096	0.467	2,802
5	6,000	0.437	2,622	0.386	2,316
Present Value of Net Cash Inflows			18,762		17,556
less Capital Outlay			18,000		18,000
Net Present Value			£762		£–444

Table 12.11 shows that cash flows for Project B when discounted at 18% provide a net present value of £0.762 million. To find the IRR (where the net present value is zero), in this case a higher discount is required. The result of increasing the rate to 21% shows that the net present value is negative at £–0.444 million. The internal rate of return must therefore fall between 18% and 21% and can be found approximately by linear interpolation.

$$IRR = d_1 + [n_1 \div (n_1 + n_2) \times s]$$

Where: d_1 = lower dcf; d_2 = higher dcf; n_1 = NPV at lower dcf; n_2 = NPV at higher dcf; $s = d_2 - d_1$

Therefore the IRR for Project B is calculated as follows:

$$IRR = 18 + (762 \div 1,206 \times 3)$$

$$= 18 + 1.9$$

$$= 19.9\%$$

Similar calculations carried out for Projects A, C and D produce the following results shown alongside that for Project B:

	Project A	Project B	Project C	Project D
Internal Rate of Return %	6.1	19.9	0	17.5

The approximations of the IRR% in this case are fairly accurate and in fact those obtained from using both a computer and a programmable calculator were 6%, 19.9%, 0% and 17.4% for Projects A, B, C and D respectively.

The results achieved from using manual calculations for the IRR produce satisfactory results provided that the difference between the two discount rates is not too large (e.g. greater than 5%). However, it is preferable to use a computer or programmable calculator which allow the user to change any of the figures with relative ease.

One major problem with the IRR is that it may be impossible to provide a clear cut solution to projects that have irregular cash flows. In such a situation there may not be an internal rate of return, or if there is, it may not be unique.

12.6   Using Annuity Tables

In addition to the arithmetical tables which provide a stream of discount factors it is also possible to obtain arithmetical tables which give cumulative discount factors over a specific period of time. These tables which are included in *pages 333 and 334*, are referred to as annuity tables because they convert a lump sum into a stream of equal annual payments. To find out the total present value of £100 over 10 years we could undertake 10 individual calculations in a similar manner to that illustrated in the last chapter. Alternatively, we can achieve the same result from a single calculation by multiplying £100 by the cumulative discount factor found from the annuity tables.

Before we go any further it might help to consider the benefit of using cumulative discount factors in appraising potential investment opportunities. From *Table 12.12* we can identify the cumulative discount factors at 10% for any period between one and five years. If we return to Project B we can calculate the present value of the net cash inflows at 10% in one operation:

£6 million   x   3.790   =   £22.740 million

This is a quicker method than that used before, see *Table 12.6*, where five multiplications were required! However, this method can only be used where the annual cash flows are equal.

Table 12.12 Discount Factors at 10%

Period	Discount Factors at 10%	Cumulative Discount Factors at 10%
1	0.909	0.909
2	0.826	1.735
3	0.751	2.486
4	0.683	3.169
5	0.621	3.790

A final point regarding the cumulative discount factors. Compare the figures we have just used in *Table 12.12* above with the corresponding figures in *Appendix A*. The slight difference is due to rounding and for the calculation of further examples we will use the figures from *Appendix A*.

Example – Using Annuity Tables

We will continue to make use of Project B, (as we already know the answer) and use the cumulative discount factors to calculate the following:

1. The internal rate of return given a capital outlay of £18 million, average annual savings of £6 million and a five year life.

2. The minimum average annual savings for the project to be acceptable on economic grounds, given a cost of capital (discount rate) of 20%, a capital outlay of £18 million and a five year life.

3. The maximum capital outlay worth expending on such a project, given only that the cost of capital is 20%, average annual savings are £6 million, and the expected life is five years.

1. Calculate the Internal Rate of Return

First, we calculate the cumulative discount factor as follows:

Capital Outlay ÷ Average Annual Savings

£18 million ÷ £6 million = 3.000

Second, we use the table in *Appendix A* and check the cumulative discount factors on the line for a five year life until we obtain a value which is close to the 3.000. In this case we will see that a figure of 2.991 is the closest and this represents the cumulative discount factors at 20%. With the use of interpolation, say between 19% and 20% it is possible to arrive at rates correct to one decimal place.

2. Calculate the Minimum Average Annual Savings

We are given a cost of capital and the life of the project therefore we refer to *Appendix A* and extract the cumulative discount factors at 20% for a period of five years which give 2.991. The minimum average annual savings is found from:

Capital Outlay   ÷   Cum Discount Factors

£18 million   ÷   2.991   =   £6.018 million

In this case, we conclude that if the capital outlay is expected to be £18 million and the company's cost of capital is 20% then the project will need to provide a minimum average annual savings of £6.018 million for five years.

3. Calculate the Maximum Capital Outlay

We follow the same procedure as in 2. above and obtain a cumulative discount factor of 2.991. The maximum capital outlay is found from:

Average annual savings   x   the cumulative discount factor

£6 million   x   2.991   =   £17.946 million

Here we conclude that if the average annual savings for five years are expected to be £6 million and the company's cost of capital is 20% then a maximum capital outlay of £17.946 million can be spent.

12.7 Project Appraisal in Practice

Many studies of project appraisal practice have been undertaken. Most have been orientated towards the practices of large organisations to which the following general observations apply:

1 The most frequently used technique is the payback period. This is often in conjunction with other techniques, but it may be used on its own for smaller projects.

2 When a discounted cash flow technique is used it is more likely to be the internal rate of return method rather than the net present value method.

3 Qualitative judgement is regarded as important.

4 The accounting rate of return is used despite potential ambiguities in definition.

5 The use of techniques is guided by standard procedures, usually in the form of a capital budgeting manual of practice.

In addition to these five observations relating to the techniques, three others are noteworthy however, they are outside the scope of this book:

❏ Inflation adjustments are made in appraising projects using rates applicable to specific inputs although the use of a single general rate is also practised.

❏ Adjustments for taxation are made to take account of the tax benefits i.e. allowances on capital projects and the tax liabilities i.e. payments due on any savings (profits).

❏ A formal analysis of risk is a standard pre-decision control procedure in many organisations, most often in the form of testing the sensitivity of key inputs and underlying economic assumptions.

One important question which emerges from the observations from the studies of practice is – 'Why the IRR is far more popular than the theoretically preferred NPV technique'? This has been attributed to a number of reasons, such as the appeal of a percentage to managers who, apparently, would be far less comfortable with interpreting a NPV calculation. Using IRR calculations a ranking of projects can be obtained without the need for knowledge of the company's required rate of return although, as indicated in the last section, this ranking may be inferior to that provided by NPV calculations. Associated with there being no need for a predetermined cut-off rate is the political appeal of the IRR. One recognised feature of the appraisal process is the potential for playing the system by ensuring that projects which have acquired the personal commitment of management always meet or exceed the prescribed hurdle rate. If the hurdle is not formally communicated then perhaps this problem can be removed. Certainly our observations of practice have found some confirmation of this view in some organisations. In such cases, the IRR usually in conjunction with other techniques, is prescribed for use below corporate level. At corporate level, however, where the desired hurdle is known the NPV technique may play a more significant role.

12.1   The management team of U. Dunnit Limited have four projects for consideration. In the past, they have evaluated projects against simple payback. The following information is available:

	Project A £	Project B £	Project C £	Project D £
Capital Outlay	65,000	140,000	30,000	160,000
Net Cash Inflows:				
Year 1	30,000	45,000	20,000	35,000
Year 2	20,000	45,000	10,000	35,000
Year 3	15,000	45,000	10,000	55,000
Year 4	10,000	45,000		55,000
Year 5	10,000	45,000		65,000

REQUIRED

1.   Evaluate the projects using each of the following methods:

a   Simple payback.

b   Accounting rate of return.

c   Net present value and profitability index. Assuming a cost of capital of 6%.

d   Internal rate of return (using the DCF tables given below), for the project with the best profitability index.

2.   Write a report to the Chairman of the management team explaining each of the evaluation methods. You are also required to make a recommendation on the method(s) which should be used by the company for future project evaluation.

12.2   A company is considering the purchase of a new machine to extend its range of products and have obtained the following information:

Capital Outlay   £390,000

Profit Forecast:–	£
Year 1	60,000
Year 2	45,000
Year 3	21,000
Year 4	12,000
Year 5	12,000

The profit before taxation figures are stated after charging £24,000 per annum of factory overheads allocated to the project.

The scrap value of the machine at the end of the fifth year will be £60,000.

The management of the company will approve the project provided that it will result in a minimum return of 10% per annum.

REQUIRED

1.   Advise the company management whether they should proceed with the project on the basis of the above figures.

2.   Suggest what other factors should be taken into consideration before a final decision is made.

12.3   The senior engineer of Maxifly Limited has submitted a project to install equipment to manufacture a new type of fishing rod. The following information is available:–

Capital Outlay	£480,000
Life of Project	5 years
Profit Forecast:	£
Year 1	32,000
Year 2	48,000
Year 3	60,000
Year 4	120,000
Year 5	48,000

The scrap value of the equipment is estimated to be £80,000 and will be received at the end of year five.

The company uses the straight-line method of depreciation. The company's cost of capital is 14 per cent.

REQUIRED

1.   Calculate the net present value and the simple payback period for the project.

2.   Although discounted cash flow is widely considered to be a superior method of investment appraisal, the simple payback method has still been shown to be the most popular method in practice. Suggest reasons why this may be the case.

12.4   D.R. Afty Ltd., make a range of wooden doors for the building industry. The production engineer has investigated replacing three existing machines with either the latest models, or a multipurpose model.

The following data has been collected:

Machine type	Existing machines		Proposed models	
	Original capital cost £	Operating expenses per year £	Capital cost £	Operating expenses per year £
Cutting	20,000	15,000	27,000	9,000
Planing	30,000	25,000	35,000	17,000
Sanding	10,000	5,000	12,000	2,000
Multipurpose model			132,000	16,000

Assume all machines to have a 10 year life.

The cost of capital within the company is 15%.

Ignore taxation.

REQUIRED

Which proposal should be accepted and why?

12.5   Given that an outlay of £90,000 is required to produce savings over 5 years as follows:

Year 1   £40,000

Year 2   £35,000

Year 3   £30,000

Year 4   £25,000

Year 5   £20,000

1.   Calculate simple payback.

2.   Calculate accounting rate of return.

12.6   A capital project has the following data:

Capital outlay   £130,000

Savings:

Year 1   £60,000

Year 2   £50,000

Year 3   £40,000

Year 4   £30,000

Year 5   £20,000

Cost of capital   12%

1.   Calculate simple payback.

2.   Calculate Net Present Value.

12.7   A project requires a capital outlay of £150 million.

The project is expected to have a useful economic life of five years and the organisation's cost of capital is 10%. The present costs incurred are £150 million per year. If the project were implemented it is estimated that future costs would be £100 million per year. (ignore inflation and taxation)

Calculate the net present value.

12.8   A machine with a purchase price of £70,000 is estimated to eliminate manual operations costing £20,000 per year. The machine will last five years and have no residual value at the end of its life.

REQUIRED

1.   Calculate the internal rate of return.

2.   Calculate the annual saving necessary to achieve a 12% internal rate of return.

3.   Calculate the net present value and the profitability index if the company's cost of capital is 10%.

References

Bliss, J.H., 'The story told by the financial and operating statements', *Management and Administration*, Vol. 7, No. 1, January, pp.25–30, 1924.

B.I.M. Study Group, 'Accounting Ratios', *Accountancy*, July, pp.267–271, 1956.

Cadbury Report, Financial Aspects of Corporate Governance, 1992.

Dobson, R.W., 'Return on capital', *Management Accounting*, November, pp.438–447, 1967.

Horngren, C.T., *Accounting for management contol*, Second Edition, Prentice Hall, 1970.

Parker, R.H., *Understanding company financial statements*, Pelican Books, 1975.

%	1	2	3	4	5	6	7	8	9	10
Period										
1	0.990	0.980	0.971	0.962	0.952	0.943	0.935	0.926	0.917	0.909
2	0.980	0.961	0.943	0.925	0.907	0.890	0.873	0.857	0.842	0.826
3	0.971	0.942	0.915	0.889	0.864	0.840	0.816	0.794	0.772	0.751
4	0.961	0.924	0.888	0.855	0.823	0.792	0.763	0.735	0.708	0.683
5	0.951	0.906	0.863	0.822	0.784	0.747	0.713	0.681	0.650	0.621
6	0.942	0.888	0.837	0.790	0.746	0.705	0.666	0.630	0.596	0.564
7	0.933	0.871	0.813	0.760	0.711	0.665	0.623	0.583	0.547	0.513
8	0.923	0.853	0.789	0.731	0.677	0.627	0.582	0.540	0.502	0.467
9	0.914	0.837	0.766	0.703	0.645	0.592	0.544	0.500	0.460	0.424
10	0.905	0.820	0.744	0.676	0.614	0.558	0.508	0.463	0.422	0.386
11	0.896	0.804	0.722	0.650	0.585	0.527	0.475	0.429	0.388	0.350
12	0.887	0.788	0.701	0.625	0.557	0.497	0.444	0.397	0.356	0.319
13	0.879	0.773	0.681	0.601	0.530	0.469	0.415	0.368	0.326	0.290
14	0.870	0.758	0.661	0.577	0.505	0.442	0.388	0.340	0.299	0.263
15	0.861	0.743	0.642	0.555	0.481	0.417	0.362	0.315	0.275	0.239
16	0.853	0.728	0.623	0.534	0.458	0.394	0.339	0.292	0.252	0.218
17	0.844	0.714	0.605	0.513	0.436	0.371	0.317	0.270	0.231	0.198
18	0.836	0.700	0.587	0.494	0.416	0.350	0.296	0.250	0.212	0.180
19	0.828	0.686	0.570	0.475	0.396	0.331	0.277	0.232	0.194	0.164
20	0.820	0.673	0.554	0.456	0.377	0.312	0.258	0.215	0.178	0.149

%	11	12	13	14	15	16	17	18	19	20
Period										
1	0.901	0.893	0.885	0.877	0.870	0.862	0.855	0.847	0.840	0.833
2	0.812	0.797	0.783	0.769	0.756	0.743	0.731	0.718	0.706	0.694
3	0.731	0.712	0.693	0.675	0.658	0.641	0.624	0.609	0.593	0.579
4	0.659	0.636	0.613	0.592	0.572	0.552	0.534	0.516	0.499	0.482
5	0.593	0.567	0.543	0.519	0.497	0.476	0.456	0.437	0.419	0.402
6	0.535	0.507	0.480	0.456	0.432	0.410	0.390	0.370	0.352	0.335
7	0.482	0.452	0.425	0.400	0.376	0.354	0.333	0.314	0.296	0.279
8	0.434	0.404	0.376	0.351	0.327	0.305	0.285	0.266	0.249	0.233
9	0.391	0.361	0.333	0.308	0.284	0.263	0.243	0.225	0.209	0.194
10	0.352	0.322	0.295	0.270	0.247	0.227	0.208	0.191	0.176	0.162
11	0.317	0.287	0.261	0.237	0.215	0.195	0.178	0.162	0.148	0.135
12	0.286	0.257	0.231	0.208	0.187	0.168	0.152	0.137	0.124	0.112
13	0.258	0.229	0.204	0.182	0.163	0.145	0.130	0.116	0.104	0.093
14	0.232	0.205	0.181	0.160	0.141	0.125	0.111	0.099	0.088	0.078
15	0.209	0.183	0.160	0.140	0.123	0.108	0.095	0.084	0.074	0.065
16	0.188	0.163	0.141	0.123	0.107	0.093	0.081	0.071	0.062	0.054
17	0.170	0.146	0.125	0.108	0.093	0.080	0.069	0.060	0.052	0.045
18	0.153	0.130	0.111	0.095	0.081	0.069	0.059	0.051	0.044	0.038
19	0.138	0.116	0.098	0.083	0.070	0.060	0.051	0.043	0.037	0.031
20	0.124	0.104	0.087	0.073	0.061	0.051	0.043	0.037	0.031	0.026

% Period	21	22	23	24	25	26	27	28	29	30
1	0.826	0.820	0.813	0.806	0.800	0.794	0.787	0.781	0.775	0.769
2	0.683	0.672	0.661	0.650	0.640	0.630	0.620	0.610	0.601	0.592
3	0.564	0.551	0.537	0.524	0.512	0.500	0.488	0.477	0.466	0.455
4	0.467	0.451	0.437	0.423	0.410	0.397	0.384	0.373	0.361	0.350
5	0.386	0.370	0.355	0.341	0.328	0.315	0.303	0.291	0.280	0.269
6	0.319	0.303	0.289	0.275	0.262	0.250	0.238	0.227	0.217	0.207
7	0.263	0.249	0.235	0.222	0.210	0.198	0.188	0.178	0.168	0.159
8	0.218	0.204	0.191	0.179	0.168	0.157	0.148	0.139	0.130	0.123
9	0.180	0.167	0.155	0.144	0.134	0.125	0.116	0.108	0.101	0.094
10	0.149	0.137	0.126	0.116	0.107	0.099	0.092	0.085	0.078	0.073
11	0.123	0.112	0.103	0.094	0.086	0.079	0.072	0.066	0.061	0.056
12	0.102	0.092	0.083	0.076	0.069	0.062	0.057	0.052	0.047	0.043
13	0.084	0.075	0.068	0.061	0.055	0.050	0.045	0.040	0.037	0.033
14	0.069	0.062	0.055	0.049	0.044	0.039	0.035	0.032	0.028	0.025
15	0.057	0.051	0.045	0.040	0.035	0.031	0.028	0.025	0.022	0.020
16	0.047	0.042	0.036	0.032	0.028	0.025	0.022	0.019	0.017	0.015
17	0.039	0.034	0.030	0.026	0.023	0.020	0.017	0.015	0.013	0.012
18	0.032	0.028	0.024	0.021	0.018	0.016	0.014	0.012	0.010	0.009
19	0.027	0.023	0.020	0.017	0.014	0.012	0.011	0.009	0.008	0.007
20	0.022	0.019	0.016	0.014	0.012	0.010	0.008	0.007	0.006	0.005

% Period	31	32	33	34	35	36	37	38	39	40
1	0.763	0.758	0.752	0.746	0.741	0.735	0.730	0.725	0.719	0.714
2	0.583	0.574	0.565	0.557	0.549	0.541	0.533	0.525	0.518	0.510
3	0.445	0.435	0.425	0.416	0.406	0.398	0.389	0.381	0.372	0.364
4	0.340	0.329	0.320	0.310	0.301	0.292	0.284	0.276	0.268	0.260
5	0.259	0.250	0.240	0.231	0.223	0.215	0.207	0.200	0.193	0.186
6	0.198	0.189	0.181	0.173	0.165	0.158	0.151	0.145	0.139	0.133
7	0.151	0.143	0.136	0.129	0.122	0.116	0.110	0.105	0.100	0.095
8	0.115	0.108	0.102	0.096	0.091	0.085	0.081	0.076	0.072	0.068
9	0.088	0.082	0.077	0.072	0.067	0.063	0.059	0.055	0.052	0.048
10	0.067	0.062	0.058	0.054	0.050	0.046	0.043	0.040	0.037	0.035
11	0.051	0.047	0.043	0.040	0.037	0.034	0.031	0.029	0.027	0.025
12	0.039	0.036	0.033	0.030	0.027	0.025	0.023	0.021	0.019	0.018
13	0.030	0.027	0.025	0.022	0.020	0.018	0.017	0.015	0.014	0.013
14	0.023	0.021	0.018	0.017	0.015	0.014	0.012	0.011	0.010	0.009
15	0.017	0.016	0.014	0.012	0.011	0.010	0.009	0.008	0.007	0.006
16	0.013	0.012	0.010	0.009	0.008	0.007	0.006	0.006	0.005	0.005
17	0.010	0.009	0.008	0.007	0.006	0.005	0.005	0.004	0.004	0.003
18	0.008	0.007	0.006	0.005	0.005	0.004	0.003	0.003	0.003	0.002
19	0.006	0.005	0.004	0.004	0.003	0.003	0.003	0.002	0.002	0.002
20	0.005	0.004	0.003	0.003	0.002	0.002	0.002	0.002	0.001	0.001

%	1	2	3	4	5	6	7	8	9	10
Period										
1	0.990	0.980	0.971	0.962	0.952	0.943	0.935	0.926	0.917	0.909
2	1.970	1.942	1.913	1.886	1.859	1.833	1.808	1.783	1.759	1.736
3	2.941	2.884	2.829	2.775	2.723	2.673	2.624	2.577	2.531	2.487
4	3.902	3.808	3.717	3.630	3.546	3.465	3.387	3.312	3.240	3.170
5	4.853	4.713	4.580	4.452	4.329	4.212	4.100	3.993	3.890	3.791
6	5.795	5.601	5.417	5.242	5.076	4.917	4.767	4.623	4.486	4.355
7	6.728	6.472	6.230	6.002	5.786	5.582	5.389	5.206	5.033	4.868
8	7.652	7.325	7.020	6.733	6.463	6.210	5.971	5.747	5.535	5.335
9	8.566	8.162	7.786	7.435	7.108	6.802	6.515	6.247	5.995	5.759
10	9.471	8.983	8.530	8.111	7.722	7.360	7.024	6.710	6.418	6.145
11	10.368	9.787	9.253	8.760	8.306	7.887	7.499	7.139	6.805	6.495
12	11.255	10.575	9.954	9.385	8.863	8.384	7.943	7.536	7.161	6.814
13	12.134	11.348	10.635	9.986	9.394	8.853	8.358	7.904	7.487	7.103
14	13.004	12.106	11.296	10.563	9.899	9.295	8.745	8.244	7.786	7.367
15	13.865	12.849	11.938	11.118	10.380	9.712	9.108	8.559	8.061	7.606
16	14.718	13.578	12.561	11.652	10.838	10.106	9.447	8.851	8.313	7.824
17	15.562	14.292	13.166	12.166	11.274	10.477	9.763	9.122	8.544	8.022
18	16.398	14.992	13.754	12.659	11.690	10.828	10.059	9.372	8.756	8.201
19	17.226	15.678	14.324	13.134	12.085	11.158	10.336	9.604	8.950	8.365
20	18.046	16.351	14.877	13.590	12.462	11.470	10.594	9.818	9.129	8.514

%	11	12	13	14	15	16	17	18	19	20
Period										
1	0.901	0.893	0.885	0.877	0.870	0.862	0.855	0.847	0.840	0.833
2	1.713	1.690	1.668	1.647	1.626	1.605	1.585	1.566	1.547	1.528
3	2.444	2.402	2.361	2.322	2.283	2.246	2.210	2.174	2.140	2.106
4	3.102	3.037	2.974	2.914	2.855	2.798	2.743	2.690	2.639	2.589
5	3.696	3.605	3.517	3.433	3.352	3.274	3.199	3.127	3.058	2.991
6	4.231	4.111	3.998	3.889	3.784	3.685	3.589	3.498	3.410	3.326
7	4.712	4.564	4.423	4.288	4.160	4.039	3.922	3.812	3.706	3.605
8	5.146	4.968	4.799	4.639	4.487	4.344	4.207	4.078	3.954	3.837
9	5.537	5.328	5.132	4.946	4.772	4.607	4.451	4.303	4.163	4.031
10	5.889	5.650	5.426	5.216	5.019	4.833	4.659	4.494	4.339	4.192
11	6.207	5.938	5.687	5.453	5.234	5.029	4.836	4.656	4.487	4.327
12	6.492	6.194	5.918	5.660	5.421	5.197	4.988	4.793	4.611	4.439
13	6.750	6.424	6.122	5.842	5.583	5.342	5.118	4.910	4.715	4.533
14	6.982	6.628	6.302	6.002	5.724	5.468	5.229	5.008	4.802	4.611
15	7.191	6.811	6.462	6.142	5.847	5.575	5.324	5.092	4.876	4.675
16	7.379	6.974	6.604	6.265	5.954	5.668	5.405	5.162	4.938	4.730
17	7.549	7.120	6.729	6.373	6.047	5.749	5.475	5.222	4.990	4.775
18	7.702	7.250	6.840	6.467	6.128	5.818	5.534	5.273	5.033	4.812
19	7.839	7.366	6.938	6.550	6.198	5.877	5.584	5.316	5.070	4.843
20	7.963	7.469	7.025	6.623	6.259	5.929	5.628	5.353	5.101	4.870

%	21	22	23	24	25	26	27	28	29	30
Period										
1	0.826	0.820	0.813	0.806	0.800	0.794	0.787	0.781	0.775	0.769
2	1.509	1.492	1.474	1.457	1.440	1.424	1.407	1.392	1.376	1.361
3	2.074	2.042	2.011	1.981	1.952	1.923	1.896	1.868	1.842	1.816
4	2.540	2.494	2.448	2.404	2.362	2.320	2.280	2.241	2.203	2.166
5	2.926	2.864	2.803	2.745	2.689	2.635	2.583	2.532	2.483	2.436
6	3.245	3.167	3.092	3.020	2.951	2.885	2.821	2.759	2.700	2.643
7	3.508	3.416	3.327	3.242	3.161	3.083	3.009	2.937	2.868	2.802
8	3.726	3.619	3.518	3.421	3.329	3.241	3.156	3.076	2.999	2.925
9	3.905	3.786	3.673	3.566	3.463	3.366	3.273	3.184	3.100	3.019
10	4.054	3.923	3.799	3.682	3.571	3.465	3.364	3.269	3.178	3.092
11	4.177	4.035	3.902	3.776	3.656	3.543	3.437	3.335	3.239	3.147
12	4.278	4.127	3.985	3.851	3.725	3.606	3.493	3.387	3.286	3.190
13	4.362	4.203	4.053	3.912	3.780	3.656	3.538	3.427	3.322	3.223
14	4.432	4.265	4.108	3.962	3.824	3.695	3.573	3.459	3.351	3.249
15	4.489	4.315	4.153	4.001	3.859	3.726	3.601	3.483	3.373	3.268
16	4.536	4.357	4.189	4.033	3.887	3.751	3.623	3.503	3.390	3.283
17	4.576	4.391	4.219	4.059	3.910	3.771	3.640	3.518	3.403	3.295
18	4.608	4.419	4.243	4.080	3.928	3.786	3.654	3.529	3.413	3.304
19	4.635	4.442	4.263	4.097	3.942	3.799	3.664	3.539	3.421	3.311
20	4.657	4.460	4.279	4.110	3.954	3.808	3.673	3.546	3.427	3.316

%	31	32	33	34	35	36	37	38	39	40
Period										
1	0.763	0.758	0.752	0.746	0.741	0.735	0.730	0.725	0.719	0.714
2	1.346	1.331	1.317	1.303	1.289	1.276	1.263	1.250	1.237	1.224
3	1.791	1.766	1.742	1.719	1.696	1.673	1.652	1.630	1.609	1.589
4	2.130	2.096	2.062	2.029	1.997	1.966	1.935	1.906	1.877	1.849
5	2.390	2.345	2.302	2.260	2.220	2.181	2.143	2.106	2.070	2.035
6	2.588	2.534	2.483	2.433	2.385	2.339	2.294	2.251	2.209	2.168
7	2.739	2.677	2.619	2.562	2.508	2.455	2.404	2.355	2.308	2.263
8	2.854	2.786	2.721	2.658	2.598	2.540	2.485	2.432	2.380	2.331
9	2.942	2.868	2.798	2.730	2.665	2.603	2.544	2.487	2.432	2.379
10	3.009	2.930	2.855	2.784	2.715	2.649	2.587	2.527	2.469	2.414
11	3.060	2.978	2.899	2.824	2.752	2.683	2.618	2.555	2.496	2.438
12	3.100	3.013	2.931	2.853	2.779	2.708	2.641	2.576	2.515	2.456
13	3.129	3.040	2.956	2.876	2.799	2.727	2.658	2.592	2.529	2.469
14	3.152	3.061	2.974	2.892	2.814	2.740	2.670	2.603	2.539	2.477
15	3.170	3.076	2.988	2.905	2.825	2.750	2.679	2.611	2.546	2.484
16	3.183	3.088	2.999	2.914	2.834	2.757	2.685	2.616	2.551	2.489
17	3.193	3.097	3.007	2.921	2.840	2.763	2.690	2.621	2.555	2.492
18	3.201	3.104	3.012	2.926	2.844	2.767	2.693	2.624	2.557	2.494
19	3.207	3.109	3.017	2.930	2.848	2.770	2.696	2.626	2.559	2.496
20	3.211	3.113	3.020	2.933	2.850	2.772	2.698	2.627	2.561	2.497

Appendix B – Sources of company information

The following are examples of sources of company information which can be found in most university/college libraries, local reference libraries, and in some company libraries. The list of necessity is selective. However, you should experiment by using any library to which you have access to find out details about a particular company or topic.

KOMPASS   (Annual publication in three volumes)

Volumes I Products and Services: Classifies 45,000 UK companies according to their products and services.   A useful volume for purchasing, but for the purpose of financial analysis can provide the opportunity to identify companies in a similar industry sector.

Volume II Company Information: Arranges companies by county and town. Most entries give name and address, a list of the directors, share capital, turnover, number of employees and product codes. It also provides some basic financial data for a three year period, together with two financial ratios. This volume is useful in that it often gives entries for a number of limited companies which might form part of a larger group. It is also useful from a geographic point of view.

Volume III Parents and Subsidiaries: Lists over 40,000 parent companies and over 130,000 subsidiaries. Shows their corporate structure. This volume is similar to *Who Owns Whom*.

WHO OWN'S WHOM   (annual publication in two volumes)

Volumes are available covering: UK and Ireland, Continental Europe, North and South America and Australasia, Middle East and Africa.

For UK and Ireland two volumes provide the following:

Volume I is in two sections. Both sections show the corporate family trees of parent companies.   Section One, the largest section relates to companies registered in the UK while Section Two relates to companies registered in the Republic of Ireland.

Volume II lists subsidiaries in a bold typeface with the parent immediately below (indented and in a normal typeface).

DIRECTORY OF DIRECTORS   (annual publication in two volumes)

Volume I is an alphabetical list of the directors of the principal public and private companies in the UK, giving the names of the companies with which they are directors.

Volume II is an alphabetical list of the principal public and private companies in the UK, giving the names of their directors, together with limited financial data for some companies.

STOCK EXCHANGE YEAR–BOOK   (annual publication)

London and Dublin stock exchange companies are listed in some detail in this publication.   Information provided includes: address of registered office, registrars, names of directors, secretary, auditors, solicitors, principal bankers, and brokers.   Details of registration, including registered number, a statement of the principal activities of the company and principal subsidiaries.

Limited financial data is provided for two years including employee details. Sections also show recent dividends, capital structure, substantial shareholdings and registrars.   A final section, in some entries, gives a brief five year summary.

FT McCARTHY (included in the FT DISCOVERY package)

FT McCarthy sheets (now renamed European Business Intelligence) are produced for quoted and unquoted UK registered companies.   The service represent a collection of press cuttings which are accumulated for each company, covering write–ups in relevant newspapers and magazines.   There is also an Industry Service which is based on subjects.   This makes it possible to compare the performance and development of individual companies in their field of operation.   The service is also included in the new FT Discovery package.

THE HEMSCOTT COMPANY GUIDE

Produced by Hemmington Scott who advertise it as "The No 1 information source on UK stockmarket companies".   Basic company entries are six to a page.   This gives a brief statement of principal activities, head office with full contact details, announcements, and limited financial data for five years. Companies can subscribe to have a larger entry, up to one page.   These entries will give details of directors, registrars, brokers, auditors, financial advisers, and solicitors.   In addition, extracts from Chairperson's or Chief Executive's statements are also included.

A large section in the back of the guide provides references to Actuaries, Auditors, Financial Advisers, Financial PR Advisers, Foreign Banks, Investment Managers, International Lawyers, Pension Fund Managers, Property Advisers, Registrars, Solicitors, Stockbrokers and Venture Capital Companies.

COMPANY REGISTRATION OFFICE

The Company Registration Office, Crown Way, Maindy, Cardiff telephone 01222 380801 holds certain information on companies on microfiche. Public limited companies are required to lodge their annual return not later than 7 months after their year end, limited companies 10 months.

The contents in a packet of microfiche contains general information about the company, including details of its incorporation, articles of association and memorandum of association; also details of movements of directors. It also includes financial information for a number of years which includes profit and loss account, balance sheet, source and application of funds, notes to the accounts, director's report and the auditor's report.

To obtain microfiche for a company, it is important to have the correct company name; better still to have the registered number of the company. Access can be gained through, visiting the Companies Registration Office at Cardiff or Companies House, London search room, (Edinburgh in Scotland), by post, or by using a company search agent.

One company search agent is *Company Formations Ltd*, 82 Whitchurch Road, Cardiff CF4 3LX telephone 01222 66 65 64 who provide an additional range of company related services all separately priced. These include, Director's Report and Accounts, Annual Return, Liquidation search, Directors database search, Compay microfiche, through to a full Credit Status report. Should you wish to use this type of service contact the company for their current fees.

FAME (financial analysis made easy)

'A database containing company information. It contains detailed information on 500,000 UK and Irish companies, and summarised information on an additional 1.2 million companies. (1.7 million companies in total)

For each company there is up to 10 years of historical information. A company record typically contains: profit and loss account, balance sheet, cash flow statement, ratios and trends, SIC codes and activity information, credit score and rating, lists of directors, shareholders, subsidiaries and holding companies, registered and trading addresses and details of miscellaneous information that has been filed at Companies House.

The software allows you to search for companies that fulfill your criteria (by over 100 criteria). You can also compare companies against each other and present your results in graphs and tables. The integral analysis software is very sophisticated. Information can be downloaded for further analysis or marketing. You can also use "Addin" functionality to access FAME from within Excel or export data directly into tailor-made templates.

FAME is widely used for all types of financial analysis as well as sales and marketing projects. It is available on CD-ROM, DVD-ROM and the Internet and is updated weekly and monthly'.

SHAREFINDER COMPANY REPORTS

These reports are available by telephone, 0870 601 4600 and currently cost £8.95. The reports are aimed at investors and include a summary page, usually with a recommendation to buy, hold or sell the shares. Other sections of the report include ratings and earnings analysis, key financials at a glance, summary key financials, stock market performance, sector performance overview, corporate details, latest directors' share dealings and latest company announcements.

ICC BUSINESS RATIOS *plus*

'140 Business Ratios *plus* titles are published covering the whole of UK industry. In each report, company data is presented alphabetically with a two page spread for each showing address, trading activity, directors, subsidiaries and other company details, *plus* Profit and Loss, Balance Sheet, ICC Ratio Analysis and League Table Positions'.

Other sections of the report give Performance League Tables where companies are ranked by Size, Profitability, Efficiency, Liquidity, Gearing, Employee Performance and Growth. Also an Industry Profile i.e. an Industry Profit and Loss Account and Industry Balance Sheet. A final section Industry Comment which is a summary of the report findings, put into context of recent industry developments. Reports are typically 400 pages in length.

INTERNET

There are many good sites on the internet providing UK company information. By its very nature the internet is continually changing and evolving therefore many links no longer work. We will continue to operate our company web site **http://www.marspub.co.uk/** and post amendments/updates from time to time. We now list a few useful sites, some included just for their links.

http://profiles.wisi.com/ Historical share prices.

http://www.corporateinformation.com/ukcorp.html

http://www.bloomberg.com/uk/ukhome.html

http://finance.uk.yahoo.com/

http://www.bized.ac.uk/

http://www.northcote.co.uk/   Annual reports

http://www.icaew.co.uk/

http://www.researchindex.co.uk/

http://www.icbinc.com/   The ultimate Annual Reports service

Glossary of Terms

Absorption Costing

The practice of charging all costs, both variable and fixed, to operations, processes or products.

Accounting Period

The period of time between two reporting dates.

Accounting Policies

These are disclosed in the annual reports published by quoted companies and represent the interpretation of accounting principles and requirements adopted by the board of directors.

Accounting Principles

A number of generally accepted accounting principles are used in preparing financial statements. They are only generally accepted and do not have the force of law. You should note that sometimes they are referred to as accounting concepts and conventions.

Accounting Rate of Return

A method used to evaluate an investment opportunity that ignores the time value of money. The return generated by an investment opportunity is expressed as a percentage of the capital outlay.

Activity Based Costing (ABC)

The practice that measures the cost and performance of activities, resources and the things that consume them.

Age Analysis

A statement analysing the transactions that make up debtor/creditor balance into discreet 'ageing' periods.

Amortisation

The writing-off of a fixed asset over a time period. It is often used in conjunction with intangible assets, e.g. goodwill.

Annual Report

A report issued to shareholders and other interested parties which normally includes a chairman's statement, report of the directors, review of operations, financial statements and associated notes.

Annuity

A series of payments of an equal, or constant, amount of money at fixed intervals for a specified number of periods.

Balance Sheet

A statement showing the financial position of a company in terms of its assets and liabilities at a specified point in time.

Bank Borrowings

Includes bank overdraft and bank loans.

Budget

A financial and/or quantitative statement, prepared and approved prior to a defined period of time, of the policy to be pursued during that period for the purpose of attaining a given objective.

Capital Investment Appraisal

The evaluation of proposed capital projects. Sometimes referred to as project appraisal.

Capital Structure

The composition of a company's sources of long-term funds e.g. equity and debt.

Cash flow statement

A statement that UK and US companies are required to include in their published accounts. Such statements analyse cash flows under three types of activity:

Investing activities

Financial activities

Operating activities.

Chairperson's Statement

A statement by the chairman of a company, normally included as part of the annual report, and which contains reference to important events.

Common–Size Analysis

A method of analysis by which data in the profit and loss account and the balance sheet are expressed as a percentage of some key figure.

Compounding

A technique for determining a future value given a present value, a time period and an interest rate.

Contribution

The difference between the sales revenue and the marginal cost of sales.

Contribution per unit

The difference between the selling price and the marginal cost per unit.

Cost Allocation

Where an item of cost can be allocated directly to a cost centre.

Cost Apportionment

Where an item of cost cannot be allocated directly to a cost centre. Apportionment requires that a range of bases are used which is fair across all cost centres e.g. floor area, machine hours, plant value.

Cost Centre

A location, person or item(s) of equipment that costs may be ascertained and used for the purpose of cost control.

Cost of Capital

The cost of long-term funds to a company.

Cost of Sales

The costs that are attributable to the sales made. It is usually before the deduction of selling, distribution and administration costs.

Cost Unit

A normal unit of quantity of a product, service or time in relation to which costs may be ascertained or expressed e.g. per 100, per tonne.

Creditors: amounts owing within one year

The amounts of money owed and payable by the business within one year.

Creditors: amounts owing after more than one year

Long–term loans and other liabilities payable after one year.

Current Assets

Those assets of a company that are reasonably expected to be realised in cash, or sold, or consumed during the normal operating cycle of the business. They include stock, debtors, short term investments, bank and cash balances.

Current Liabilities

Those liabilities which a company may rely upon to finance short-term activities. They include creditors, bank overdraft, proposed final dividend, and current taxation.

Current Ratio

A measure of short-term solvency. It is calculated as current assets divided by current liabilities. It gives an indication of a company's ability to pay its way within one year.

Debtors

Amounts owed to a company by its customers.

Depreciation

An accounting adjustment to take account of the diminution in value of a fixed asset over its economic life.

Discounted Cash Flow (DCF)

A technique for calculating whether a sum receivable at some time in the future is worthwhile in terms of value today. It involves discounting, or scaling-down, future cash flows.

Dividend

The proportion of the profits of a company distributed to shareholders.

Earnings Per Share

Profit before taxation divided by the weighted average number of ordinary shares in issue during the period. The calculation and result is shown by way of note in a company's annual report.

Equity

The sum of issued share capital, capital reserves and revenue reserves which is also known as shareholders' funds, or net worth.

Equity Share Capital

The share capital of a company attributable to ordinary shareholders.

First In First Out (FIFO)

The price paid for the material first taken into stock. Issues from stores are priced based on the oldest material taken into stock.

Last In First Out (LIFO)

The price paid for the material last taken into stock. Issues from stores are priced based on the most recent material taken into stock.

Fixed Assets

Those assets which an organisation holds for use within the business and not for resale. They consist of tangible assets, like land and buildings, plant and machinery, vehicles, and fixtures and fittings; and intangible assets like goodwill.

Fixed Costs

A cost that tends not to vary with the level of activity. Fixed costs are often determined by management decisions to invest in plant and equipment; once undertaken these result in period/time related costs and often bear little resemblance to activity.

Flexible Budget

A budget which, by recognising the differences in variable, semi-variable and fixed costs, changes in relation to the level of activity attained.

Floating Charge

A charge against assets as security for a debt. It is a general claim against any available asset of the company.

Gearing

Expresses the relationship between some measure of interest-bearing capital and some measure of equity capital or the total capital employed.

Goodwill

The difference between the amount paid for a company as a whole and the net value of the assets and liabilities acquired.

Income Statement

An US term for the profit and loss account.

Intangible Assets

Assets the value of which does not relate to their physical properties, e.g. goodwill and brands.

Internal Rate of Return (IRR)

The rate of discount at which the present value of the future cash flows is equal to the initial outlay, i.e. at the IRR the net present value is zero.

Interest Payable

Money payable (but not necessary paid) on interest bearing debt.

Key Ratio

A term sometimes given to the profitability ratio. In the UK this is usually defined as profit before tax plus interest payable expressed as a percentage of net capital employed.

Labour Cost Variance

The difference between the standard cost of labour allowed for the actual output less the actual wages paid.

Labour Efficiency Variance

The difference between the standard hours of labour allowed less the actual hours at the standard price.

Labour Rate Variance

The actual hours at the difference between the standard rate less the actual rate.

Labour Hour Rate

An actual or predetermined rate. Calculated by dividing the cost apportioned (to a cost centre) by the actual or forecast labour hours for the period.

Liabilities

The financial obligations owed by a company, these can be to shareholders, other providers of debt, trade creditors and other creditors.

Liquid Assets

The difference between current assets and stock.

Liquid Ratio

Liquid assets divided by current liabilities. It attempts to show a company's ability to pay its way in the short term.

Loan Capital

Finance that has been borrowed and not obtained from the shareholders.

Long-Term Liabilities

Liabilities which are not due for repayment within one year.

Machine Hour Rate

An actual or predetermined rate. Calculated by dividing the cost apportioned (to a cost centre) by the actual or forecast machine hours for the period.

Material Cost Variance

The difference between the standard cost of materials allowed for the actual output less the actual cost of materials used.

Material Price Variance

The actual quantity at the difference between the standard price less the actual price.

Material Usage Variance

The difference between the standard materials allowed less the actual quantity at the standard price.

Minority Interest

The proportion of shares in subsidiary companies which is not held by a holding company. Profit attributable to minority interests and accumulated balances are shown in the consolidated financial statements.

Net Assets

Total assets minus Current Liabilities minus Creditors: amounts owing after one year.

Net Capital Employed

The sum of fixed assets, investments, current assets minus current liabilities.

Net Current Assets

See working capital.

Net Present Value (NPV)

The difference between the discounted value of future net cash inflows and the initial outlay..

Ordinary Shares

Shares which attract the remaining profits after all other claims, and, in liquidation, which attract the remaining assets of a company after creditors and other charges have been satisfied.

Payback Period

How long it will take to recover the outlay involved in a potential investment opportunity from net cash inflows.

PE Ratio

One of the most significant indicators of corporate performance which it is widely quoted in the financial press. It is calculated by dividing the market price of a share by the earnings per share (or the total market value by the total profit attributable to shareholders), i.e.

$$\text{PE Ratio} \quad = \quad \frac{\text{Market Price of a Share}}{\text{Earnings Per Share}}$$

Present Value Rule

A rule which explains why in a world of certainty accepting all projects with a positive NPV maximises the wealth of shareholders.

Profit and Loss Account

A statement showing what profit has been made over a period and the uses to which the profit has been put.

Quoted Investments

Investments in another company which has its shares quoted on a stock exchange..

Reducing Balance Depreciation

A method of depreciation whereby the periodic amount written off is a percentage of the reduced balance. (cost less accumulated depreciation).

Relevant Data

Relevant data for decision making is *future oriented* – that is *yet to be incurred.*

Residual Value

Value generated beyond the planning period

Sales or Turnover

Income derived from the principal activities of a company, net of value added tax (VAT).

Share Capital (Issued)

The product of the total number of shares issued and the nominal value of the shares.

Shareholder's Funds

Another name for equity.

Share Premium

The excess paid for a share, to a company, over its nominal value.

Short–Termism

A term associated with managing for today rather than tomorrow and beyond.

Straight Line Depreciation

A method of depreciation whereby an equal amount is written off the value of a fixed asset over its estimated economic life.

Standard Cost

A cost prepared prior to a defined period of time; calculated in relation to a prescribed set of working conditions in respect to material quantities and prices, labour hours and rates with an appropriate share of overheads.

Standard Costing

The preparation and use of standard costs, their comparison with actual costs and the analysis of variances.

Standard Price

A predetermined price on the basis of a specification of all the factors affecting that price.

Tangible Assets

An asset having a physical identity such as land and buildings, plant and machinery, vehicles etc.

Time Value of Money

A concept which is an integral part of the discounted cash flow technique used in capital investment appraisal. It recognises that cash flows in the later years of an investment opportunity cannot be compared with cash flows in the earlier years.

Total Assets

The sum of fixed assets, investments and current assets.

Variable Cost

A cost that tends to vary directly with the level of activity.

Weighted Average Cost of Capital (WACC)

A term associated with the view that there is an optimal or ideal capital structure. It is calculated as follows:

$$\text{Weighted Average Cost of Capital} = \%\text{Debt}(K_d) + \%\text{Equity}(K_e)$$

where K_d = Cost of debt $\qquad K_e$ = Cost of equity

Working Capital

The excess of current assets (stock, debtors and cash) over current liabilities (creditors, bank overdraft etc.).

2.1

Cash

Dr.					Cr.
Mar 1	Capital	10,000	Mar 7	Equipment	3,500
Mar 9	Sales	3,000			

Capital

Dr.					Cr.
			Mar 1	Cash	10,000

Purchases

Dr.					Cr.
Mar 6	R. Matthews	2,500			

R. Matthews & Sons

Dr.					Cr.
			Mar 6	Purchases	2,500

Equipment

Dr.					Cr.
Mar 7	Cash	3,500			

Sales

Dr.					Cr.
			Mar 9	Cash	3,000

2.2

Bank

Dr.						Cr.
Oct 1	Capital	20,000	Oct 5	Motor Van		3,500
Mar 9	Sales	3,000				

Capital

Dr.					Cr.
		Oct 1	Bank		20,000

Purchases

Dr.				Cr.
Oct 2	F. Ewart & Co	3,200		

F. Ewart & Co

Dr.					Cr.
Oct 8	Returns Outwards	300	Oct 2	Purchases	3,200

Motor Van

Dr.				Cr.
Oct 5	Bank	2,500		

Returns Outwards

Dr.				Cr.
		Oct 8	F. Ewart & Co	300

2.3

Bank

May 1	Capital	3,000	May 5	Cash (contra)	500
May 15	U. Candoit	2,500	May 8	Motor Van	1,500
			May 31	DottyCom Ltd	2,000

Capital

			May 1	Bank	3,000

Purchases

May 4	DottyCom Ltd	3,000	

DottyCom Ltd

May 14	Returns Outwards	500	May 4	Purchases	3,000
May 31	Bank	2,000			

Cash

May 5	Bank (contra)	500	

Motor Van

May 8	Bank	1,500	

Sales

			May 11	U. Candoit	2,500

U. Candoit

May 11	Sales	2,500	May 15	Bank	2,500

Returns Outwards

			May 14	DottyCom Ltd	500

Furniture

May 22	B. Wise Ltd	1,500	

B. Wise Ltd

			May 22	Furniture	1,500

2.4

Bank

Aug 1	Capital	8,000	Aug 4	Cash (contra)	2,000
Aug 28	M. Istaken Ltd	4,500	Aug 31	I.T. Digital & Co	4,000

Capital

			Aug 1	Bank	8,000

Purchases

Aug 3	I.T. Digital & Co	6,000	
Aug 30	U.N. Wise Ltd	1,500	

I.T. Digital & Co

Aug 21	Returns Outwards	300	Aug 3	Purchases	6,000
Aug 31	Bank	4,000			

Cash

Aug 4	Bank (contra)	2,000	Aug 7	Furniture	1,500

Furniture

Aug 7	Cash	1,500	

Sales

			Aug 10	M. Istaken Ltd	4,500

Returns Outwards

			Aug 21	I.T. Digital & Co	300

M. Istaken Ltd

Aug 10	Sales	4,500	Aug 28	Bank	4,500

U.N. Wise Ltd

			Aug 30	Purchases	1,500

2.5

<h2 style="text-align:center">Bank</h2>

Dr.						Cr.
Nov 1	Balance b/d	20,000	Nov 13	Cash (contra)		1,000
Nov 5	Interest Received	450	Nov 16	Insurance		1,200

<h2 style="text-align:center">Capital</h2>

Dr.				Cr.
		Nov 1	Balance b/d	28,000

<h2 style="text-align:center">Cash</h2>

Dr.					Cr.
Nov 1	Balance b/d	2,000	Nov 1	Rent	800
Nov 13	Bank (contra)	1,000	Nov 13	Wages	1,400

<h2 style="text-align:center">Motor Van</h2>

Dr.			Cr.
Nov 1	Balance b/d	6,000	

<h2 style="text-align:center">Rent</h2>

Dr.			Cr.
Nov 1	Cash	800	

<h2 style="text-align:center">Interest Received</h2>

Dr.			Cr.
		Nov 5 Bank	450

<h2 style="text-align:center">Wages</h2>

Dr.			Cr.
Nov 13 Cash	1,400		

<h2 style="text-align:center">Insurance</h2>

Dr.			Cr.
Nov 16 Bank	1,200		

2.6

Bank

Dr.					Cr.
Aug 1	Balance b/d	8,000	Aug 10	Telephone	300

Capital

Dr.					Cr.
			Aug 1	Balance b/d	16,400

Cash

Dr.					Cr.
Aug 1	Balance b/d	1,400	Aug 1	Wages	600
Aug 3	Rent Received	300	Aug 6	Motor Expenses	500

Motor Van

Dr.				Cr.
Aug 1	Balance b/d	7,000		

Wages

Dr.				Cr.
Aug 1	Cash	600		

Rent Received

Dr.				Cr.
			Aug 3	Cash	300

Motor Expenses

Dr.				Cr.
Aug 6	Cash	500		

Telephone

Dr.				Cr.
Aug 10	Bank	300		

2.7

Bank

Dr.						Cr.
Aug 1	Capital	50,000	Aug 10	L. Last Ltd	11,400
Aug 14	K. Krankie	18,500	Aug 10	C. Cooke & C0	20,900
Aug 14	N. Nettle	25,000	Aug 21	Betta-Build	8,000
			Aug 31	Motor Van	15,000

Capital

Dr.					Cr.
			Aug 1	Balance b/d	50,000

Purchases

Dr.				Cr.
Aug 2	R.E. Turn Ltd	30,000		
Aug 2	L. Last Ltd	12,000		
Aug 2	C. Cooke & Co	22,000		
Aug 9	Cash	18,000		

R.E. Turn Ltd

Dr.					Cr.
Aug 18	Returns Outwards	5,000	Aug 2	Purchases	30,000

L. Last Ltd

Dr.					Cr.
Aug 10	Bank	11,400	Aug 2	Purchases	12,000
Aug 10	Discount Received	600			

C. Cooke & Co

Dr.					Cr.
Aug 10	Bank	20,900	Aug 2	Purchases	22,000
Aug 10	Discount Received	1,100			

Sales

Dr.				Cr.
	Aug 5	Cash	32,000	
	Aug 7	Sid Spice	14,000	
	Aug 7	K. Krankie	19,000	
	Aug 7	N. Nettle	30,000	

Cash

Dr.					Cr.
Aug 5	Sales	32,000	Aug 6	Wages	4,400
Aug 30	J. Jones	12,000	Aug 9	Purchases	18,000
			Aug 13	Wages	4,400

Wages

Dr.				Cr.
Aug 6	Sales	4,400		
Aug 13	Cash	4,400		

Sid Spice

Dr.					Cr.
Aug 7	Sales	14,000	Aug 27	Returns Inwards	1,200

K. Krankie

Dr.					Cr.
Aug 7	Sales	19,000	Aug 14	Bank	18,500
			Aug 14	Discount Allowed	500

N. Nettle

Dr.					Cr.
Aug 7	Sales	30,000	Aug 14	Bank	25,000
			Aug 14	Discount Allowed	800

Discount Received

Dr.					Cr.
			Aug 10	L. Last Ltd	600
			Aug 10	C. Cooke & Co	1,100

Discount Allowed

Dr.				Cr.
Aug 14	K. Krankie	500		
Aug 14	N. Nettle	800		

Shop Fixtures

Dr.				Cr.
Aug 15	Betta-Build	8,000		

Betta Build

Dr.				Cr.
Aug 21 Bank	8,000	Aug 15	Shop Fixtures	8,000

Returns Outwards

Dr.			Cr.
	Aug 18	R. E. Turn Ltd	5,000

Returns Inwards

Dr.		Cr.
Aug 27 Sid Spice	1,200	

J. Jones

Dr.			Cr.
	Aug 30	Cash	12,000

Motor Van

Dr.		Cr.
Aug 31 Bank	15,000	

Trial Balance as at 31st August

	Dr.	Cr.
Bank	38,200	
Purchases	82,000	
Cash	17,200	
Wages	8,800	
Sid Spice	12,800	
N. Nettle	4,200	
Discount Allowed	1,300	
Shop Fixtures	8,000	
Returns Inwards	1,200	
Motor Van	15,000	
Capital		50,000
R.E. Turn Ltd		25,000
Sales		95,000
Discount Received		1,700
Returns Outwards		5,000
J. Jones		12,000
	188,700	188,700

2.8

Bank

Dr.						Cr.
Jun 1	Capital	60,000	Jun 5	Motor Van	8,000
Jun 25	P. Mickelson	4,300	Jun 7	Motor Expenses	120
			Jun 21	E. Els	5,500
			Jun 21	G. Norman	4,000

Cash

Dr.						Cr.
Jun 1	Capital	5,000	Jun 4	Purchases	2,300
Jun 23	T. Woods	6,200	Jun 15	Motor Expenses	50
Jun 26	Sales	3,400	Jun 20	Drawings	1,000
			Jun 27	Drawings	2,400
			Jun 29	Postage Stamps	40

Capital

Dr.					Cr.
		Jun 1	Bank	60,000
		Jun 1	Cash	5,000

Purchases

Dr.					Cr.
Jun 2	D. Duval	50,000			
Jun 4	Cash	2,300			
Jun 11	N. Price	24,000			
Jun 11	E. Els	6,200			
Jun 11	G. Norman	4,600			

D. Duval

Dr.					Cr.
		Jun 2	Purchases	50,000

Sales

Dr.					Cr.
			Jun 3	T. Woods	6,600
			Jun 3	F. Couples	2,500
			Jun 3	P. Mickleson	4,300
			Jun 9	C. Montgomerie	2,400
			Jun 9	L. Westwood	2,600
			Jun 9	D. Clarke	6,500
			Jun 26	Cash	3,400
			Jun 30	F. Couples	4,300
			Jun 30	P. Mickleson	6,700
			Jun 30	L. Westwood	4,500

T. Woods

Dr.					Cr.
Jun 3	Sales	6,600	Jun 23	Cash	6,200
			Jun 23	Discount Allowed	400

F. Couples

Dr.					Cr.
Jun 3	Sales	2,500	Jun 19	Returns Inwards	1,100
Jun 30	Sales	4,300			

P. Mickleson

Dr.					Cr.
Jun 3	Sales	4,300	Jun 25	Bank	4,300
Jun 30	Sales	6,700			

Motor Van

Dr.					Cr.
Jun 5	Bank	8,000			

Motor Expenses

Dr.					Cr.
Jun 7	Bank	120			
Jun 15	Cash	50			

C. Montgomerie

Dr.					Cr.
Jun 9	Sales	2,400			

L. Westwood

Dr.					Cr.
Jun 9	Sales	2,600			
Jun 30	Sales	4,500			

D. Clarke

Dr.					Cr.
Jun 9	Sales	6,500			

N. Price

Dr.					Cr.
Jun 13	Returns Outwards	2,500	Jun 11	Purchases	24,000
Jun 28	Returns Outwards	4,200			

E. Els

Dr.					Cr.
Jun 21	Bank	5,500	Jun 11	Purchases	6,200
Jun 21	Discount Received	700			

G. Norman

Dr.					Cr.
Jun 21	Bank	4,000	Jun 11	Purchases	4,600
Jun 21	Discount Received	600			

Returns Outwards

Dr.					Cr.
			Jun 13	N. Price	2,500
			Jun 28	N. Price	4,200

Returns Inwards

Dr.					Cr.
Jun 19	F. Couples	1,100			

Drawings

Dr.					Cr.
Jun 20	Cash	1,000			
Jun 27	Cash	2,400			

Discount Received

Dr.				Cr.
	Jun 21	E. Els		700
	Jun 21	G. Norman		600

Discount Allowed

Dr.			Cr.
Jun 23	T. Woods	400	

Postage Stamps

Dr.			Cr.
Jun 29	Cash	40	

Trial Balance as at 30th June

	Dr.	Cr.
Bank	46,680	
Cash	8,810	
Purchases	87,100	
F. Couples	5,700	
P. Mickleson	6,700	
Motor Van	8,000	
Motor Expenses	170	
C. Montgomerie	2,400	
L. Westwood	7,100	
D. Clarke	6,500	
Returns Inwards	1,100	
Drawings	3,400	
Discount Allowed	400	
Postage Stamps	40	
Capital		65,000
D. Duval		50,000
Sales		43,800
N. Price		17,300
Returns Outwards		6,700
Discount Received		1,300
	184,100	184,100

3.1

Equipment

Dr.			Cr.
Jan 1	Balance b/d	500,000	

Provision for Depreciation – Equipment

Dr.						
1997			1997			
Dec 31	Balance c/d	115,000	Dec 31	Profit & Loss a/c	115,000	
1998			1998			
Dec 31	Balance c/d	230,000	Jan 1	Balance b/d	115,000	
			Dec 31	Profit & Loss a/c	115,000	
		230,000			230,000	
1999			1999			
Dec 31	Balance c/d	345,000	Jan 1	Balance b/d	230,000	
			Dec 31	Profit & Loss a/c	115,000	
		345,000			345,000	
2000			2000			
			Jan 1	Balance b/d	345,000	

Profit and Loss Account for the year ended 31st December

Dr.		Cr.
1997/1998/1999		
Depreciation of Equipment	115,000	

Balance Sheet as at 31 December 1999

ASSETS		LIABILITIES
Fixed Assets:		
Equipment at cost	500,000	
less Depreciation	345,000	
Net Book Value	115,000	

3.2

Equipment

Dr.					Cr.
Jan 1	Balance b/d	500,000			

Provision for Depreciation – Equipment

Dr.					Cr.
1997			1997		
Dec 31	Balance c/d	200,000	Dec 31	Profit & Loss a/c	200,000
1998			1998		
Dec 31	Balance c/d	320,000	Jan 1	Balance b/d	200,000
			Dec 31	Profit & Loss a/c	120,000
		320,000			320,000
1999			1999		
Dec 31	Balance c/d	392,000	Jan 1	Balance b/d	320,000
			Dec 31	Profit & Loss a/c	72,000
		392,000			392,000
2000			2000		
			Jan 1	Balance b/d	392,000

Profit and Loss Account for the year ended 31st December

Dr.			Cr.
1997			
Depreciation of Equipment	200,000		
1998			
Depreciation of Equipment	120,000		
1999			
Depreciation of Equipment	72,000		

Balance Sheet as at 31 December 1999

ASSETS		LIABILITIES
Fixed Assets:		
Equipment at cost	500,000	
less Depreciation	392,000	
Net Book Value	108,000	

3.3

Albert Doe & Sons

Dr.						Cr.
Mar 1	Balance b/d	900	Mar 4	Bad Debts a/c		900

Barney Brothers

Dr.						Cr.
Aug 1	Balance b/d	3,500	Aug 18	Bad Debts a/c		3,500

Jim Cunning

Dr.						Cr.
Oct 1	Balance b/d	1,700	Oct 7	Bad Debts a/c		1,700

Bad Debts Account

Dr.						Cr.
Mar 4	A. Doe & Sons	900	Dec 31	Profit & Loss a/c		6,100
Aug 18	Barney Brothers	3,500				
Oct 7	Jim Cunning	1,700				
		6,100				6,100

Profit and Loss Account for the year ended 31st December

Dr.			Cr.
Bad Debts Account	6,100		

3.4

Blight & Co

Dr.						Cr.
Feb 1	Balance b/d	3,300	Feb 19	Bad Debts a/c		3,300

B. Dreadenough

Dr.						Cr.
May 1	Balance b/d	800	May 6	Bad Debts a/c		800

H. Hardup Ltd

Dr.						Cr.
Sept 1	Balance b/d	6,000	Sept 15	Bad Debts a/c		6,000

Bad Debts Account

Dr.						Cr.
Feb 19	Blight & Co	3,300	Dec 31	Profit & Loss a/c		10,100
May 6	B. Dreadenough	800				
Sept 15	H. Hardup Ltd	6,000				
		10,100				10,100

Profit and Loss Account for the year ended 31st December

Dr.				Cr.
Bad Debts Account	10,100			

3.5

Provision for Bad Debts Account

Dr.						Cr.
1998			1998			
Dec 31	Balance c/d	9,500	Jan 1	Balance b/d	8,000	
			Dec 31	Profit & Loss a/c	1,500	
		9,500			9,500	
1999			1999			
Dec 31	Balance c/d	11,500	Jan 1	Balance b/d	9,500	
			Dec 31	Profit & Loss a/c	2,000	
		11,500			11,500	
2000			2000			
			Jan 1	Balance b/d	11,500	

Profit and Loss Account for the year ended 31st December

Dr.			Cr.
1998			
Provision for Bad Debts	1,500		
1999			
Provision for Bad Debts	2,000		

Balance Sheet as at 31 December 1999

ASSETS		LIABILITIES
Current Assets:		
Debtors	1,150,000	
less Provision	11,500	
	1,138,500	

3.6

Provision for Bad Debts Account

Dr.						Cr.
1998				1998		
Dec 31	Balance c/d	1,200		Jan 1	Balance b/d	1,600
Dec 31	Profit & Loss a/c	400				
		1,600				1,600
1999				1999		
Dec 31	Balance c/d	1,500		Jan 1	Balance b/d	1,200
				Dec 31	Profit & Loss a/c	300
		1,500				1,500
2000				2000		
				Jan 1	Balance b/d	1,500

Profit and Loss Account for the year ended 31st December

Dr.				Cr.
1998			1998	
			Provision for Bad Debts	400
1999			1999	
Provision for Bad Debts	300			

Balance Sheet as at 31 December 1999

ASSETS			LIABILITIES	
Current Assets:				
Debtors	180,000			
less Provision	1,500			
	178,500			

3.7

Wages Account

Dr.			Cr.		
Oct 7	Bank	25,000	Oct 31	Profit & Loss a/c	109,500
Oct 14	Bank	25,000			
Oct 21	Bank	25,000			
Oct 28	Bank	25,000			
Oct 31	Balance c/d	9,500			
		109,500			109,500
Nov 4	Bank	26,000	Nov 1	Balance b/d	9,500
Nov 11	Bank	26,000	Nov 30	Profit & Loss a/c	117,000
Nov 18	Bank	26,000			
Nov 25	Bank	26,000			
Nov 30	Balance c/d	22,500			
		126,500			126,500
			Dec 1	Balance b/d	22,500

Profit and Loss Account for the period ended

Dr.		Cr.
31st October		
Wages	109,500	
31st November		
Wages	117,000	

Balance Sheet as at 31st October

ASSETS		*LIABILITIES*	
		Current Liabilities:	
		Accruals (wages due)	9,500

3.8

Rent Account

Dr.						Cr.
Jan 1	Balance b/d	2,000	Dec 31	Profit & Loss a/c	8,400
Apr 1	Bank	4,200	Dec 31	Balance c/d	2,200
Oct 1	Bank	4,400			
		10,600			10,600
Jan 1	Balance b/d	2,200			

Profit and Loss Account for the period ended 31st October

Dr.			Cr.
Rent	8,400		

Balance Sheet as at 31st October

ASSETS		LIABILITIES	
Current Assets:			
Prepayments (rent)	2,200		

Exercise 4.1

Trading Account

Opening Stock	67,700	Sales		536,300
Purchases	300,000			
	367,700			
− Closing Stock	99,200			
= Cost of Sales	268,500			
Gross Profit c/d	267,800			
	536,300			536,300

Profit and Loss Account

General Expenses	4,700	Gross Profit b/d	267,800
Rent	8,000		
Motor Expenses	14,700		
Salaries	71,200		
Insurance	7,800		
Depn. of Motor Vehicle	11,200		
Net Profit for period	150,200		
	267,800		267,800

Balance Sheet

Fixed Assets:			Owners Capital	464,500
Premises		400,000	add Profit for period	150,200
Vehicles	56,000		less Drawings	87,000
less Depn.	33,600	22,400	Closing Capital	527,700
Current Assets:			Current Liabilities:	
Stock	99,200		Creditors	103,200
Debtors	81,800		General Expenses due	500
Bank	28,000			103,700
		209,000		
		631,400		631,400

Exercise 4.2

Trading Account

Opening Stock	30,000	Sales	300,000
Purchases	200,000		
	230,000		
– Closing Stock	40,000		
= Cost of Sales	190,000		
Gross Profit c/d	110,000		
	300,000		300,000

Profit and Loss Account

Administrative costs	62,000	Gross Profit b/d	110,000
Selling Costs	19,000	Income from Investments	2,000
Audit Fee	1,000		
Interest Paid	1,000		
Prov. for Doubtful Debts	300		
Net Profit for period	28,700		
	112,000		112,000

Balance Sheet

Fixed Assets:			Owners Capital		138,300
Land and Buildings		100,000	add Profit for period		28,700
Vehicles		20,000	less Drawings		15,000
Trade Investments		20,000	Closing Capital		152,000
Current Assets:			Current Liabilities:		
Stock		40,000	Creditors		40,000
Debtors	30,000		Bank Overdraft	20,000	
less Provision	1,000	29,000	Admin costs due	2,000	22,000
Cash		5,000			62,000
		74,000			
		214,000			214,000

Exercise 4.3

Trading Account

Opening Stock	219,400	Sales	712,000
Purchases	400,000		
	619,400		
– Closing Stock	199,200		
= Cost of Sales	420,200		
Gross Profit c/d	291,800		
	712,000		712,000

Profit and Loss Account

Rent	31,200	Gross Profit b/d	291,800
Insurance	5,500		
Lighting and Heating	10,320		
Motor Expenses	39,200		
Salaries and Wages	97,000		
Sundry Expenses	16,120		
Interest Payable	15,000		
Bad Debts Written Off	6,000		
Net Profit for period	71,460		
	291,800		291,800

Balance Sheet

Fixed Assets:			Owners Capital	685,980
Buildings		545,000	add Profit for period	71,460
Motor Vehicles		70,000	less Drawings	125,560
Furniture and Fittings		79,200	Closing Capital	631,880
Current Assets:			Current Liabilities:	
Stock		199,200	Creditors	165,000
Debtors	136,200		Bank Overdraft	250,000
less Bad Debts	6,000	130,200		415,000
Insurance Prepaid		600		
Cash		22,680		
		352,680		
		1,046,880		1,046,880

Exercise 4.4

Trading Account

Opening Stock	40,000	Sales	350,000
Purchases	190,000		
	230,000		
− Closing Stock	20,000		
= Cost of Sales	210,000		
Gross Profit c/d	140,000		
	350,000		350,000

Profit and Loss Account

Rates	4,000	Gross Profit b/d	140,000
General Expenses	30,000		
Wages and Salaries	40,000		
Bad Debts written off	1,000		
Distribution Costs	25,000		
Loan Interest	10,000		
Depn. of Machinery	11,000		
Net Profit for period	19,000		
	140,000		140,000

Balance Sheet

Fixed Assets:			Owners Capital		86,000
Land and Buildings		100,000	add Profit for period		19,000
Machinery	110,000		less Drawings		17,000
less Depn.	44,000	66,000	Closing Capital		88,000
			Loan at 10%		100,000
Current Assets:			Current Liabilities:		
Stock		20,000	Creditors		38,000
Debtors		25,000	Loan Interest due		5,000
Bank		20,000			43,000
		65,000			
		231,000			231,000

Exercise 4.5

Trading Account

Opening Stock	27,600	Sales	103,200
Purchases	86,400		
	114,000		
− Closing Stock	31,200		
= Cost of Sales	82,800		
Gross Profit c/d	20,400		
	103,200		103,200

Profit and Loss Account

Discount Allowed	1,800	Gross Profit b/d	20,400
Bad Debts	1,800		
General Expenses	5,100		
Repairs to Premises	1,800		
Depreciation of Fix & Fitt	540		
Net Profit for the period	9,360		
	20,400		20,400

Partnership Appropriation Accounts

	Smith	Jones	Total
Interest on Capital	600	270	870
Salaries		3,000	3,000
Balance	3,660	1,830	5,490
	4,260	5,100	9,360

Partnership Capital Accounts

	Smith	Jones
Opening Capital	12,000	5,400
add Profit appropriation	4,260	5,100
less Drawings	1,800	4,800
Closing Capital	14,460	5,700

Balance Sheet

Fixed Assets:			Capital Accounts:	
Freehold Premises		30,000	Smith	14,460
Fixtures and Fittings	5,400		Jones	5,700
less Depreciation	1,440	3,960		20,160
Current Assets:			Current Liabilities:	
Stock		31,200	Creditors	34,800
Debtors		37,200	Bank Overdraft	48,600
Insurance prepaid		300		
Cash		900		
		103,560		103,560

Exercise 4.6

Trading Account

Opening Stock	56,000	Sales	516,000
Purchases	268,000		
	324,000		
− Closing Stock	44,000		
= Cost of Sales	280,000		
Gross Profit c/d	236,000		
	516,000		516,000

Profit and Loss Account

Overheads	60,000	Gross Profit b/d	236,000
Depreciation of Equipment	46,000		
Net Profit c/d	130,000		
	236,000		236,000

Partnership Appropriation Accounts

	Jim	Dougal	Rosie	Total
Interest on Capital	7,200	4,800	3,840	15,840
Salaries		24,000	20,000	44,000
Balance	35,080	23,387	11,693	70,160
	42,280	52,187	35,533	130,000

Partnership Capital Accounts

	Jim	Dougal	Rosie
Opening Capital	60,000	40,000	32,000
add Profit appropriation	42,280	52,187	35,533
less Drawings	36,000	28,000	20,000
Closing Capital	66,280	64,187	47,533

Balance Sheet

Fixed Assets:			Capital Accounts:	
Equipment	220,000		Jim	66,280
less Depreciation	82,000	138,000	Dougal	64,187
			Rosie	47,533
				178,000
Current Assets:			Current Liabilities:	
Stock		44,000	Creditors	64,000
Debtors		48,000		
Bank		12,000		
		242,000		242,000

Exercise 4.7

Income and Expenditure Account

Wages	63,750	Subscriptions	74,250
General Expenses	3,750	Social Takings	23,750
Insurance	2,500		
Rates	3,750		
Printing and Stationery	2,500		
Depreciation of Furn.&Equip.	9,375		
Surplus to Capital a/c	12,375		
	98,000		98,000

Balance Sheet

Fixed Assets:			Opening Capital Fund		125,000
Premises		75,000	add Surplus for period		12,375
Equipment	37,500		Closing Capital Fund		137,375
less Depreciation	9,375	28,125			
Current Assets:			Current Liabilities:		
Subs in arrears	1,250		Creditors	2,500	
Cash	36,250		Subs paid in advance	750	
		37,500			3,250
		140,625			140,625

Exercise 4.8

Bar Trading Account

Opening Stock	5,400	Sales		58,800
Purchases	46,500			
	51,900			
− Closing Stock	3,600			
= Cost of Sales	48,300			
Wages − Bar attendant	3,000			
Sundry Bar Expenses	720			
Profit from Bar	6,780			
	58,800			58,800

Income and Expenditure Account

Wages	69,000	Profit from Bar	6,780
Insurance	2,880	Subscriptions	90,600
Rates	2,100	Locker Rents	3,600
Printing and Stationery	1,200		
Depreciation of Equipment	840		
Surplus to Capital a/c	24,960		
	100,980		100,980

Balance Sheet

Fixed Assets:			Opening Capital Fund		128,100
Premises		108,000	add Surplus for period		24,960
Equipment	22,750		Closing Capital Fund		153,060
less Depreciation	6,790	15,960			
Current Assets:			Current Liabilities:		
Stock − Bar	3,600		Creditors − Bar Pur.	1,500	
Subs in arrears	1,500		Subs paid in adv.	2,100	
Insurance in adv	1,320		Sundry bar expenses	420	
Cash	26,700				4,020
		33,120			
		157,080			157,080

In order to reduce the space required for vertical layouts, we have provided these answers using two sided Trading Account, Profit and Loss Account, Profit and Loss Appropriation Account and Balance Sheet.

Exercise 5.1

Trading Account

Opening Stock	54,000	Sales	540,000
Purchases	360,000		
	414,000		
– Closing Stock	72,000		
= Cost of Sales	342,000		
Gross Profit c/d	198,000		
	540,000		540,000

Profit and Loss Account

Administrative costs	108,000	Gross Profit b/d	198,000
Selling Costs	34,200	Rent Received	2,000
Audit Fee	1,800	Income from Investments	3,600
Interest Paid	2,160	Prov. for Doubtful Debts	300
Depreciation of Vehicles	5,000		
Net Profit for the period	52,740		
	203,900		203,900

Balance Sheet

Fixed Assets:			Capital and Reserves:		
Land and Buildings		234,000	Issued Share Capital		180,000
Vehicles	36,000		Profit and Loss Account		147,140
less Depn.	5,000	31,000	Shareholder's Fund		327,140
Trade Investments		36,000			
Current Assets:			Current Liabilities:		
Stock		72,000	Creditors		72,000
Debtors	54,000		Bank Overdraft		36,000
less Provision	500	53,500	Interest due		360
Cash		9,000			108,360
		134,500			
		435,500			435,500

Exercise 5.2

Trading Account

Opening Stock	189,000	Sales	1,890,000
Purchases	1,260,000		
	1,449,000		
– Closing Stock	252,000		
= Cost of Sales	1,197,000		
Gross Profit c/d	693,000		
	1,890,000		1,890,000

Profit and Loss Account

Interest Paid	6,300	Gross Profit b/d	693,000
Discount Allowed	12,200	Income from Investments	12,600
Selling Costs	119,700	Discount Received	22,200
Audit Fee	6,100		
Bad Debts written off	4,400		
Administration costs	380,900		
Net Profit for the period	198,200		
	727,800		727,800

Balance Sheet

Fixed Assets:			Capital and Reserves:	
Land and Buildings		819,000	Issued Share Capital	630,000
Vehicles		126,000	Profit and Loss Account	516,200
Trade Investments		114,000	Shareholder's Fund	1,146,200
Current Assets:			Current Liabilities:	
Stock		252,000	Creditors	252,000
Debtors	185,400		Bank Overdraft	126,000
less Bad Debt	800	184,600	Admin Costs due	2,900
Cash		31,500		380,900
		468,100		
		1,527,100		1,527,100

Exercise 5.3

Trading Account

Opening Stock	281,400	Sales	4,410,000
Purchases	2,604,000		
	2,885,400		
– Closing Stock	325,500		
= Cost of Sales	2,559,900		
Gross Profit c/d	1,850,100		
	4,410,000		4,410,000

Profit and Loss Account

Rent and Rates	151,200	Gross Profit b/d	1,850,100
Directors Remuneration	115,500	Income from Investments	8,400
Office Expenses	102,900		
Heating and Lighting	58,800		
Sales Expenses	114,800		
Insurance	35,700		
Wages and Salaries	700,200		
Auditors Remuneration	25,000		
Depn. of Equipment	176,400		
Depn. of Vehicles	42,000		
Provision for Bad Debts	14,700		
Interest on Loan at 10%	14,700		
	1,551,900		
Net Profit c/d	306,600		
	1,858,500		1,858,500

Profit and Loss Appropriation Account

Corporation Tax	126,000	Net Profit b/d	306,600
Ordinary Dividend	40,000	P&L a/c opening	277,200
Preference Dividend	8,400		
P&L a/c Closing	409,400		
	583,800		583,800

Balance Sheet

Fixed Assets:			Capital and Reserves:		
Equipment	882,000		Issued Share Capital		420,000
less Depn.	495,600	386,400	Profit and Loss Account		409,400
Vehicles	168,000		Preference Share Capital		105,000
less Depn.	126,000	42,000	Shareholder's Fund		934,400
Investments Quoted		58,800	Long-Term Loan at 10%		147,000
Current Assets:			Current Liabilities:		
Stock		325,500	Creditors		144,900
Debtors	630,000		Wages due		25,200
less Provision	31,500	598,500	Interest on Loan due		14,700
Rates paid in advance		6,300	Corporation Tax		126,000
Bank		14,700	Dividend Proposed		40,000
		945,000			350,800
		1,432,200			1,432,200

Exercise 5.4

Trading Account

Opening Stock	1,206,000	Sales	18,900,000
Purchases	11,160,000		
	12,366,000		
– Closing Stock	1,395,000		
= Cost of Sales	10,971,000		
Gross Profit c/d	7,929,000		
	18,900,000		18,900,000

Profit and Loss Account

Administrative Expenses	441,000	Gross Profit b/d	7,929,000
Bad Debts written off	98,000	Income from Investments	36,000
Directors Remuneration	495,000		
Heating and Lighting	252,000		
Insurance	126,000		
Marketing and Selling	270,000		
Rent and Rates	675,000		
Wages and Salaries	3,150,000		
Depn. of Equipment	756,000		
Depn. of Vehicles	180,000		
Provision for Bad Debts	63,000		
Interest on Loan at 10%	75,600		
Net Profit c/d	1,383,400		
	7,965,000		7,965,000

Profit and Loss Appropriation Account

Corporation Tax	540,000	Net Profit b/d	1,383,400
Interim Dividend	36,000	P&L a/c opening	1,188,000
Final Dividend	135,000		
P&L a/c Closing	1,860,400		
	2,571,400		2,571,400

Balance Sheet

Fixed Assets:			Capital and Reserves:		
Equipment	3,780,000		Issued Share Capital		2,250,000
less Depn.	2,124,000	1,656,000	Profit & Loss Account		1,860,400
Vehicles	720,000		Shareholder's Fund		4,110,400
less Depn.	540,000	180,000			
Investments Quoted		252,000	Long-Term Loan at 12%		630,000
Current Assets:			Current Liabilities:		
Stock		1,395,000	Creditors		621,000
Debtors	2,700,000		Interest on Loan due		75,600
less Bad Debt	26,000		Corporation Tax		540,000
less Provision	135,000	2,539,000	Final Dividend		135,000
Insurance prepaid		27,000			1,371,600
Bank		63,000			
		4,024,000			
		6,112,000			6,112,000

Exercise 5.5

Trading Account

Opening Stock	270,000	Sales	2,700,000
Purchases	1,710,000		
	1,980,000		
– Closing Stock	360,000		
= Cost of Sales	1,620,000		
Gross Profit c/d	1,080,000		
	2,700,000		2,700,000

Profit and Loss Account

Marketing & Selling Costs	540,000	Gross Profit b/d	1,080,000
Administration Costs	203,400	Rent Received	18,000
Audit Fee	9,000		
Rates	9,000		
Depn. of Equipment	36,000		
Depn. of Vehicles	18,000		
Bad Debts write off	9,000		
Provision for Bad Debts	1,800		
Net Profit c/d	271,800		
	1,098,000		1,098,000

Profit and Loss Appropriation Account

Corporation Tax	58,500	Net Profit b/d	271,800
Dividend at 8%	21,744	P&L a/c opening	387,000
P&L a/c Closing	578,556		
	658,800		658,800

Balance Sheet

Fixed Assets:			Capital and Reserves:		
Land and Buildings		1,080,000	Issued Share Capital		855,000
Equipment	360,000		Profit and Loss Account		578,556
less Depn.	72,000	288,000	Shareholder's Fund		1,433,556
Vehicles	180,000				
less Depn.	108,000	72,000			
Current Assets:			Current Liabilities:		
Stock		360,000	Creditors		360,000
Debtors	270,000		Bank Overdraft		180,000
less Bad Debts	9,000		Administration costs due		32,400
less Provision	19,800	241,200	Corporation Tax		58,500
Cash		45,000	Dividend Proposed		21,744
		646,200			652,644
		2,086,200			2,086,200

Exercise 5.6

Trading Account

Opening Stock	402,000	Sales	6,300,000
Purchases	3,720,000		
	4,122,000		
– Closing Stock	465,000		
= Cost of Sales	3,657,000		
Gross Profit c/d	2,643,000		
	6,300,000		6,300,000

Profit and Loss Account

Advertising	90,000	Gross Profit b/d	2,643,000
Directors Remuneration	165,000	Income from Investments	12,000
Electricity	84,000		
Insurance	42,000		
Office Expenses	147,000		
Rent and Rates	225,000		
Wages and Salaries	1,074,000		
Depn. of Equipment	252,000		
Depn. of Vehicles	60,000		
Auditors Fees	36,000		
Provision for Bad Debts	21,000		
Interest on Loan at 12%	21,000		
Net Profit c/d	438,000		
	2,655,000		2,655,000

Profit and Loss Appropriation Account

Corporation Tax	180,000	Net Profit b/d	438,000
Interim Dividend	12,000	P&L a/c opening	396,000
Final Dividend	75,000		
P&L a/c Closing	567,000		
	834,000		834,000

Balance Sheet

Fixed Assets:			Capital and Reserves:		
Equipment	1,260,000		Issued Share Capital		750,000
less Depn.	708,000	552,000	Profit and Loss Account		567,000
Vehicles	240,000		Shareholder's Fund		1,317,000
less Depn.	180,000	60,000			
Investments Quoted		84,000	Long-Term Loan at 12%		210,000
Current Assets:			Current Liabilities:		
Stock		465,000	Creditors		207,000
Debtors	900,000		Auditors Fee		36,000
less Provision	45,000	855,000	Interest on Loan due		21,000
Insurance prepaid		9,000	Corporation Tax		180,000
Bank		21,000	Final Dividend		75,000
		1,350,000			519,000
		2,046,000			2,046,000

Exercise 6.1

Fixed Assets	?	Issued Share Capital	110,000
		Profit and Loss Account	140,000
		Shareholder's Fund or Equity	250,000
		Long Term Loans	?
Current Assets:		Current Liabilities:	
Stock	210,000	Creditors	170,000
Debtors	105,000	Bank Overdraft	70,000
Cash	45,000		
	360,000		240,000

a. Total Borrowings = £250,000 x 0.72 = £180,000
   Long Term Loans = £180,000 – £70,000 = **£110,000**

b. Total Liabilities = £250,000 + £110,000 + £240,000 = £600,000
   Fixed Assets = £600,000 – £360,000 = **£240,000**

c. Current Ratio = £360,000 ÷ £240,000 = **1.50 to 1**

d. Return on Net Assets = £48,000 ÷ (£240,000 + £360,000 – £240,000) x 100 = **13.3%**

Exercise 6.2

Premises	9,000	Issued Share Capital	1,000
Vehicle	6,000	Profit and Loss Account	9,000
		Shareholder's Fund or Equity	10,000
		Long Term Loans	9,000
Current Assets:		Current Liabilities:	
Stock	16,000	Creditors	16,000
Debtors	9,000	Bank Overdraft	6,000
Cash	1,000		
	26,000		22,000

1. Profitability, key ratio = (£500 + £3,500) ÷ (£15,000 + £26,000 – £22,000) x 100 = **21.1%**

2. Profit Margin ratio = (£500 + £3,500) ÷ £25,500 x 100 = **15.7%**

3. Sales Generation Ratio = £25,500 ÷ (£15,000 + £26,000 – £22,000) = **1.34 to 1**

4. Current Ratio = £26,000 ÷ £22,000 = **1.18 to 1**

5. Liquid or Acid Test Ratio = (£26,000 – £16,000) ÷ £22,000 = **0.45 to 1**

6. Stock Turn = £20,000 ÷ £16,000 = **1.25 times**

7. Debtor weeks = £9,000 ÷ (£25,500 ÷ 52) = **18.4 weeks**

8. Borrowings Ratio = (£9,000 + £6,000) ÷ £10,000 = **1.50 to 1**

9. Income Gearing = £3,500 ÷ (£500 + £3,500) x 100 = **87.5%**

Exercise 6.3

Fixed Assets	90,000	Issued Share Capital	50,000
		Profit and Loss Account	20,000
		Shareholder's Fund or Equity	70,000
		Long Term Loans	50,000
Current Assets:		Current Liabilities:	
Stock	50,000	Creditors	40,000
Debtors	30,000	Bank Overdraft	20,000
Cash	10,000		
	90,000		60,000

1. Profitability, key ratio = (£22,000 + £8,000) ÷ (£90,000 + £90,000 – £60,000) x 100 = **25%**
2. Profit Margin ratio = (£22,000 + £8,000) ÷ £700,000 x 100 = **4.3%**
3. Sales Generation Ratio = £700,000 ÷ (£90,000 + £90,000 – £60,000) = **5,83 to 1**
4. Current Ratio = £90,000 ÷ £60,000 = **1.50 to 1**
5. Liquid or Acid Test Ratio = (£90,000 – £50,000) ÷ £60,000 = **0.67 to 1**
6. Stock Turn = £480,000 ÷ £50,000 = **9.6 times**
7. Debtor weeks = £30,000 ÷ (£700,000 ÷ 52) = **2.2 weeks**
8. Borrowings Ratio = (£50,000 + £20,000) ÷ £70,000 = **1.00 to 1**
9. Income Gearing = £8,000 ÷ (£22,000 + £8,000) x 100 = **26.7%**

Exercise 6.4

Premises	3,000	Issued Share Capital	200
Vehicle	1,500	Profit and Loss Account	2,800
	4,500	Shareholder's Fund or Equity	3,000
		Long Term Loans	1,800
Current Assets:		Current Liabilities:	
Stock	4,500	Creditors	5,000
Debtors	2,500	Bank Overdraft	2,000
Cash	300		
	7,300		7,000

1. Profitability, key ratio = (£200 + £700) ÷ (£4,500 + £7,300 – £7,000) x 100 = **18.8%**
2. Profit Margin ratio = (£200 + £700) ÷ £8,000 x 100 = **11.3%**
3. Sales Generation Ratio = £8,000 ÷ (£4,500 + £7,300 – £7,000) = **1.67 to 1**
4. Current Ratio = £7,300 ÷ £7,000 = **1.04 to 1**
5. Liquid or Acid Test Ratio = (£7,300 – £4,500) ÷ £7,000 = **0.40 to 1**
6. Stock Turn = £6,300 ÷ £4,500 = **1.4 times**
7. Debtor weeks = £2,500 ÷ (£8,000 ÷ 52) = **16.3 weeks**
8. Borrowings Ratio = (£1,800 + £2,000) ÷ £3,000 = **1.27 to 1**
9. Income Gearing = £700 ÷ (£200 + £700) x 100 = **77.8%**

Exercise 6.5

Land and Buildings		Issued Share Capital	100,000
Equipment	110,000	Profit and Loss Account	50,000
		Shareholder's Fund or Equity	150,000
		Long Term Loans	160,000
Current Assets:		Current Liabilities:	
Stock	150,000	Creditors	220,000
Debtors	250,000	Bank Overdraft	80,000
Cash	20,000	Accruals (wages)	20,000
	420,000		320,000

a. Total Liabilities = £150,000 + £160,000 + £320,000 = £630,000
Land and Buildings = £630,000 – £420,000 – £110,000 = **£100,000**

b. Gearing Ratio = (£160,000 + £80,000) ÷ £150,000 = **1.60 to 1**

c. Current Ratio = £420,000 ÷ £320,000 = **1.31 to 1**

d. Return on Net Assets = (£210,000 + £420,000 – £320,000) x 15 ÷ 100 = **£46,500**

Exercise 6.6 (suggestions for possible movements)

General points:

❏ This is not an answer to a specific question, it is simply suggestions/pointers to help with interpretation.

❏ List all the ratios in a table showing the annual results side by side.

❏ Interpret each ratio in turn. Then provide a summary for each group of ratios e.g. profitability.

❏ Where you have three years or more, look at the overall movement i.e. from the earliest to the latest year.

❏ Alternatively, where there is a substantial change in one year, interpret that movement.

❏ Your aim in interpretation is to show the examiner that you understand these ratios.

❏ Tip for interpretation Use the ratio to help you. Has the numerator increased or decreased? Has the denominator increased or decreased? What might have caused the numerator and/or denominator to increase or decrease?

Profitability Ratios

Key Profitability Ratio
Profit as a percentage of Capital Employed.
Profit can be taken either as Profit before Taxation or Profit before Taxation plus Interest Payable.
Capital Employed can be taken either as Total Assets less Current Liabilities or simply Total Assets.

○ An absolute ratio, the higher the better.

○ Shows whether a company has achieved higher or lower profits than in previous year(s), and/or against competitors. Does not give any indication why there is a movement in the ratio. Must interpret profit margin and sales generation ratios to identify reason(s) for movements.

Average Profit Margin Ratio
Profit as a percentage of Sales.
Profit can be taken either as Profit before Taxation or Profit before Taxation plus Interest Payable.

○ Shows the average profit generated by a company.

○ Can hide high profit and loss making parts of a company.

○ Try to identify reasons for any change.

○ For example, should a company increase its profit margins on its products, the ratio should increase. If a company reduced its costs the profit margin ratio increase. If a company increased its selling prices the profit margin ratio would increase.

○ An increase in the profit margin ratio could also be due to a change in the mix of products making up the total sales. For example, a company could be selling more higher margin lines and less of lower margin lines. This could be a redistribution of their own products and/or products that it had acquired when purchasing new businesses.

Sales Generation Ratio
Sales divided by Capital Employed.
Capital Employed can be taken either as Total Assets less Current Liabilities or simply Total Assets.

○ Known as the asset utilisation or sales generation ratio.

○ Shows the amount of sales in £'s generated by each £ of capital employed.

○ An increase in the ratio could be due to an increase in sales and/or a reduction in the capital employed. For example, if a company reduced it profit margins in order to try to obtain additional market share; sales should increase, therefore, given that the capital employed remained constant there would be an increase in the ratio.

○ Similarly, if a company disposed of under-utilised assets, given that the sales remained constant there would be an increase in the ratio.

○ Should a company pursue an expansion policy, capital employed should increase and sales should also increase. However, sales might lag behind the increases in capital employed.

Current Ratio
Current Assets divided by Current Liabilities.

○ Gives an indication how a company might be able to pay its way in the short to medium term. i.e. three months to one year.

○ Does not consider a company's ability to generate or attract finance.

○ Interpretation should be against industry averages and/or historic trends for the ratio.

○ A ratio of 1.50 to 1 means that the current liabilities are covered once plus an additional 50%.

○ Movement in a ratio from 1.50 to 1.25 should be interpreted without the 1.00 (i.e. unity). Therefore, the additional cover has fallen from 50% down to 25%.

Liquid Ratio (or Acid Test)
Liquid Assets divided by Current Liabilities.
Liquid assets exclude stock.

○ Gives an indication how a company might be able to meet its short term obligations.

○ Can be influenced by movements in bank overdrafts.

○ Interpretation should be against industry averages and/or historic trends for the ratio.

○ When trying to decide an appropriate level for this ratio you should take into account, the average movement in the working capital cycle, how profitable or loss making and the level of gearing. For example if the movement in the working capital cycle is say 6 weeks, the company is making higher than average profits for the industry and it is low geared then a low ratio might be in order.

Stock Turn
Cost of Sales divided by Stock.

○ The average number of times in a year that a company turns over its stock. e.g. a stock turn of 5 times means that a company holds approximately 10 weeks stock.

○ Interpretation should be against industry averages and/or historic trends for the ratio.

○ Movements in the ratio should be confirmed by undertaking a similar analysis within product groups.

○ Too much of a company's resources tied up in stock means idle facilities in the working capital cycle, also the physical cost of holding stock and the possibility of obsolescence.

Debtor Weeks
Debtors divided by Average Weekly (or Daily) Sales.

○ The debtor collection period.

○ The length of time it takes in weeks (or days) for a company to collect its debts.

○ This is linked to a company's ability to generate sales.

○ The aim is to achieve a balance between sales and bad debts.

○ Interpretation should be against industry averages and/or historic trends for the ratio.

○ Too much of a company's resources tied up in debtors means idle facilities in the working capital cycle including the possibility of increases in bad debts.

Borrowings Ratio

Total Borrowings divided by Equity.
Total Borrowings include both long-term debt and bank overdraft (i.e. all interest bearing debt).

o   Shows the number of times total borrowings (or interest bearing debt) exceeds equity.

o   A ratio of < 0.5 would be considered low gearing, while > 1.0 is considered to be in the high gearing region.

o   It is important to achieve an appropriate level of gearing. For example, a company that is low geared might not be making best use of debt finance (if it is cheaper than equity finance).

o   Movement in this ratio is an important factor.

Income Gearing Ratio

Interest Payable as a percentage of (Profit before Tax + Interest Payable).

o   The previous ratio showed the level of gearing. This ratio shows whether a company can afford its level of gearing.

o   Profit before tax plus interest payable represents the available profits.

o   A level of 25% is considered ideal. This allows that a company's interest payments are covered four times.

Exercise 6.7

Premises	300	Issued Share Capital	400
Vehicle	200	Profit and Loss Account	800
	500	Shareholder's Fund or Equity	1,200
Current Assets:		Current Liabilities:	
Stock	2,100	Creditors	2,000
Debtors	1,200	Bank Overdraft	800
Cash	200		
	3,500		2,800
	4,000		4,000

1.   Profitability, key ratio = (£200 + £100) ÷ (£500 + £3,500 – £2,800) x 100 = **25%**

2.   Profit Margin ratio = (£200 + £100) ÷ £3,500 x 100 = **8.6%**

3.   Sales Generation Ratio = £3,500 ÷ (£500 + £3,500 – £2,800) = **2.92 to 1**

4.   Current Ratio = £3,500 ÷ £2,800 = **1.25 to 1**

5.   Liquid or Acid Test Ratio = (£3,500 – £2,100) ÷ £2,800 = **0.50 to 1**

6.   Stock Turn = £2,000 ÷ £2,100 = **0.95 times**

7.   Debtor weeks = £1,200 ÷ (£3,500 ÷ 52) = **17.8 weeks**

Exercise 6.8

1. Profitability Ratios	1995	1996	1997	1998	1999
	£000s	£000s	£000s	£000s	£000s
PBIT	12,000	15,000	19,500	28,600	35,000
Net Assets	37,000	83,000	93,000	109,000	125,000
Total Assets	102,000	147,000	160,000	179,000	225,000
Sales	90,000	118,000	124,000	140,000	170,000
PBIT / Net Assets %	32.43	18.07	20.97	26.24	28.00
PBIT / Sales %	13.33	12.71	15.73	20.43	20.59
Sales / Net Assets (times)	2.43	1.42	1.33	1.28	1.36
PBIT / Total Assets %	11.76	10.20	12.19	15.98	15.56
PBIT / Sales %	13.33	12.71	15.73	20.43	20.59
Sales / Total Assets (times)	0.88	0.80	0.78	0.78	0.76

2. **Liquidity Ratios**	1995	1996	1997	1998	1999
	£000s	£000s	£000s	£000s	£000s
Current Assets	76,000	77,000	80,000	83,000	90,000
Current Liabilities	65,000	64,000	67,000	70,000	100,000
Stock	50,000	50,000	51,000	52,000	58,000
Debtors	24,000	25,000	26,000	28,000	24,000
Sales	90,000	118,000	124,000	140,000	170,000
Cost of Sales	78,000	103,000	104,500	111,400	135,000
Current Ratio (times)	1.17	1.20	1.19	1.19	0.90
Liquid Ratio (times)	0.40	0.42	0.43	0.44	0.32
Cost of Sales/Stock (times)	1.56	2.06	2.05	2.14	2.33
Debtors/A.W.S. (weeks)	13.9	11.0	10.9	10.4	7.3

3. **Gearing Ratios**	1995	1996	1997	1998	1999
	£000s	£000s	£000s	£000s	£000s
Total Borrowing	30,000	38,000	38,000	41,000	65,000
Equity	18,000	57,000	67,000	80,000	92,000
Interest Paid	3,000	3,000	3,500	3,600	10,000
P.B.I.T.	12,000	15,000	19,500	28,600	35,000
Total Borrowing/Equity	1.67	0.67	0.57	0.51	0.71
Interest Payable/PBIT %	25.0	20.0	17.9	12.6	28.6

Exercise 6.9

Preparatory work:

Current Assets	=	1.75 x £125,000	=	£218,750
Liquid Assets	=	1.05 x £125,000	=	£131,250
Stock (CA – LA)	=	£218,750 – £131,250	=	£87,500
Fixed Assets (TA – CA)	=	£258,750 – £218,750	=	£50,000
Net Assets (TA – CL)	=	£258,750 – £125,000	=	£133,750
Net Current Assets (CA – CL)	=	£218,750 – £125,000	=	£93,750
Net Profit	=	£93,750 x 20%	=	£18,750
Gross Profit	=	£18,750 + £33,250	=	£52,000
Sales	=	£52,000 ÷ 20 x 100	=	£260,000
Cost of Sales	=	£260,000 + £52,000	=	£208,000
Debtors	=	£260,000 ÷ 52 x 12	=	£60,000

H.O. Ratio Limited
Profit and Loss Account for the year ended 31st October 200X

	£
Sales	260,000
Cost of Sales	–208,000
Gross Profit	52,000
Expenses	–33,250
Net Profit	18,750

H.O. Ratio Limited
Balance Sheet as at 31st October 200X

	£		£	
Issued Share Capital	125,000	Fixed Assets		50,000
Profit and Loss Account	18,750			
Shareholder's Fund or Equity	143,750			
Current Liabilities:	125,000	Current Assets:		
		Stock	87,500	
		Debtors	60,000	
		Cash	71,250	
				218,750
	268,750			268,750

7.1   **A.   Overhead analysis sheet**

Works Overhead	Basis for apportionment	Total	Shop1	Shop 2
Indirect Labour	Direct Labour	8,400	3,360	5,040
Salaries	Direct Labour	42,000	16,800	25,200
Depreciation	Plant Value	18,900	7,560	11,340
Maintenance	Technical Estimate	19,600	12,000	7,600
Rent and Rates	Floor Area	32,200	16,100	16,100
Totals		121,100	55,820	65,280

B.   Overhead absorption rates

Shop 1: $\dfrac{\text{Overheads}}{\text{Labour hours}} = \dfrac{£55,820}{12,000 \text{ hours}} = £4.65$ per Labour Hour

Shop 2: $\dfrac{\text{Overheads}}{\text{Labour hours}} = \dfrac{£65,280}{18,000 \text{ hours}} = £3.63$ per Labour Hour

C.   Estimated product cost

		JOBS	
		A1127	A1131
Direct Materials		184.00	262.00
Direct Labour	Shop 1 (22hrs x £5.00 = £110.00)	90.00	110.00
Direct Labour	Shop 2	0	98.00
Outwork		99.00	55.00
Prime Cost		373.00	525.00
Overheads	Shop 1 (22hrs x £4.65 = £102.30)	83.70	102.30
	Shop 2	0	50.82
Product Cost		456.70	678.12

7.2   **A.   Overhead analysis sheet**

Works Overhead	Basis for apportionment	Total	Shop1	Shop 2
Indirect Labour	Direct Labour	12,000	3,000	9,000
Salaries	Direct Labour	30,000	7,500	22,500
Depreciation	Plant Value	16,600	6,200	10,400
Maintenance	Technical Estimate	14,000	4,400	9,600
Rent and Rates	Floor Area	20,000	6,667	13,333
Totals		92,600	27,767	64,833

B.   Overhead absorption rates

Shop 1: $\dfrac{\text{Overheads}}{\text{Labour hours}} = \dfrac{£27,767}{5,000 \text{ hours}} = £5.55 \text{ per Labour Hour}$

Shop 2: $\dfrac{\text{Overheads}}{\text{Labour hours}} = \dfrac{£64,833}{15,000 \text{ hours}} = £4.32 \text{ per Labour Hour}$

C.   Estimated product cost

		JOBS	
		E102	E110
Direct Materials		71.80	228.04
Direct Labour	Shop 1 (12hrs x £7.50 = £90.00)	120.00	90.00
Direct Labour	Shop 2	0	84.00
Outwork		65.00	40.00
Prime Cost		256.80	442.04
Overheads	Shop 1 (12hrs x £5.55 = £66.60)	88.80	66.60
	Shop 2	0	34.56
Product Cost		345.60	543.20

7.3	Direct Materials	544	£5.00	2,720
	Direct Labour	220	£6.00	1,320
	Variable Overhead	220	£18.00	3,960
	Total Variable Cost			8,000
	Fixed Overhead		50%	4,000
	Total Cost			12,000
	Profit		30%	3,600
	Quote Price			£15,600

7.4	Direct Materials						200.00
	Direct Labour	Shop 1	5 hrs	x	£7.00	35.00	
	Direct Labour	Shop 2	3 hrs	x	£5.00	15.00	50.00
	Overheads	Shop 1	10 hrs	x	£12.00	120.00	
	Overheads	Shop 2	3 hrs	x	£1 0.00	30.00	150.00
	Manufacturing Cost						400.00
	Administration Costs				30%		120.00
	Total Costs						520.00
	Profit				20%		104.00
							£624.00

7.5	Basis of Apportionment	Methods of Absorption
	Floor Area	Percentage of Materials
	Plant Value	Percentage of Labour
	Machine Hours	Labour Hour Rate
	Number of Employees	Machine Hour Rate
	Labour Hours	
	Technical Estimate	

7.6	Direct Materials	550	£4.00	2,200
	Direct Labour	220	£9.00	1,980
	Variable Overhead	220	£30.20	6,644
	Total Variable Cost			10,824
	Fixed Overhead		66.7%	7,216
	Total Cost			18,040
	Profit		30%	5,412
	Quote Price			£23,452

7.7	Direct Materials					144.00
	Direct Labour	Machine Shop	1 hr x	£6.00	6.00	
	Direct Labour	Assembly	2 hrs x	£5.00	10.00	16.00
	Overheads	Machine Shop	4 hrs x	£2.50	10.00	
	Overheads	Assembly	2 hrs x	£4.00	8.00	18.00
	Manufacturing Cost					178.00
	Administration Costs			25%		44.50
	Delivery Charges					30.00
	Total Costs					252.50
	Profit			15%		37.88
						£290.38

7.8 **a. Traditional Overhead Apportionment**

Fixed Factory Overheads ÷ Total Machine Hours
£525,000 ÷ 120,000 = £4.375 per machine hour

	A1123		A1139
Cost per component (£4.375 x 4hrs)	£17.50	(£4.375 x 4hrs)	£17.50

Overhead costs absorbed

(5,000 x £17.50)	**£87,500**	(25,000 x £17.50)	**£437,500**

b. ABC method of apportionment

Volume related rate:
£250,000 ÷ 120,000 machine hours = £2.08333 per machine hour

Purchasing related rate:
£125,000 ÷ 500 purchase orders = £250 per purchase order

Setup related rate:
£150,000 ÷ 190 setups = £789.474 per setup

		A1123		A1139
Volume costs	(20,000 x £2.08333)	41,667	(100,000 x £2.08333)	208,333
Purchasing costs	(150 x £250)	37,500	(350 x £250)	87,500
Setup costs	(70 x £789.474)	55,263	(120 x £789.474)	94,737
		134,430		**390,570**

8.1

Sales (70,000 units)	210,000	30.00	30.00	31.20
less Variable Costs	140,000	20.00	21.00	20.00
= Contribution	70,000	10.00	9.00	11.20
less Fixed Costs	40,000			
= Profit	£30,000			

1. BEP Units £40,000 ÷ £10 = **4,000 units**

2a. BEP fixed costs increase by 10%
£44,000 ÷ £10 = **4,400 units**

2b. BEP variable costs increase by 5%
£40,000 ÷ £9 = **4,444 units**

2c. BEP selling price increase by 4%
£40,000 ÷ £11.2 = **3,571 units**

2d. No change, break even as 1. above i.e. **4,000 units**

8.2

Sales (30,000 units)	750,000	25.00	25.00	23.00
less Variable Costs	450,000	15.00	16.00	15.00
= Contribution	300,000	10.00	9.00	8.00
less Fixed Costs	200,000			
= Profit	£100,000			

1. BEP Units £200,000 ÷ £10 = **20,000 units**
BEP Sterling 20,000 x £25 = **£500,000**

2. BEP variable costs increase to £16
£200,000 ÷ £9 = **22,222 units**

3. BEP Units £235,000 ÷ £10 = 23,500 units
BEP Sterling 23,500 x £25 = **£587,500**

4. Minimum Selling Price (refer to formula sheet)
[(£200,000 + £70,000) ÷ 30,000] + £15.00 = **£24.00**

5. Volume of Sales (refer to formula sheet)
   (£200,000 + £100,000) ÷ £8 = **37,500 units**

6. BEP Units £40,000 ÷ £10 = **4,000 units**

8.3

Sales		6,000,000	300.00	280.00	280.00
Materials	2,200,000				
Labour	640,000				
Variable Prod. Costs	160,000				
Total Variable Costs		3,000,000	150.00	150.00	156.00
Contribution		3,000,000	150.00	130.00	124.00
Fixed Prod. Costs	1,440,000				
Selling & Admin.	1,960,000				
Total Fixed Costs		3,400,000			
Profit		− 400,000			

1. BEP Units £3,400,000 ÷ £150.00 = **22,667 units**

2. BEP Units £3,400,000 ÷ £130.00 = **26,154 units**

3. Contribution (60,000 ÷ 2) x £130.00   3,900,000
   Fixed Costs   3,400,000
   Profit   **500,000**

4. Contribution   (60,000 x £124.00)   7,440,000
   Fixed Costs (2 x £3,400,000 x 1.10)   7,480,000
   Profit / loss   **− 40,000**

   Break even point (units)   = $\dfrac{£7,480,000}{£124.00}$

                               =   **60,323 units**

8.4 a.

Sales (5,500 units)	462,000	84.00	84.00
less Variable Costs	220,000	40.00	44.00
= Contribution	242,000	44.00	40.00
less Fixed Costs	195,000		
= Profit	**£47,000**		

b. BEP Units £195,000 ÷ £44 = 4,432 units

BEP Sterling 4,432 x £84 = **£372,288**

c. BEP variable costs + 10%

£195,000 ÷ £40 = **4,875 units**

8.5

1.	Standard £	Super £	Deluxe £	Total £
Selling Price	300.00	375.00	550.00	
Direct Material	90.00	120.00	160.00	
Direct Labour	45.00	45.00	90.00	
Variable Overhead	20.00	30.00	50.00	
Variable Costs	155.00	195.00	300.00	
Contribution Per Unit	145.00	180.00	250.00	
Sales Volume (units)	4,000	3,000	1,000	
Contribution Margin	580,000	540,000	250,000	1,370,000
Fixed Costs				1,000,000
Profit				370,000

2. Choice – Reduce Selling Price of Deluxe by £75.00

Contribution Per Unit	£250.00 – £75.00	=	£175.00
Volume Change	1,000 x 1.50	=	1,500 units
Contribution Margin	1,500 x £175.00	=	£262,500
Profit Increase	£262,500 – £250,000	=	**£12,500**

Choice – Drop Deluxe, increase production of Super (i.e. highest contribution)

	Standard	Super	Total
Extra Volume Super [1]		2,000	
Contribution Per Unit		£180.00	
	£	£	£
Extra Contribution		360,000	360,000
Contribution Margin	580,000	540,000	1,120,000
			1,480,000
Fixed Costs [2]			1,000,000
Profit			480,000

[1]   £90.00 x 1,000 units ÷ £45.00 = 2,000 units

Profit Increase   £480,000 – £370,000 = **£110,000**

8.6	a.				
		Sales (25,000 units)	625,000	25.00	25.00
		less Variable Costs	375,000	15.00	15.00
		= Contribution	250,000	10.00	10.00
		less Fixed Costs	200,000		260,000
		= Profit	**£50,000**		

b.   BEP Units £200,000 ÷ £10 = 20,000 units
      BEP Sterling   20,000 x £25 = **£500,000**

c.   Minimum Selling Price
      [(£260,000 + £50,000) ÷ 25,000] + £15.00 = **£27.40**

8.7

Sales (5,500 units)	1,750,000	35.00	35.00	35.00	38.00
less Variable Costs	1,300,000	26.00	23.00	26.00	26.00
= Contribution	450,000	9.00	12.00	9.00	12.00
less Fixed Costs	350,000				
= Profit	£100,000				

a. BEP Units £350,000 ÷ £9 = 38,889 units
    BEP Sterling 38,889 x £35 = **£1,361,115**

b. BEP variable costs decrease to £23.00
    £350,000 ÷ £12 = **29,167 units**

c. BEP Units £370,000 ÷ £9 = 41,111 units
    BEP Sterling 41,111 x £35 = **£1,438,885**

d. Minimum Selling Price
    [(£350,000 + £120,000) ÷ 50,000] + £26.00 = **£35.40**

e. Volume of Sales
    (£350,000 + £100,000) ÷ £12 = **37,500 units**

f. BEP Units £60,000 ÷ £9 = **6,667 units**

8.8   a.

Sales (35,000 units)	840,000	24.00	24.00
less Variable Costs	560,000	16.00	16.00
= Contribution	280,000	8.00	8.00
less Fixed Costs	200,000		260,000
= Profit	**£80,000**		

b. BEP Units £200,000 ÷ £8 = 25,000 units
    BEP Sterling 25,000 x £24 = **£600,000**

c. Minimum Selling Price
    [(£260,000 + £80,000) ÷ 35,000] + £16.00 = **£25.71**

8.9

Sales (70,000 units)	2,940,000	42.00	42.00	42.00	45.00
less Variable Costs	2,310,000	33.00	30.00	33.00	33.00
= Contribution	630,000	9.00	12.00	9.00	12.00
less Fixed Costs	490,000				
= Profit	£140,000				

a. BEP Units £490,000 ÷ £9 = 54,444 units
   BEP Sterling 54,444 x £42 = **£2,286,648**

b. BEP variable costs decrease to £30
   £490,000 ÷ £12 = **40,834 units**

c. BEP Units £550,000 ÷ £9 = 61,111 units
   BEP Sterling 61,111 x £42 = **£2,566,662**

d. Minimum Selling Price
   [(£490,000 + £180,000) ÷ 70,000] + £33.00 = **£42.57**

e. Volume of Sales
   (£490,000 + £140,000) ÷ £12 = **52,500 units**

f. BEP Units £72,000 ÷ £9 = **8,000 units**

9.1   1.   Statement showing Bristol and Reading Depots making losses

		Swindon	Bristol	Reading	Total
Sales Volume		67,000	22,000	10,000	99,000
	£	£	£	£	£
Sales Revenue	**22.00**	**1,474,000**	**484,000**	**220,000**	**2,178,000**
Direct Material	6.50	435,500	143,000	65,000	643,500
Direct Labour	3.40	227,800	74,800	34,000	336,600
Variable Overhead	5.10	341,700	112,200	51,000	504,900
Selling and distribution:					
Variable		117,920	48,400	26,400	192,720
Fixed		70,000	60,000	60,000	190,000
Factory Fixed Costs		169,192	55,556	25,252	250,000
Total Costs		**1,362,112**	**493,956**	**261,652**	**2,117,720**
Profit / Loss		111,888	− 9,956	− 41,652	60,280

2a.   Statement showing effect of closure of Bristol and Reading Depots

		Swindon	Total
Sales Volume		67,000	67,000
	£	£	£
Sales Revenue	22.00	1,474,000	1,474,000
Direct Material	6.50	435,500	435,500
Direct Labour	3.40	227,800	227,800
Variable Overhead	5.10	341,700	341,700
Selling and Distribution:			
Variable		117,920	117,920
Fixed		70,000	70,000
Contribution to Factory Fixed		281,080	281,080
Factory Fixed Costs			250,000
Profit / Loss			31,080

2b. Statement showing effect of closure of the Reading depot

		Swindon	Bristol		Total
Sales Volume		67,000	22,000		89,000
	£	£	£	£	
Sales Revenue	22.00	1,474,000	484,000		1,958,000
Direct Material	6.50	435,500	143,000		578,500
Direct Labour	3.40	227,800	74,800		302,600
Variable Overhead	5.10	341,700	112,200		453,900
Selling and Distribution:					
Variable		117,920	48,400		166,320
Fixed		70,000	60,000		130,000
Contribution to Factory Fixed		281,080	45,600		326,680
Factory Fixed Costs					250,000
Profit / Loss					76,680

9.2   1. Best use of scarce resources – ranking

	A	B	C	D	E	F	G
Sales	7,000	2,000	2,000	4,000	6,000	2,000	4,000
Variable Costs	6,000	1,400	1,700	3,500	4,000	1,200	2,600
Contribution	1,000	600	300	500	2,000	800	1,400
Machine hours	40	20	20	60	80	20	120
Contribution per Machine hour	25.00	30.00	15.00	8.33	25.00	40.00	11.67
Ranking	3=	2	5	7	3=	1	6

2. Product income statement (for a single week)

	F	B	A	E	Total
Machine Hours	20	20	40	80	160
	£	£	£	£	£
Sales	2,000	2,000	7,000	6,000	17,000
Materials	600	800	4,000	3,000	8,400
Labour	600	600	2,000	1,000	4,200
Variable Costs	1,200	1,400	6,000	4,000	12,600
Contribution	800	600	1,000	2,000	4,400
Fixed Costs (£115,440 ÷ 52)					2,220
Profit					2,180

9.3   1.   Order from regular customer

			£
Direct Materials	100	£40.00	4,000
Direct Labour	240	£5.00	1,200
Variable Overhead	240	£15.00	3,600
Total Variable Cost			8,800
Fixed Overhead		62.5%	5,500
Total Cost			14,300
Profit		20%	2,860
Quote Price			£17,160

2.   Labour in short supply

Contribution per labour hour   (£780,000 − £400,000) ÷ 10,000 = £38.00

Total Variable Cost	£8,800
Contribution to Fixed and Profit (240 hrs x £38.00)	£9,120
Quote Price	£17,920

3.   Check the considerations (in the text) when arriving at a price for a special order.

In this case we could quote any figure above Total Variable Cost i.e. £8,801+. The assumption being that the company has covered its fixed costs from the existing customer base and any amount above total variable cost will go straight to profit.

9.4   1.   Variable costs of making cartons:

	£ p.a.
Direct materials	84,000
Direct labour	18,000
Electricity (power costs)	4,500
Repairs to plant	3,000
	109,500
Cost of buying in cartons:	
360,000 cartons at £325 per 1,000	117,000
additional storage costs	9,000
	126,000

The variable costs of making the cartons is less than the cost of buying in the cartons, therefore Mars Packers Ltd should continue to produce their own cartons.

9.5

	A	B	C	D
Sales	14,000	4,000	4,000	8,000
Variable Costs	12,000	2,800	3,400	6,400
Contribution	2,000	1,200	600	1,600
Labour hours	80	40	40	80
Contribution per Labour hr	25	30	15	20
Ranking	2	1	4	3

9.6   Relevant costs which would be eliminated if electric motors were bought-in.

	£
Direct Materials	16,000
Direct Labour	24,000
Variable Production Overhead	16,000
Fixed Production Overhead	12,000
	£68,000
Cost of buying in cartons:	
32,000 motors at £2.50 per unit	80,000
less Rent Received	8,000
	£72,000

The relevant costs of manufacture are less than the cost of buying the electric motors from Wedge Ltd, therefore the company should continue to produce their own motors.

9.7   1. Production capacity   240,000 ÷ 0.60 =   400,000 units

       Therefore, increase in capacity/sales   =   160,000 units

	Total p.a. £	Per unit £
Sales		9.60
Variable Costs		7.80
Contribution	288,000	1.80
Additional Fixed Costs	150,000	
Increase in Profit	138,000	

9.8 Best use of scarce resources – determine labour hours

	A	B	C	D	E	F
Units	400	1,000	300	800	500	300
Labour Cost per Unit	40.00	90.00	90.00	50.00	70.00	90.00
Labour Cost	16,000	90,000	27,000	40,000	35,000	27,000
Labour Hours [1]	2,000	11,250	3,375	5,000	4,375	3,375

[1] labour cost divided by £8.00 per hour

Best use of scarce resources – ranking

	A	B	C	D	E	F
Units	400	1,000	300	800	500	300
Contribution Per Unit	140.00	295.00	265.00	185.00	195.00	275.00
Contribution	56,000	295,000	79,500	148,000	97,500	82,500
Labour Hours	2,000	11,250	3,375	5,000	4,375	3,375
Contribution per Labour Hour	28.00	26.22	23.56	29.60	22.29	24.44
Ranking	2	3	5	1	6	4

Product income statement

	D	A	B	F	C	Total
Labour Hours	5,000	2,000	11,250	3,375	3,375	25,000
	£	£	£	£	£	£
Sales	384,000	168,000	570,000	171,000	153,000	
Materials	164,000	76,000	160,000	45,000	39,000	
Labour	40,000	16,000	90,000	27,000	27,000	
Variable Overhead	32,000	20,000	25,000	16,500	7,500	
Total Variable Costs	236,000	112,000	275,000	88,500	73,500	
Contribution	148,000	56,000	295,000	82,500	79,500	661,000
Fixed Overheads [2]						300,000
Profit						361,000

[2]   Fixed Overheads   =   Labour Rate x Hours x 1.50
                                  =   £8.00 x 25,000 x 1.5
                                  =   £300,000

9.9

	A	B	C	D
Sales	16,000	6,000	6,000	10,000
Variable Costs	13,000	3,800	4,400	7,400
Contribution	3,000	2,200	1,600	2,600
Labour hours	80	40	40	80
Contribution per Labour hr	37.5	55	40	32.5
Ranking	3	1	2	4

9.10   WITHOUT RESTRICTION

	A	B	C	D	Total
Amill (Kgs) [1]	2,700	5,184	3,240	11,520	
Selling Price (£)	3.24	4.92	4.62	6.00	
Variable Costs (£)	1.80	2.76	2.28	4.20	
Contribution Per kg (£)	1.44	2.16	2.34	1.80	
Volume	18,000	21,600	18,000	28,800	
	£	£	£	£	£
Contribution	25,920	46,656	42,120	51,840	166,536
Fixed Costs					30,000
Profit					136,536

[1]   Calculation to find the amount of Amill used for Product A

£0.90 ÷ £6.00 x 18,000 = 2,700 kgs

CONTRIBUTION PER UNIT OF LIMITING FACTOR

	A	B	C	D
Contribution £	25,920	46,656	42,120	51,840
AMILL (kgs)	2,700	5,184	3,240	11,520
Contribution Per Kg of Limiting Factor	9.60	9.00	13.00	4.50
Ranking	2	3	1	4

WITH RESTRICTION

	C	A	B	D	Total
Contribution Per Kg (£)	2.34	1.44	2.16	1.80	
Volume (2)	18,000	18,000	21,600	2,190	
	£	£	£	£	£
Contribution £	42,120	25,920	46,656	3,942	118,638
Fixed Costs					30,000
Profit					88,638

(2) Calculation to determine the balance of Amill to produce/sell Product D.

Product	C	3,240
	A	2,700
	B	5,184
		11,124
Product	D	876
		12,000

Kgs of Product D $= 876 \div 11,520 \times 28,800 = 2,190$

9.11   **Budget forecast and special order**

	Price/Rate	£	£
Sales (125,000 units)	25.00		3,125,000
Sales (35,000 units)	18.00		630,000
Total Sales Revenue			3,755,000
Direct Materials	4.00	640,000	
Direct Labour	7.00	1,120,000	
Variable Overhead	2.00	320,000	
Fixed Overhead		420,000	
Total Production Cost			2,500,000
= Gross Margin			1,255,000
Selling Costs			200,000
			1,055,000

Differential

	Price/Rate	£	£
Sales (35,000 units)	18.00		630,000
Direct Materials	4.00	140,000	
Direct Labour	7.00	245,000	
Variable Overhead	2.00	70,000	
Total Production Costs			455,000
= Gross Margin			175,000

9.12   **Marginal cost of Production**

	£	Jan £	£	Feb £
Sales Volume		160,000		195,000
Production Volume		190,000		175,000
Closing Stock Volume		30,000		10,000
Sales		10,816,000		13,182,000
Opening Stock	0		1,092,000	
Factory Costs	6,916,000		6,370,000	
	6,916,000		7,462,000	
less Closing Stock	1,092,000		364,000	
		5,824,000		7,098,000
Contribution		4,992,000		6,084,000
less Factory Overheads		975,000		975,000
		4,017,000		5,109,000

Absorption Cost of Production

	£	Jan £	£	Feb £
Sales Volume		160,000		195,000
Production Volume		190,000		175,000
Closing Stock Volume		30,000		10,000
Sales		10,816,000		13,182,000
Opening Stock	0		1,242,000	
Variable Costs	7,866,000		7,245,000	
	7,866,000		8,487,000	
less Closing Stock	1,242,000		414,000	
		6,624,000		8,073,000
Gross Profit		4,192,000		5,109,000

10.1   E. TEE Ltd
        CASH BUDGET
        for the quarter ending 31st March 200X

	Jan £	Feb £	Mar £
Part A			
Receipts:			
Sales	216,000	144,000	132,000
Cash Sales	36,000	33,000	30,000
Fixtures and Fittings			1,500
Sub Total A	252,000	177,000	163,500
Part B			
Payments:			
Creditors	87,750	58,500	117,000
Overhead Expense	28,500	26,500	31,500
Wages	60,000	51,000	52,000
Computer		37,500	
Sub Total B	176,250	173,500	200,500
Part C			
Balance (A–B)	75,750	3,500	– 37,000
Part D			
Balance b/f	30,000	105,750	109,250
Balance c/f	105,750	109,250	72,250

10.2   DREAM Ltd
        CASH BUDGET
        for the six months ending 30th June 200X

	Jan £	Feb £	Mar £	Apr £	May £	Jun £
Part A Receipts:						
Sales	0	20,000	40,000	40,000	50,000	60,000
Sub Total A	0	20,000	40,000	40,000	50,000	60,000
Part B Payments:						
Raw Materials	0	12,000	12,000	12,000	18,000	18,000
Wages	8,000	8,000	8,000	12,000	12,000	12,000
Rent	10,000			10,000		
Heat and Light			5,000			5,000
Other Expenses	10,000	10,000	10,000	10,000	10,000	10,000
Capital Equipment	5,000	5,000	5,000	5,000	5,000	5,000
Sub Total B	33,000	35,000	40,000	49,000	45,000	50,000
Part C						
Balance (A–B)	–33,000	–15,000	0	–9,000	5,000	10,000
Part D						
Balance b/f	25,000	–8,000	–23,000	–23,000	–32,000	–27,000
Balance c/f	–8,000	–23,000	–23,000	–32,000	–27,000	–17,000

DREAM Ltd
BUDGETED PROFIT & LOSS ACCOUNT
for the six months ended 30th June 200X

	£	£
Sales		300,000
Raw Materials	90,000	
Wages and Salaries	60,000	
Rent	20,000	
Heat and Light	10,000	
Other Expenses	60,000	
Depreciation (50,000 x 25% ÷ 2)	6,250	
		246,250
Net Profit		53,750

DREAM Ltd
BUDGETED BALANCE SHEET
as at 30th June 2000X

	£	£	£
Fixed Assets:	Cost	Depn.	N.B.V.
Plant and Machinery	50,000	6,250	43,750
Current Assets:			
Debtors		90,000	
Cash		0	
		90,000	
less Current Liabilities:			
Creditors	38,000		
Bank Overdraft	17,000	55,000	35,000
			78,750
financed as follows:			
Issued Share Capital			25,000
Profit and Loss Account			53,750
			78,750

10.3   ALASTAIR DRYANT
       CASH BUDGET
       for the four months ending 30th April 200X

	Jan £	Feb £	Mar £	Apr £
Part A Receipts:				
Sales		4,500	6,000	9,000
Cash Sales	4,500	6,000	9,000	10,000
Sub Total A	4,500	10,500	15,000	19,000
Part B Payments:				
Raw Materials	0	0	8,400	7,200
Wages and Expenses	2,700	3,600	5,400	6,000
Fixed Expenses	1,800	1,800	1,800	1,800
Managers Salary	2,000	2,000	2,000	2,000
Machinery	0	12,000	12,000	12,000
Sub Total B	6,500	19,400	29,600	29,000
Part C				
Balance (A–B)	–2,000	–8,900	–14,600	–10,000
Part D				
Balance b/f	25,000	23,000	14,100	–500
Balance c/f	23,000	14,100	–500	–10,500

Calculation of purchases and creditors:

	Jan £	Feb £	Mar £	Apr £
Sales	9,000	12,000	18,000	20,000
Materials: 40%	3,600	4,800	7,200	8,000
Purchases				
January	3,600			
February	4,800			
March		7,200		
April			8,000	
May				8,000

Calculation of expenses:
Fixed expenses of £2,200 less £400 per month depreciation.

10.4   P.C Ltd

CASH BUDGET

for the six months to 31st December 200X

	Jul £	Aug £	Sep £	Oct £	Nov £	Dec £
Part A Receipts:						
Sales	70,000	40,000	40,000	50,000	70,000	80,000
Sub Total A	70,000	40,000	40,000	50,000	70,000	80,000
Part B Payments:						
Creditors	40,000	25,000	15,000	39,000	46,000	60,000
Wages	5,000	7,000	8,000	10,000	6,000	4,000
Capital Equipment		40,000				
Fixed Costs	5,000	5,000	5,000	5,000	5,000	5,000
Dividend	10,000					
Sub Total B	60,000	77,000	28,000	54,000	57,000	69,000
Part C						
Balance (A–B)	10,000	–37,000	12,000	–4,000	13,000	11,000
Part D						
Balance b/f	0	10,000	–27,000	–15,000	–19,000	–6,000
Balance c/f	10,000	–27,000	–15,000	–19,000	–6,000	5,000

Calculation to determine purchases:

	Jul £000	Aug £000	Sep £000	Oct £000	Nov £000	Dec £000
Sales	50	70	80	100	60	40
– Gross profit	15	21	24	30	18	12
= Cost of sales	35	49	56	70	42	28
+ Closing stock	200	190	180	170	170	160
	235	239	236	240	212	188
– Opening stock	220	200	190	180	170	170
= Purchases	15	39	46	60	42	18

10.5   Thrust Limited – Cash Budget, for the quarter ending 30th September
200X

	July £	Aug. £	Sept. £
Part A Receipts:			
Sales	260,650	241,250	194,000
Loan Stock		30,000	
Sub Total A	260,650	271,250	194,000
Part B Payments:			
Purchases	60,000	55,000	80,000
Wages	46,250	32,500	33,750
Research and Development	9,000	12,500	13,500
Administration Costs	25,000	30,000	25,000
Production Costs	25,000	20,000	18,000
Taxation		110,000	
Dividend	50,000		
Capital Expenditure			40,000
Commissions	5,800	4,900	3,600
Sub Total B	221,050	264,900	213,850
Part C: Balance (A–B)	39,600	6,350	–19,850
Part D			
Balance b/f	30,000	69,600	75,950
Balance c/f	69,600	75,950	56,100

Calculation of Sales:

	May	June	July	Aug.	Sept.
Sales (£)	240,000	290,000	245,000	180,000	170,000
In month 20%			49,000	36,000	34,000
1 month 50%			145,000	122,500	90,000
2 months 30%			72,000	87,000	73,500
			266,000	245,500	197,500
less cash discount 5%			–2,450	–1,800	–1,700
cash discount 2%			–2,900	–2,450	–1,800
			260,650	241,250	194,000

10.6   FINDINGS Ltd
       CASH BUDGET
       for the quarter ending 30th April 200X

	Jan £	Feb £	Mar £	Apr £
Part A Receipts:				
Sales [1]	10,800	71,700	120,560	105,880
Sub Total A	10,800	71,700	120,560	105,880
Part B Payments:				
Purchases	–	62,000	50,000	40,000
Labour	34,000	34,000	26,000	36,000
Capital Expenditure	180,000		20,000	
Production Expenses [2]	8,500	5,500	4,500	5,500
Administration Expenses	9,200	7,200	7,200	7,200
Selling and Distribution	7,500	8,500	7,000	9,500
Sub Total B	239,200	117,200	114,700	98,200
Part C				
Balance (A–B)	–228,400	–45,500	5,860	7,680
Part D				
Balance b/f	0	–228,400	–273,900	–268,040
Balance c/f	–228,400	–273,900	–268,040	–260,360

[1] Calculation of sales

	Jan £	Feb £	Mar £	Apr £
Sales	120,000	130,000	84,000	132,000
10%	12,000	13,000	8,400	13,200
1 month 50%	–	60,000	65,000	42,000
2 months 40%	–	–	48,000	52,000
	12,000	73,000	121,400	107,200
less cash discount 10%	– 1,200	– 1,300	– 840	– 1,320
	10,800	71,700	120,560	105,880

(2) Calculation of production costs

	Jan £	Feb £	Mar £	Apr £
Production Costs	7,000	8,000	7,000	8,000
deduct Depreciation	−1,500	−1,500	−1,500	−1,500
deduct Monthly Charge	−1,000	−1,000	−1,000	−1,000
add Cash Payment	4,000			
	8,500	5,500	4,500	5,500

11.1	Standard Hours times Standard Rate			Actual Hours times Standard Rate			Actual Hours times Actual Rate		
	Hrs	Rate	£	Hrs	Rate	£	Hrs	Rate	£
1	9,000	4.00	36,000	6,000	4.00	24,000	6,000		26,400
2	6,000	4.50	27,000	7,000	4.50	31,500	7,000		34,650
3	6,000	6.00	36,000	7,000	6.00	42,000	7,000		46,200
			99,000			97,500			107,250

Labour Efficiency Variance   Labour Rate Variance

£1,500   − £9,750

Labour Cost Variance

− £8,250

11.2	Standard Qty times Standard Price			Actual Qty times Standard Price			Actual Qty times Actual Price		
	Qty	Price	£	Qty	Price	£	Qty	Price	£
A	5,390	0.70	3,773	5,200	0.70	3,640	5,200	0.84	4,368
B	1,400	0.28	392	1,300	0.28	364	1,300	0.35	455
C	3,500	0.49	1,715	3,700	0.49	1,813	3,700	0.42	1,554
D	420	2.80	1,176	450	2.80	1,260	450	2.50	1,125
			7,056			7,077			7,502

Material Usage Variance   Material Price Variance

− £21   − £425

Material Cost Variance

− £446

11.3a

	Standard Qty times Standard Price			Actual Qty times Standard Price			Actual Qty times Actual Price		
	Qty	Price	£	Qty	Price	£	Qty	Price	£
A	240	3.00	720	230	3.00	690	230	2.50	575
B	360	7.50	2,700	370	7.50	2,775	370	7.00	2,590
			3,420			3,465			3,165

Material Usage Variance   Material Price Variance

– £45   £300

Material Cost Variance

£255

11.3b

	Standard Hours times Standard Rate			Actual Hours times Standard Rate			Actual Hours times Actual Rate		
	Hrs	Rate	£	Hrs	Rate	£	Hrs	Rate	£
1	120	8.00	960	130	8.00	1,040	130	7.50	975
2	60	10.00	600	58	10.00	580	58	10.00	580
			1,560			1,620			1,555

Labour Efficiency Variance   Labour Rate Variance

– £60   £65

Labour Cost Variance

£5

11.4

	Standard Qty times Standard Price			Actual Qty times Standard Price			Actual Qty times Actual Price		
	Qty	Price	£	Qty	Price	£	Qty	Price	£
A	30,000	0.75	22,500	32,000	0.75	24,000	32,000	0.80	25,600
B	20,000	1.50	30,000	16,000	1.50	24,000	16,000	1.80	28,800
			52,500			48,000			54,400

Material Usage Variance   Material Price Variance

£4,500   –£6,400

Material Cost Variance

–£1,900

11.5

Standard Hours times Standard Rate			Actual Hours times Standard Rate			Actual Hours times Actual Rate		
Hrs	Rate	£	Hrs	Rate	£	Hrs	Rate	£
300	6.00	1,800	360	6.00	2,160	360	5.00	1,800

Labour Efficiency Variance   Labour Rate Variance

– £360   £360

Labour Cost Variance

£0

11.6

Standard Qty times Standard Price			Actual Qty times Standard Price			Actual Qty times Actual Price		
Qty	Price	£	Qty	Price	£	Qty	Price	£
300	3.00	900	250	3.00	750	250	4.00	1,000

Material Usage Variance   Material Price Variance

£150   – £250

Material Cost Variance

– £100

11.7

Standard Qty times Standard Price			Actual Qty times Standard Price			Actual Qty times Actual Price		
Qty	Price	£	Qty	Price	£	Qty	Price	£
1,250	5.00	6,250	1,100	5.00	5,500	1,100	5.20	5,720

Material Usage Variance   Material Price Variance

£750   − £220

Material Cost Variance

£530

11.8

Standard Qty times Standard Price			Actual Qty times Standard Price			Actual Qty times Actual Price		
Qty	Price	£	Qty	Price	£	Qty	Price	£
A	30,000	3.75	112,500	32,000	3.75	120,000	32,000	4.00	128,000
B	20,000	7.50	150,000	16,000	7.50	120,000	16,000	9.00	144,000
			262,500			240,000			272,000

Material Usage Variance   Material Price Variance

£22,500   −£32,000

Material Cost Variance

−£9,500

12.1

Payback period – Project A = 3 years

	£		
Capital Outlay	– 65,000		
Cash Inflows:	Annual	Annual to payback	Cumulative to payback
	£	£	£
Year 1	30,000	30,000	30,000
Year 2	20,000	20,000	50,000
Year 3	15,000	15,000	65,000

Payback period – Project B = 3.1 years

	£		
Capital Outlay	– 18,000		
Cash Inflows:	Annual	Annual to payback	Cumulative to payback
	£	£	£
Year 1	45,000	45,000	45,000
Year 2	45,000	45,000	90,000
Year 3	45,000	45,000	135,000
Year 4	45,000	5,000	140,000

Payback period – Project C = 2 years

	£		
Capital Outlay	– 30,000		
Cash Inflows:	Annual	Annual to payback	Cumulative to payback
	£	£	£
Year 1	20,000	20,000	20,000
Year 2	10,000	10,000	30,000

Payback period – Project D = 3.6 years

	£		
Capital Outlay	– 160,000		
Cash Inflows:	Annual	Annual to payback	Cumulative to payback
	£	£	£
Year 1	35,000	35,000	35,000
Year 2	35,000	35,000	70,000
Year 3	55,000	55,000	125,000
Year 4	55,000	35,000	160,000

Accounting rate of return

	A £	B £	C £	D £
Net Cash Inflows	85,000	225,000	40,000	245,000
less Capital Outlay	65,000	140,000	30,000	160,000
Profit over the Life of each Project	20,000	85,000	10,000	85,000
Life (years)	5	5	2	5
Average Annual Profit	4,000	17,000	5,000	17,000
Accounting Rate of Return	6.2%	12.1%	16.7%	10.6%

Accounting rate of return: calculations for Project A

Project A = 4,000 ÷ 65,000 x 100 = 6.2%

Net present value – Project A   Profitability Index = 1.14

Year	Cash flows £	DCF factor 6.0%	Present value £
1	30,000	0.943	28,290
2	20,000	0.890	17,800
3	15,000	0.840	12,600
4	10,000	0.792	7,920
5	10,000	0.747	7,470
Present Value of Cash Inflows			74,080
less Capital Outlay			65,000
Net Present Value			9,080

Net present value – Project B   Profitability Index = 1.35

Year	Cash flows £	DCF factor 6.0%	Present value £
1	45,000	0.943	42,435
2	45,000	0.890	40,050
3	45,000	0.840	37,800
4	45,000	0.792	35,640
5	45,000	0.747	33,615
Present Value of Cash Inflows			189,540
less Capital Outlay			140,000
Net Present Value			49,540

Net present value – Project C   Profitability Index = 1.21

Year	Cash flows £	DCF factor 6.0%	Present value £
1	20,000	0.943	18,860
2	10,000	0.890	8,900
3	10,000	0.840	8,400
Present Value of Cash Inflows			36,160
less Capital Outlay			30,000
Net Present Value			6,160

Net present value – Project D   Profitability Index = 1.27

Year	Cash flows £	DCF factor 6.0%	Present value £
1	35,000	0.943	33,005
2	35,000	0.890	31,150
3	55,000	0.840	46,200
4	55,000	0.792	43,560
5	65,000	0.747	48,555
Present Value of Cash Inflows			202,470
less Capital Outlay			160,000
Net Present Value			42,470

Internal rate of return – Project B only

Year	Cash Flows £	DCF Factor 17%	Present Value £	DCF Factor 19%	Present Value £
1	45,000	0.855	38,475	0.840	37,800
2	45,000	0.731	32,895	0.706	31,770
3	45,000	0.624	28,080	0.593	26,685
4	45,000	0.534	24,030	0.499	22,455
5	45,000	0.456	20,520	0.419	18,855
Present Value of Cash Inflows			144,000		137,565
less Capital Outlay			140,000		140,000
Net Present Value			+ 4,000		− 2,435

$$\text{Internal Rate of Return} \quad = \quad 17 + \frac{4,000}{(4,000 + 2,435)} \times 2$$

$$= \quad 17 + 1.2$$

$$= \quad 18.2\%$$

12.2

Convert profit to cash flows:

Year	Profit		Overhead		Depn [1]		Cash flow
	£		£		£		£
1	60,000	+	24,000	+	66,000	=	150,000
2	45,000	+	24,000	+	66,000	=	135,000
3	21,000	+	24,000	+	66,000	=	111,000
4	12,000	+	24,000	+	66,000	=	102,000
5	12,000	+	24,000	+	66,000	=	102,000

[1] $\text{Depreciation} \quad = \quad \dfrac{(\text{Capital Outlay} - \text{Residual Value})}{\text{Life}}$

Year	Cash flows [2]	DCF factor	Present value
	£	10 %	£
1	150,000	0.909	136,350
2	135,000	0.826	111,510
3	111,000	0.751	83,361
4	102,000	0.683	69,666
5	162,000	0.621	100,602
Present Value of Cash Inflows			501,489
less Capital Outlay			390,000
Net Present Value			111,489

[2] The residual value of £60,000 is added to the cash flow for year 5 to give £162,000.

12.3

Convert profit to cash flows:

Year	Profit		Depn [1]		Cash flow
	£		£		£
1	32,000	+	80,000	=	112,000
2	48,000	+	80,000	=	128,000
3	60,000	+	80,000	=	140,000
4	120,000	+	80,000	=	200,000
5	48,000	+	80,000	=	128,000

[1] Depreciation = £400,000 ÷ 5 = £80,000

Net Present Value:

Year	Cash flows [2] £	DCF factor 14 %	Present value £
1	112,000	0.877	98,224
2	128,000	0.769	98,432
3	140,000	0.675	94,500
4	200,000	0.592	118,400
5	208,000	0.519	107,952
Present Value of Cash Inflows			517,508
less Capital Outlay			480,000
Net Present Value			37,508

[2] The residual value of £80,000 is added to the cash flow for year 5 to give £208,000.

Payback period:

	£		
Capital Outlay	− 480,000		
Cash Inflows:	Annual	Annual to payback	Cumulative to payback
	£	£	£
Year 1	112,000	112,000	112,000
Year 2	128,000	128,000	240,000
Year 3	140,000	140,000	380,000
Year 4	200,000	100,000	480,000

Payback period   =   3.5 years

12.4

Replace existing machines:

	Outlay £	Annual Savings £
Cutting machine	27,000	6,000
Planing machine	35,000	8,000
Sanding machine	12,000	3,000
	74,000	17,000

		£
Present Value of Cash Inflows	(£17,000 x 5.019) =	85,323
less Capital Outlay		74,000
Net Present Value		11,323
Profitability Index	(85,323 ÷ 74,000)	1.15

Replace existing machines with a multipurpose machine:

Annual Savings £45,000 – £16,000 = £29,000

		£
Present Value of Cash Inflows	(£29,000 x 5.019) =	145,551
less Capital Outlay		132,000
Net Present Value		13,551
Profitability Index	(145,551 ÷ 132,000)	1.10

Choose the option with the highest Profitability Index i.e. 1.15

12.5   **1.   Payback period:**

	£'000		
Capital Outlay	– 90,000		
Cash Inflows:	Annual	Annual to payback	Cumulative to payback
	£'000	£'000	£'000
Year 1	40,000	40,000	40,000
Year 2	35,000	35,000	75,000
Year 3	30,000	15,000	90,000

Payback period   =   2 years 6 months

2.   Accounting rate of return:

	£
Net Cash Inflows	150,000
less Capital Outlay	90,000
Profit over the Life of Project	60,000
Life (years)	5
Average Annual Profit	12,000

Accounting Rate of Return   =   12,000 ÷ 90,000 x 100   =   13.3%

12.6   **1.   Payback period**

	£'000		
Capital Outlay	– 130,000		
Cash Inflows:	Annual	Annual to payback	Cumulative to payback
	£'000	£'000	£'000
Year 1	60,000	60,000	60,000
Year 2	50,000	50,000	110,000
Year 3	40,000	20,000	130,000

Payback period   =   2 years 6 months

2. Net present value

Year	Cash flows £000	DCF factor 12 %	Present value £000
1	60,000	0.893	53,580
2	50,000	0.797	39,850
3	40,000	0.712	28,480
4	30,000	0.636	19,080
5	20,000	0.567	11,340
Present Value of Cash Inflows			152,330
less Capital Outlay			130,000
Net Present Value			22,330

12.7

			£m
Present Value of Cash Inflows	(£50m x 3.791)	=	189.55
less Capital Outlay			150.00
Net Present Value			39.55
Profitability Index	(189.55 ÷ 150.00)		1.26

12.8 This answer uses annuity tables

1. Internal Rate of Return

Capital Outlay ÷ Annual Savings = £70,000 ÷ £20,000 = 3.500

Consult annuity tables for a 5 year life. 3.517 is equal to 13%, therefore internal rate of return is approximately **13%**.

2. Annual savings to achieve a 12% internal rate of return

Capital Outlay ÷ Annuity at 12% = £70,000 ÷ 3.605 = **£19,417**

3. Net present value and profitability index

			£
Present Value of Cash Inflows	(£20,000 x 3.791)	=	75,820
less Capital Outlay			70,000
Net Present Value			5,820
Profitability Index	(£75,820 ÷ £70,000)		1.08

Index

A

B

C

Guildford College
Learning Resource Centre

Please return on or before the last date shown
This item may be renewed by telephone unless overdue

- 7 APR 200	1 2 MAY 2004	3 0 JUN 2005
2 x SEP 2003	1 0 JUN 2004	
- 7 NOV 2003		0 8 JUL 2005
	1 5 DEC 2004	
- 8 JAN 2004		- 2 NOV 2005
	2 2 FEB 2005	- 7 DEC 2005
- 8 MAR 2004	7 MAR 2005	
2 9 MAR 2004		3 0 JAN 2006
- 6 MAY 2004	- 5 MAY 2005 2 FEB 2006	
	- 6 JUN 2005	0 7 JUN 2006

Class: _____ 657 ROB

Title: _____ Accounting Principles for Non-Accounting
_____ Students
Author: _____ ROBERTSON   2 8 JUN 2006

2 0 NOV 2006 1 7 OCT 2006